SCREEN/PLAY

SCREEN/PLAY

Derrida and Film Theory

Peter Brunette and David Wills

Princeton University Press
Princeton, New Jersey

Library of Congress Cataloging-in-Publication Data

Brunette, Peter.
Screen/play : Derrida and film theory /
Peter Brunette and David Wills.
p.   cm.
Bibliography: p.
Includes index.
ISBN 0–691–05572–6 (alk. paper) ISBN 0–691–00846–9 (pbk.)
1. Motion pictures. 2. Film criticism. 3. Derrida, Jacques.
I. Wills, David, 1953–   . II. Title.
PN1995.B764   1989
791.43'01—dc20   89–33404
CIP

Earlier versions of portions of this book originally appeared as "Toward a Deconstructive Theory of Film," *Studies in the Literary Imagination* 19,
1 (Spring 1986), 55–71; "Un Ecran déchiré," *Hors
cadre*, no. 4 (Spring 1986), 75–91; and "Theories
of Spectacle/Spectacles of Theory," *Iconics* (1987),
65–82. Permission to reprint sections of these articles is gratefully acknowledged.

Publication of this book has been aided by the
Whitney Darrow Fund of Princeton University Press

This book has been composed in Linotron Bembo

Printed in the United States of America
by Princeton University Press,
Princeton, New Jersey

To Lynne, finally, and to the memory of three good friends: Gianfranco DeLisio (1945–84), Frank DiFederico (1933–87), and S. Eric Molin (1929–87)

—P.B.

To Roberta

—D.W.

CONTENTS

Preface   ix

CHAPTER ONE   Introduction   3

CHAPTER TWO   Derrida and Contemporary Film Studies   33

CHAPTER THREE   Film as Writing: From Analogy to Anagram   60

CHAPTER FOUR   The Frame of the Frame   99

CHAPTER FIVE   Black and Blue   139

CHAPTER SIX   Cinema and the Postal   172

Works Cited   199

Index   207

PREFACE

The pages that follow constitute an attempt to apply the work of French philosopher Jacques Derrida, generally restricted thus far to literary and philosophical questions, to considerations of film theory. We want to make clear at the outset, however, that despite the fact that what has come to be known as deconstruction in America has been primarily concerned with the interpretation of texts, we have not been especially interested, at least not in the present volume, in producing a series of deconstructive readings of films. It is our experience that unless they are elaborated or understood in a theoretical context, many so-called deconstructive interpretations do not ultimately differ greatly from their New Critical counterparts. We wish rather to begin the process of "translation" of Derrida's work to Anglo-American film theory by offering a certain reading of his texts, especially those written since *Glas* (1974), that have, for a variety of reasons, been largely neglected by English-speaking literary theorists. Hence, with the exception of chapter 5, in which we offer readings of two films (readings that are, however, in no way meant to be "how-to" demonstrations of a normative deconstructive methodology), we have for the most part chosen to avoid discussing individual film texts. We have preferred instead to offer a tentative rationalization for a certain perspective on contemporary film theory, and for a certain novel way of approaching film texts *anagrammatically*, as it were, that has been repressed because of the challenges it offers to the traditional institutional supports for interpretation. We hope that as the argument proceeds, the reasons for such decisions will become clearer. In any case, we have been conscious throughout of having perhaps the first or, more likely, the second or third word on the relation of deconstruction and film, but hardly the last. It is our hope that in the future we or others, in other books, will be able to apply more specifically the general, somewhat abstract elaborations of Derrida's work offered here.

This book had its beginning, one lovely spring day in 1984, on the bright, tidy lawn of one of the colleges at the University of Toronto. We had met earlier in the week as participants on what may very well have been the first panel on deconstruction and film theory ever held in North America. (Coincidentally, Jacques Derrida was on campus at the same time, leading a workshop on translation, and because the coffee was better at *our* conference—at least according to him—we got to see a lot of him.)

After a few days, each of us finally admitted his desire to write something more substantial on Derrida and film theory, and we decided, with some trepidation, that it might be a good idea to pool our efforts. That first heady planning session on the lawn, some five hours long, gave us our initial outline and a belief that it could be done, in spite of the fact that at the time one of us was teaching in Australia, the other in the United States. Our first thanks, then, must go to the University of Toronto and to the organizers of the "Semiotics of Cinema" conference, Teresa de Lauretis and Cam Tolton, for bringing us together.

We also want to thank Devon Hodges, Dana Polan, and David Rodowick for helpful comments on various versions of the manuscript. Special thanks are due to Joanna Hitchcock of Princeton University Press, who supported our project wholeheartedly from the start.

Peter Brunette is also grateful to J. Hillis Miller for guiding him through his initial immersion in the rigors of Derridean thought in a 1977 NEH Summer Seminar for College Teachers. In addition, he wants to thank the enthusiastic participants in his own NEH Summer Seminar, on film theory, that was offered in 1983 at New York University, as well as the graduate students at George Mason University who have taken his seminars in literary and film theory since 1980. They have all taught him a lot. Furthermore, he is grateful to Northwestern University and the School of Criticism and Theory for a fellowship in 1982 and to the NEH for a fellowship in 1987–1988, which, although granted for another project, enabled him to complete his share of the present book as well.

David Wills would like to acknowledge the support of James Cook University during sabbatical leave and thank it for a Special Research Grant in 1984. The Head of the Department of Modern Languages, Keith Sinclair, was helpful in getting the project off the ground. Summer grants were provided by the Louisiana State University Center for French and Francophone Studies as well as the University Council on Research. Warm thanks are due to Nat Wing, Chairman of the Department of French and Italian at Louisiana State University, for his interest and encouragement. The response received from attentive listeners at various institutions in Australia during August 1988 was instrumental in bringing into focus the final version of certain sections of the manuscript.

P.B.
Arlington, Virginia

D.W.
New Orleans, Louisiana

November 1988

SCREEN/PLAY

CHAPTER ONE

INTRODUCTION

The work of French philosopher Jacques Derrida has already had a profound influence on literary studies in the English-speaking world. It is beginning to have a similar effect on Anglo-American analytical philosophy, and the name, at least, now has a certain currency within literate circles in general. Yet Derrida's influence on film studies has so far been minimal. It is this state of affairs that we wish to examine in what follows; we would also like to suggest ways in which Derridean thinking and what has come to be known as deconstruction might contribute to our understanding of certain crucial questions in the domain of film theory and criticism.

Strictly speaking, of course, "deconstruction" and "Derrida" are not synonymous. In fact, commentators like Rodolphe Gasché have complained that deconstruction as it is practiced in America, most obviously by what has misleadingly come to be called the "Yale School," departs significantly from Derrida's own work.[1] Christopher Norris suggests that the lingering influence of American New Criticism might vitiate the "total revaluation of interpretative theory and practice"[2] that deconstruction promises, and it has become almost automatic to assume that deconstruction in America necessarily domesticates the political force of Derrida's writings.[3] Derrida himself has expressed reserve at the use of the term:

[1] See Gasché's "Deconstruction as Criticism," *Glyph 6* (Baltimore: The Johns Hopkins University Press, 1979), 177–216.

[2] *Deconstruction: Theory and Practice* (London and New York: Methuen, 1982), 17.

[3] See, for example, Terry Eagleton, *Literary Theory: An Introduction* (Minneapolis: University of Minnesota Press, 1983), 143–48; or more recently Colin MacCabe's "Foreword" to Gayatri Spivak, *In Other Worlds: Essays in Cultural Politics* (New York: Routledge, 1987), where he calls deconstruction–U.S. style a "Reagan kind of radical theory" (xi). The question is also raised by various participants at the Cerisy colloquium, published as *Les Fins de l'homme: A partir du travail de Jacques Derrida* (Paris: Galilée, 1981), 278–81, 526–29. Derrida accepts here that "a certain literary criticism [in America], which finds its point of departure in his work but doesn't question its practices, can contribute to an institutional closure which serves dominant economic and political interests" (529).

For me, it was a word in a chain with many other words—such as trace or differance—as well as with a whole elaboration which is not limited only to a lexicon, if you will. . . . this word which I had written only once or twice (I don't even remember where exactly) all of a sudden jumped out of the text and was seized by others who have since determined its fate in the manner you well know. Faced with this, I myself then had to justify myself, to explain, to try to get some leverage . . . the word by itself bothered me . . . for me "deconstruction" was not at all the first or the last word, and certainly not a password or slogan for everything that was to follow.[4]

On the other hand he has refused to arbitrate between authorized and unauthorized versions or uses of his work, in spite of the reproach to which this refusal has laid him open, preferring instead to make the questions of "ownership," "inheritance," "seal," and "signature" major topics of address in his writing.[5] Obviously, the problem with insisting upon a distinction between Derrida and deconstruction, in spite of the loose and often ill-informed use of the latter term, is that an appeal is inevitably, if unconsciously, being made to a "correct" or "true" Derrida or deconstruction, as opposed to a cheap or not-so-cheap imitation of it. Such a gesture remains firmly within the logocentric will to truth that Derrida has been at pains to identify and critique.

This does not mean that it is not important to continue to argue painstakingly the sense of Derrida's work, the matter of what he means or wants to say. Derrida himself is committed to this process, and in debates such as that with John Searle, the Speech Act theorist,

---

[4] *The Ear of the Other*, ed. Christie V. McDonald, trans. Peggy Kamuf and Avital Ronell (New York: Schocken Books, 1985), 86. Later, in answer to the comment that he seems to have "repudiated" the term, Derrida replies that it is his strength or weakness not to repudiate: "whether it's my luck or my naiveté, I don't think I have ever repudiated anything. . . . The fortune, let's say, of the word has surprised me. If I had been left all to myself, if I had been left alone with that word, I would not have given it as much importance. But finally, rightly or wrongly, I still believe in what was bound up with this word—I am not against it" (142). In fact Derrida uses the word "deconstruction" more liberally than he suggests here. He offers perhaps the most concise explanation of it, one that is also sensitive to its uses and abuses, in a recently published article concerning the proposed translation of the word into Japanese. See "Lettre à un ami japonais," in *Psyché: Inventions de l'autre* (Paris: Galilée, 1987), 387–93.

[5] See, inter alia, "Limited Inc.," *Glyph 2* (Baltimore: The Johns Hopkins University Press, 1977), 162–254; "Plato's Pharmacy," in *Dissemination*, trans. Barbara Johnson (Chicago: University of Chicago Press, 1982), 61–171; "To Speculate—on 'Freud,' " in *The Post Card: From Socrates to Freud and Beyond*, trans. Alan Bass (Chicago: University of Chicago Press, 1987), 257–409.

or more recently that over the apartheid question[6] he has unrelentingly corrected the reading to which something he has written has been subjected. There is nothing contradictory about this; or rather, it is a paradox which, for all his emphasis on it, Derrida has never suggested that we can avoid. Certainly no single speaking subject can do so by the simple fiat of his or her utterances. What is always involved here, interminably and interminably paradoxically, is the question of reading. The fact that there is never a final true reading—certainly not by an author of her or his own work—in no way reduces our reliance on, our managing of, and our playing with a complex system of protocols of reading. By reading "loosely," "against the grain," "parodically," or "irresponsibly"—some of which deconstructionists might claim to do, and all of which Derrida might be said to have done within the limits of a carefully developed logic and for certain strategic ends—one is nevertheless still reading and calling for the reply of yet another reading.

To return to our point then: since what we are involved with here is nothing more nor less than a reading of the work of Derrida in the context of film studies, we would argue both for and against the assimilation of Derrida with deconstruction, but always within the terms of reading practices, ours and those of others. For example, deconstructionists in America have up to this point shown little evidence of having read the specific form that Derrida's writing has taken since *Glas*, originally published in 1974. Though the recent appearance of that text in English[7] may bring about a change, they have so far chosen to emulate the earlier Derrida, the Derrida of the rigorously close textual analysis that demonstrates the inevitable double binds of logocentrism without attempting to "rewrite" these double binds in the language of *différance*. By this we mean that in Derrida's later work there is something of a shift from the description and explanation of *différance* (to take but one word) in discursive terms to a putting into effect of the "other" conceptual and ludic side of language that the sense of *différance*

---

[6] On Speech Act theory, see Derrida, "Signature Event Context," in *Margins of Philosophy*, trans. Alan Bass (Chicago: University of Chicago, 1982), 307–30; John R. Searle, "Reiterating the Differences: A Reply to Derrida," *Glyph 1* (Baltimore: The Johns Hopkins University Press, 1977), 198–208; and Derrida, "Limited Inc." For the apartheid controversy, see Derrida, "Racism's Last Word," *Critical Inquiry* 12 (Autumn 1985), 290–99; Ann McClintock and Rob Nixon, "No Names Apart: The Separation of Word and History in Derrida's 'Le Dernier Mot du Racisme,'" and Derrida, "But, beyond . . . (Open Letter to Ann McClintock and Rob Nixon)," *Critical Inquiry* 13 (Autumn 1986), 140–70.

[7] *Glas*, trans. John P. Leavey and Richard Rand (Lincoln: University of Nebraska Press, 1986).

opens up. We do not hold to a rigorous separation of these two Derridas and shall have more to say about these different styles, modes, or moments of deconstruction in the course of our discussion. In the meantime, however, keeping in mind the reservation that we are always involved in a reading of Derrida's texts, we shall use his name and the name "deconstruction" interchangeably.

Though the basic outlines of Derrida's thought have been conveniently mapped in an ever proliferating number of books, several very worthwhile and each having its own merits,[8] it may be useful for the present discussion to attempt a brief and inevitably reductive summary of its major concerns. A consideration of Derrida may begin from diverse starting points, but a potentially fruitful way of approaching deconstruction is as a radicalization of Saussure's insights into the nature of language, and specifically into the nature of the sign itself and the relation between signifier and signified. Saussure's already radical formulation—that nothing in language is meaningful in and of itself, but only as it *differs* from other elements within the system—was powerful enough to keep him from pursuing its full implications, as Derrida clearly shows in *Of Grammatology* (see especially pp. 27–73). Derrida sees this as an almost inadvertent breach[9] of what he calls the "metaphysics of presence," that system of thought common to the Western tradition since Socrates holding that that which is, is that which is present or capable of being present. Also called into question is the attendant logocentrism of this metaphysics, which is that system of concepts such as "truth," "good," "nature," and so on, which are regarded, throughout the entire history of Western thought, as being

---

[8] See, for example, Jonathan Culler, *On Deconstruction* (Ithaca: Cornell University Press, 1982); Christopher Norris, *Deconstruction: Theory and Practice* and *Derrida* (Cambridge: Harvard University Press, 1987); Vincent Leitch, *Deconstructive Criticism: An Advanced Introduction* (New York: Columbia University Press, 1983); Barbara Johnson, "Translator's Introduction," in *Dissemination*, vii–xxiii; Gayatri Chakravorty Spivak, "Translator's Preface," in Derrida, *Of Grammatology* (Baltimore: The Johns Hopkins University Press, 1974), ix–xc; and for the "later" Derrida, Gregory Ulmer, *Applied Grammatology* (Baltimore: The Johns Hopkins University Press, 1985).

[9] As we warned, this summary risks being reductive, and our own brief formulations greatly oversimplify the issues. What we call here an "inadvertent breach" evokes the whole problem of the extent to which a discourse controls and remains aware of what it utters, as well as the sense in which deconstruction cannot be reduced to a simple correction of errors in thinking. These questions have been elaborated at length by Derrida in *Of Grammatology* itself, particularly in the pages on his approach to Rousseau's text (157–64, "The Exorbitant. Question of Method") and in *The Ear of the Other* (85–87). We continue to refer the reader to more lengthy discussions of these general concerns in both Derrida and his commentators, while we shall ourselves develop in the pages to follow the specific questions we see as relating to film.

whole, internally coherent, consistent, and originary. Invariably these concepts are seen to have opposites ("falsehood," "evil," "culture") that are always presented as in some way harmful, deficient, deformed, or secondary, in short as a falling away from the fullness and self-sufficiency of the primary term. What Derrida has done is to show that, just as in Saussure's analysis of language, these concepts can only function *because* of their opposites, which then must inevitably be seen as constituting them.

Perhaps a homely example will make this clear. If there were only day, around the clock, and never night, the idea of day would not have any sense. It needs an opposite, paradoxically, in order to exist, because a thing, idea, or event can only be said to exist, or function *significantly* within a system, insofar as it differs from something else. To repeat, if there were *only* day (without night to differ from it), we would not be able to conceptualize such a thing as "day." If this is the case, then this thing, idea, or event cannot ever be whole, self-contained, and uncontaminated by an "outside," because it depends for its very existence on that which it is *not*. Every concept, in other words, has its opposite somehow inscribed within it, in the form of what Derrida calls a "trace," which, like a footprint, is paradoxically there and, as a sign of an absence, not there at the same time. Western logic's grounding principle of noncontradiction (something cannot simultaneously be "A" and "not-A") is thus challenged. Our very reluctance to give up the principle of noncontradiction is evidence of how tenacious a hold the metaphysics of presence has on our consciousness and on the way in which we conceptualize reality.

Obviously, such a calling into question of entrenched conceptions has enormous consequences. If truth, for example, depends upon error and is in some way constituted by it, then what will be the status of the truth claims that all intellectual disciplines need in order to function? If unity has disunity already within it, what are the possibilities for unified expression (including that which we are attempting here)?[10] Or even for making sense, if non-sense is there all along? The reply is not that nothing ever makes sense any longer but rather that nothing makes sense only within the simplistic and commonsense idea of making sense, that is, in terms of a straightforward and uninterrupted com-

---

[10] We would not want to pretend that there is not some paradox in our own exercise, seeking as we are, especially at this early stage, to present a unitary representation of a "system" of ideas. What we hope is different about our particular reading of Derrida—not the reading that we "own" but the one that we are practicing—lies in the matters to which we address it, the new contextualization we are effecting by bringing his work to bear on film theory.

munication of an intact message from a sender to a receiver. What were previously conceived of as accidental threats to normal sense making— such as what the language of communications science calls "noise," the residue of conflicting etymologies within a word, or the possible breaches in the solidity of context (for the more language one adds to "clarify" a given utterance, the greater the chances of indetermination of sense)—cannot be rigorously excluded from the sense-making process. Nor can they be easily relegated to secondary positions within a hierarchy of sense-making processes, given that the idea of a central, straightforward common sense has no validity or priority in and of itself.

As Derrida describes it, all versions of Western thinking have attempted to repress this sense of the "other" that is at the very heart of whatever is seen as being whole, meaningful, self-sufficient, originary, and true. His entire project can be described (again, only reductively) as an attempt to analyze the elaborate variations that have been wrought throughout the history of Western civilization on this single theme. As we shall see, the history of film theory has its own unique strategies for eliding this breach as well. What Derrida calls the "logic of the supplement" is perhaps the chief form of this strategy, and it is often imported into any discussion when the inevitable cracks and fissures of the unified argument begin to appear. It is this idea that has formed the basis of the most general application of deconstruction in literary studies and that has recently been imported into other fields.[11]

The classic example, which Derrida evokes in *Of Grammatology* (144–57), is Rousseau's distinction between nature (which of course Rousseau favors) and culture or education (which he is against, since it is held to corrupt nature). At a certain point in his argument, however, Rousseau is led to say, paradoxically, that the "real" nature of human beings can only be brought forward through education. Elsewhere Rousseau suggests, in a similar vein, that since he does not express himself very well in person, the "real" Rousseau can actually only appear in the written form. Measured against speech, however, writing is historically considered another one of the secondary, distorted, incomplete entities constituting the "other." As a further corollary Derrida discusses Rousseau's treatment of masturbation as a "dangerous supplement" to "proper" sexuality, rendered necessary by the absence

---

[11] See for instance the work of Critical Legal Theorists: J.M. Balkin, "Deconstructive Practice and Legal Theory," *Yale Law Review* 96 (1987), 743–86; Gerald E. Frug, "The Ideology of Bureaucracy in American Law," *Harvard Law Review* 97 (1984), 1277–1388; Gary Peller, "The Metaphysics of American Law," *California Law Review* 73 (1985), 1151–1290; and the special edition of *Stanford Law Review* 36, nos. 1–2 (1984).

of the sexual partner. As Derrida points out, however, the difference between masturbation and sexual intercourse can never be clear–cut, given the fact that intercourse also depends upon a certain "auto–affection" that effectively renders the other absent. What we have in each case is the idea of something supposedly exterior, foreign, or opposite to what is favored or desired coming to replace and supplant the latter; but in each case the supplement also acts as a correction to a problem or deficiency within the system. So the question arises as to whether what is supposedly foreign to the system was not in fact part of it, as potential or constitutive force, from the beginning, and not just an accident that befell it along the way. Derrida's strategy, then, by pointing to what suddenly appears as an obvious contradiction and by showing how such a contradiction is, or can be, generalized at various levels throughout the text, is to overturn and displace these hierarchies that rule—and enable—our system of thought. He thus identifies the inevitable presence of the other or opposite within the supposedly whole or pure term. In most of his analyses he finds a key word or phrase—an ambiguity within a word such as *pharmakon* (both "poison" and "remedy") or *suppléer* (Fr. "to supplement" [which in English also has contradictory senses] and "to supplant") or an idea relegated to a footnote or secondary example such as Kant's *parergon*[12]—that neatly encapsulates the "logic of the supplement" and that can usually be taken in two opposing senses, allowing him to reveal the difference that breaks into the order of the same.

In *Of Grammatology* Derrida makes the speech versus writing oppositional relation something of a paradigm for the operations of logocentrism in general. The fact that writing in its literal sense has been systematically treated, by any number of thinkers from Plato to Rousseau and Saussure, as a derivative corruption of the natural language that is speech, becomes the basis for an elaboration of "writing" in a much wider sense. Writing becomes the model for all linguistic operations, including speech, to the extent that they always involve a dependence on the difference, spacing, and rupture that the speech model occludes. Writing thus comes to stand for otherness in general.

Truth in our thinking has always been implicitly or explicitly tied to the *logos* or spoken word, relying as it does on the commonsense model we referred to above. In this model, a speaking subject has the illusion of forming speech in total simultaneity with thought, thus ap-

[12] See "Plato's Pharmacy," in *Dissemination*; and "Parergon," in *The Truth in Painting*, trans. Geoff Bennington and Ian McLeod (Chicago: University of Chicago Press, 1987), 15–147.

parently collapsing the space between the signifier and the signified in a self-contained fullness. Similarly, these thoughts are instantly conveyed to the listener in a manner that once again promotes the illusion of directness, appearing to suppress the gap, however minute, of representation. Meaning here travels within a closed circuit; it is protected from interference, it remains intact. The model is therefore underwritten by the idea of presence; it is presence that insures the unimpeded operation of the system. But the model is also underwritten by the idea of the breath, the life-giving force that profits from its metonymic relation to the voice to endow that voice with an added sense of naturalness and that thus bolsters the model with a concept of being that has always been fundamental to philosophical inquiry.

The voice, in conjunction with the breath, also acts in philosophical thinking as a form of origin. Philosophical inquiry is as committed to an explanation of the origin as it is to discovery of truth and so becomes caught in a paradox. The origin, to have absolute meaning as such, must reside outside of language, untouched by the error, dispute, and interpretation that pervade language. Philosophy wants to conceive of an origin that is beyond reproach, and to be true it must be a fullness, an ideal self-presence. By confining references to language to the model based on the voice, by transferring the "guilt" of language's failures to writing, that other language, philosophy, is thus able to speak as though an intact truth or origin had been preserved despite the fall into language. As Derrida has pointed out, only recourse to some sort of transcendental metaphysics can make this possible; only by implying that there is an outside to language where such paradoxes are resolved can philosophy claim to be speaking not nonsense but truth.

In making writing the scapegoat for the things that language does not want to recognize as part of itself, things like distancing rather than presence and difference rather than sameness, spoken language conceals the very paradoxes that constitute it. For difference does not suddenly appear in the case of writing; as Saussure insisted, difference constitutes all language. Without oppositional difference, in other words, language is simply a continuum of unintelligible garble. It is from this basis that Derrida argues that writing constitutes spoken language rather than vice versa. What he means is that the things that are identified in writing as being derived, supplemental to natural language, or as being the results of a falling away from the origin are in fact the very things that constitute any language, even the most natural. The commonsensical hierarchy of speech over writing is thus reversed and, in the process, displaced.

The strength of Derrida's strategy (and also the reason behind so much of the criticism it has attracted) lies in his carrying the critique or radical application of Saussure's ideas well beyond their presumed limits. For, as we have suggested, he reads Saussure—whose work represents a privileged but by no means unique moment—as opening possibilities that are never fully exploited. Rather than simply correcting Saussure or remaining within the terms Saussure prescribes, Derrida takes the materiality of the signifier and a radicalized principle of difference as the bases for a whole series of interventions in the operations of language. Derrida insists that language is institution and convention against and beyond structuralism's claims to that end, and those claims are shown to betray, however partially, a desire for language that would on the contrary be natural utterance. But once the full extent of language as conventionality is conceded, the terms of that convention are open to debate; once language is shown to be institution, discussion about language inevitably revolves around the operations of that institution and the possibilities of subverting it.

Before turning to the context of film theory, we should point out once again, at the risk of repeating ourselves, an aspect of Derrida's work that is commonly elided, namely that his critique insists on being a double operation. It is not content to analyze logocentrism purely on its own terms, that is, by means of a straightforward discursive exercise that inevitably implies its own truth claims. By the same token, however, Derrida argues that there is no way of simply stepping outside of logocentrism, for in an important sense it makes meaning possible while reducing its range of operations. What that leaves for the deconstructionist is a range of strategies designed to work on the edges of logocentrism, to resist its reductive impulse not just by critique but also by radical practice. This side of the enterprise is often referred to as its practice of "erasure," discussed by Gayatri Spivak in some detail in her introduction to the translation of *Of Grammatology*. The interventions that deal with etymological determinations, for example, or the pitting of a supposed literal level of language against a supposed metaphorical level, may be seen as part of this practice. This is followed by an operation in which words within the text are treated as having been crossed out so that they can be read as both there and not there, an operation that, like the term deconstruction itself (from Ger. *Destruktion*), Derrida borrows from Heidegger. These are all strategic resistances to logocentrism's will to truth and centrality of meaning.

While continuing a minute and careful deconstruction of logocentrism, Derrida concurrently develops a new lexicon, some of whose elements we have already mentioned. But it must be said, the moment it is written, that this new lexicon is *not* a new lexicon but a series of words written under erasure, attempts to move toward a new conceptualization without at the same time imposing a new set of hierarchical truths. *Différance* is the first or the most often repeated of those words, and in an interview that appeared only five years after *Of Grammatology* was originally published in France and that therefore refers primarily to the terms used in that text, Derrida is careful to point out the limits of this word as a supposed key concept. In describing his project as that of writing "[in] the space in which is posed the question of saying and meaning," he calls *différance* a gamble or game, whose consequence is to prevent "any word, any concept, any major enunciation from coming to summarize and to govern from the theological presence of a center the movement and textual spacing of differences."[13] Already the term *différance* is only one of a number of terms, and it is promised that there will be more, designed as shorthand for the whole operation of deconstruction—its critical moment and its experimental moment: "To be entangled in hundreds of pages of a writing simultaneously insistent and elliptical, imprinting, as you saw, even its erasures, carrying off each concept into an interminable chain of differences, surrounding or confusing itself with so many precautions, references, notes, citations, collages, supplements—this . . . is not, you will agree, the most assured of exercises" (*Positions*, 14). In short, the aim of Derrida's critique is to work through, to unpack the operations of logocentrism, the functions by which Western thinking has assured its sameness and repressed its otherness, but in such a way as to avoid falling back into a system of analysis that does nothing but repeat, in practice, those very same pitfalls. Derrida's analysis would be differ*ant*, not just different, for the apparent singularity of such an oppositional tactic only amounts in the end to more of the same.

Différance, then, is a radical attempt at otherness. It is first of all double—a "double science" as the title of one of Derrida's essays suggests[14]—both painstakingly analytical and, for want of a better word, experimental. But second, by virtue of its experimental phase (concurrent and not successive), it subverts its scientificity and throws the terms of its discursive mode back into play. Third, through the neologisms of the experimental mode, it breaks ground that opens upon the permanently unutterable, the impossibility of any simple

[13] Derrida, *Positions*, trans. Alan Bass (Chicago: University of Chicago Press, 1981), 14; translation modified.

[14] "The Double Session," in *Dissemination*, 172–286.

otherness that is not always also constituted by its opposite; it becomes a working over of the margins and borders. And fourth, the cumbersome, even prosaic nature of those neologisms or wordplays is such that what we have just called the unutterable or the impossible are refused transcendence; they remain locked awkwardly into the discursive practices that were the point of departure for the exercise.

Finally, it is important to remember that Derridean deconstruction arises, quite simply, from that first movement, mentioned above, namely the division of the centralizing function of the Western philosophical tradition into a double science, the fact that it is made to cohabit with another mode of discourse. It is a simple apposition—placing within the same discursive space two ideas previously made to obey a strict hierarchy—or, at most, the rehabilitation of what a singularizing discourse refused to accept as part of itself that achieves the tactical results of deconstruction. But those results are surprising, for as we have just seen, a double science, even one that is only the folding in upon itself of a single science, very quickly becomes not double but triple, quadruple, and so on. Once the center no longer holds, the possibilities of otherness quickly proliferate. The task of deconstruction becomes one of defining (and constantly redefining) without containing those possibilities, hence the variety of practices to which it resorts.

In later texts what we are calling the experimental mode of Derrida's enterprise takes off more systematically in other directions, especially by means of the problematic of the frame and the signature, in order to further interrogate the terms of the relation a text, an event, a concept, or a supposed entity has with its outside—hence a further deflection from centrality. For instance, the idea of signature can easily be seen as an instance of the same problematic that describes the operation of language. In signing, just as in speaking, one seeks by apparently natural means to ensure ownership of and thus control over one's utterance. But for Derrida, just as speech is revealed to partake of the structure of writing, itself possessing the difference it finds in writing, so the signature does not function as assurance of authority, authorship, and authenticity, without also representing a dispersal or dissemination of originary meaning. We shall be returning to this matter in detail as well as to the idea of the frame, for, as the word suggests, it is of primary importance for us in discussion of film and the visual arts.

In later texts also, often in the context of "signatory" writing—*Glas* is exemplary here—Derrida goes further in subverting the self-present meaning of language by means of wordplay. This takes place at the level of the word as signifier, where he exploits what Saussure described as the arbitrary nature of its relation with a signified, and also at the level of relations between pieces of text. In *Glas*, for instance, Hegel and Genet are placed next to each other in columns on opposing pages, and any number of possible cross-references echo against one another without being systematically codified. Again, however, this is not so very different, at least not structurally, from the practice of bringing a footnote to bear on the supposed central thesis of a text of philosophy,[15] for such a practice is underwritten by the radical notion of context—the possibility that every utterance can be lifted from one context and grafted onto another—which is defined in one of the first texts by Derrida to gain a wide English readership, "Signature Event Context." Even though this aspect of Derrida's work has aroused a great deal of antagonism, none of these strategies should be taken for gratuitous play on his part. Rather, they are all part of a carefully worked out and extensively elaborated set of ideas obeying its own rigorous if complex logic. The point, in other words, is that the concept of "play" must itself be interrogated concerning its bases, limits, and strategies. Not to do so would on the one hand encourage a Romantic type of play for its own sake and, on the other, remain within the bounds of a logocentric discourse that presupposes a subsequent and necessary return to the "serious" as that which is prior and proper:

> There is another attitude—let us call it obscurantist—that one may adopt toward play which consists in throwing in the towel and saying: "Okay, that's a game. It's gratuitous, play for the sake of play; it means nothing, it's pure expenditure." I would be very wary of this temptation, even though it might fascinate me. I am very wary of it because it would be at this moment that one risks falling short of the scientific, theoretical demand and failing in one's responsibility to try to comprehend what play signifies, what strategies, interests, and investments are at work in play. . . . Philosophy has always made play into an activity, the activity of a subject manipulating objects. As soon as one interprets play in the sense of playing, one has already been dragged into the space of classical philosophy where play is dominated by meaning . . . and consequently something that surpasses and orients it. (*The Ear of the Other*, 67–68, 69)

Play in the sense that Derrida uses it should also be understood as the "give," or margin of movement, that exists within the system of logocentrism as in a well-worn machine. This is its own space of play that

[15] Cf. "Parergon," in *The Truth in Painting*.

it would have confined to the margins but that Derrida exploits or finds active within the central workings of the system itself.

———————

Having given some overview of Derrida's critical strategies, let us now turn our attention to the narrower context of film theory. Interestingly, the term "deconstruction" was in fact used in the early seventies by a group of critics associated with the journal *Cahiers du cinéma*. These critics sought to analyze the ideological determinations of the cinematic apparatus in response to others who, maintaining an instrumentalist approach, insisted that the camera was not an ideological apparatus but an ideologically neutral instrument. It was held to be a machine that relied on scientific principles and that was not constructed according to an ideology of representation. Writers like Pleynet, Comolli, Narboni, Oudart, and Baudry, in the pages of *La Nouvelle critique*, *Cahiers*, and *Cinéthique*, thus undertook a series of analyses designed to reveal the ideological underpinnings of the emergence of monocular perspective (and hence photography and cinema), the practice of deep focus, the introduction of sound and color, the lack of theorization of the chemical processes of cinema in favor of optics, and so on.[16] Although their work remained fairly strictly within a Marxist perspective and a Marxist conception of ideology—inspired by Althusser and Macherey among others[17]—their research clearly in-

———————

[16] See for example Jean-Louis Comolli and Jean Narboni's editorial in *Cahiers du cinéma*, no. 216 (1969), "Cinema/Ideology/ Criticism," in *Movies and Methods: An Anthology*, ed. Bill Nichols (Berkeley: University of California Press, 1976), 22–30; the collective text, in *Cahiers du cinéma*, no. 223 (1970) entitled "John Ford's *Young Mr. Lincoln*," in Nichols, *Movies and Methods*, 492–529; Jean-Louis Comolli, "Technique and Ideology: Camera, Perspective, Depth of Field (Part I)," in *Movies and Methods Volume II: An Anthology*, ed. Bill Nichols (Berkeley: University of California Press, 1985), 40–57; and parts 3 and 4, in *Narrative, Apparatus, Ideology: A Film Theory Reader*, ed. Philip Rosen (New York: Columbia University Press, 1986), 421–43. (A recent article challenges the epistemological continuity that is widely held to exist between the *camera obscura* and photography. See Jonathan Crary, "Techniques of the Observer," *October*, no. 45 [Fall 1988], 3–35.) The term "deconstructionist" was also more loosely used by a group of avant-garde filmmakers in France at the time. See Metz's discussion in the interview "Sur mon travail," in *Essais sémiotiques* (Paris: Editions Klincksieck, 1977), 167–72. Metz attributes the term to Kristéva rather than to Derrida.

[17] Althusser's idea of the "symptomatic" reading, derived from Freud and Lacan and which he applied to Marx's text to challenge the traditional treatment of a homogeneous system of thought, points forward to Derrida's deconstructive reading strategies. See Louis Althusser and Etienne Balibar, *Reading Capital*, trans. Ben Brewster (London: Verso, 1979), 28. Derrida calls Althusser's readings "decisive" in his discussion of Marxism in *Positions*, 62–64.

troduced a form of analysis aimed at uncovering and revalorizing factors that a dominant history of cinema, obeying a dominant ideology
of realism, had obscured or repressed. What has come to be known as
Derridean deconstruction has a more specific form and goes further
than the sort of correction of misconceptions that the *Cahiers* cinematic
deconstructionists practiced,[18] but our point here is that there existed
previously in film studies an opening toward Derridean theory that
remained within the contexts of Marxism and psychoanalysis[19] prominent to this day.

Certainly most contemporary post-structuralist film criticism and
theory continues, for better or worse, to be based on the strong re-
reading of Freud initiated by Jacques Lacan. Although one hears the
term "deconstructive" more and more frequently applied to film criticism based on the Lacanian model (and even to formalist studies
stressing nothing more radical than a modernist self-reflexivity), there
have only been a few scattered attempts to apply more properly speaking deconstructive strategies (in the Derridean sense) to film. The
work of Marie-Claire Ropars-Wuilleumier[20] is the single notable exception and as such will be the focus of further discussion. What we
want to do in the remainder of this chapter is to consider why Lacan's
work has been so much more influential than Derrida's in film studies,
exactly reversing the situation that has prevailed, at least until very
recently, in American literary criticism,[21] and to indicate briefly what
we see as some of the shortcomings of the Lacanian model. Our purpose here is not to replace one orthodoxy with another but to examine
ways in which an application of Derridean thought to film theory

    [18] It is interesting that one of the models Marx himself refers to in order to describe
ideology as an obfuscation and inversion of reality is the camera obscura. For an analysis
of this from a Derridean perspective see Sarah Kofman, *Camera obscura: De l'idéologie*
(Paris: Galilée, 1973).
    [19] Oudart's work on "suture," for instance, translated in *Screen* ("Cinema and Suture,"
Screen 18, no. 4 [1977–78], 35–77) and complemented by Stephen Heath's important
essay ("On Suture" in *Questions of Cinema* [Bloomington: Indiana University Press,
1981]), also forms part of the work of these deconstructionists. Heath returns to a number of these ideas in the essays in *Questions of Cinema*, especially in "Narrative Space."
    [20] See especially her book, *Le Texte divisé* (Paris: Presses Universitaires de France,
1981).
    [21] Besides the great number of articles written in this area, see for example Juliet
Flower MacCannell, *Figuring Lacan: Criticism and the Cultural Unconscious* (Lincoln: University of Nebraska Press, 1986); Shoshana Felman, *Jacques Lacan and the Adventure of*
Insight (Cambridge: Harvard University Press, 1987); Jane Gallop, *The Daughter's Seduc*
tion: Feminism and Psychoanalysis (Ithaca: Cornell University Press, 1982) and *Reading*
Lacan (Ithaca: Cornell University Press, 1985).

might help us out of certain theoretical impasses (and perhaps lead us to new, more productive ones).

Probably the most fruitful use of Lacanian psychoanalysis has been the challenging of the myth of the unified, coherent, intentional self. Out of this investigation a powerful critique of the dynamics of the spectator's assumption of cinematic realism has evolved, complementing the critique of the ideological determinations of the apparatus mentioned above.[22] We can now see more clearly how subjects are positioned and constructed through the representation of reality as unproblematic and given, and this of course has important political implications. One can no longer doubt that at least partly because of the work of "realistic" Hollywood films, which inculcate a certain predetermined reality in the spectator and which create that spectator as subject, the world is seen as natural rather than constructed and therefore as beyond the reach of political change. As we shall see later, Derrida's version of post-structuralist thought has also provoked grave doubts concerning the unitary model of the subject in Western intellectual history.

Since the cinematic experience, with its apparently (and misleadingly) privileged relationship to reality, is usually described as more "immediate" and "total" than the experience of literature, it becomes important to chart the psychological relation of spectator to film text as accurately as possible. The illusionism promoted and intermittently achieved in the movie theater thus quite properly becomes more crucial than the question of illusionism in literary studies. Furthermore, since much of Lacanian theory is based on the model of the mirror stage, the illusory fullness of the imaginary, and the problematizing of vision as the subject is introduced to castration and thus to the symbolic, Lacan's emphasis on the visual has seemed particularly appropriate to the study of film.

Another result of this concern for investigating the spectator's psychological relation to the film has been to make most film theorists de facto reader-response critics, focusing on the mechanics of reception rather than on the recalcitrant particulars of the text itself. In spite of this emphasis, however, the reigning models of reception have remained surprisingly unsophisticated in social, national, and racial terms. Unconsciously perhaps, the precritical humanist assumption of most conventional film criticism, which sees film as more popular,

---

[22] See Kaja Silverman, *The Subject of Semiotics* (New York: Oxford University Press, 1983); Stephen Heath, *Questions of Cinema*; Colin MacCabe, *Tracking the Signifier* (Minneapolis: University of Minnesota Press, 1985); and various uncollected articles by Heath and MacCabe that originally appeared in *Screen* in the 1970s.

more universal, and thus presumably connected to what is "most basic" in all of us, still seems to be at work. This assumption then leads to a further assumption, namely that all readers of film are the same. Feminist theorists have been the exception here, challenging the positioning of the spectator of classic film as male, but beyond this few Lacanian critics have bothered to make distinctions among viewers.

In any case, one troublesome problem with the Lacanian model has been the apparent grounding of his system within the Oedipal triangle and most especially the founding opposition between the imaginary and the symbolic. A close reading of Lacan will show that these two fields are in fact complicated modes that continuously interpenetrate one another and are by no means meant to constitute some sort of developmental teleology, an engrossing narrative that has a subject "grow out" of the imaginary to live (happily or not) ever after in the symbolic. Nevertheless, especially in the early stages of the importation of Lacanian thought into film studies, not enough attention was paid to Lacan's problematizing of these "stages" and the terms tended to rigidify, in ordinary usage, into a grounding dualism (or triad, if Lacan's concept of the "real" is included), which, with its attendant implied hierarchy, would obviously be susceptible to a Derridean deconstruction. For Derrida it is the concept of dissemination, which we will discuss further at a later stage, that disturbs and escapes Lacan's conceptual triad (*Positions*, 84). In his critique of Lacan's seminar on Poe's "The Purloined Letter" Derrida has further criticized what he calls Lacan's "telos of 'full speech' in its essential tie to Truth"—the latter a concept far from self-evident for Derrida—as well as Lacan's untheorized adoption of Hegelian and Heideggerian idealist conceptuality and vocabulary (*Positions*, 107–9).[23]

[23] See the original context of Derrida's comments, namely "Le Facteur de la vérité" on Lacan's seminar on "The Purloined Letter" (*The Post Card*, 411–96). In her essay on this debate Barbara Johnson suggests that Lacan is less univocal and grounded than Derrida makes him out to be, asking: "Does the fact that psychoanalysis is a technique based on verbal interlocution automatically reduce it to a logocentric error? Is it not equally possible to regard what Lacan calls 'full speech' as being *full* precisely of what Derrida calls *writing*?" (Johnson, *The Critical Difference* [Baltimore: The Johns Hopkins University Press, 1980], xx). Derrida in turn makes some informal comments on Johnson's remarks to his correspondent(s) in "Envois" (*The Post Card*, 149–52).

Derrida's debate with Lacan, itself long and complicated, should not obscure the range of relations his work has with psychoanalysis. We return to this matter in our final chapter, but a brief summary of these links might be in order here: (1) the idea of deconstructive criticism as a type of symptomatic reading of the text's unconscious; (2) the writing on Freud—"Freud and the Scene of Writing" in *Writing and Difference*, trans. Alan Bass (Chicago: University of Chicago Press, 1978), 196–231, and the major text "To Speculate—On 'Freud' " in *The Post Card*; (3) the association with the work of Nicolas Abraham and Maria Torok, whose research, notably on the Wolf Man's vocabu-

Clearly it is within feminist theory that Lacan's model of sexual difference has been most useful, especially in terms of the ways in which
the symbolic manifests itself linguistically. However, his grounding of
the Oedipal struggle and accession to the symbolic in the exchange of
the phallus and in forms of castration anxiety, no matter how vocifer-
ously his disciples insist upon the distinction between phallus and penis
(constituting the former as a structural relation rather than as the male
sexual organ), has quite properly created difficulties for feminists trying to decenter phallocentrism in all its forms.[24] In a summation representative of the feminist critique, Teresa de Lauretis writes:

> Even though castration is to be understood as referring to the
> symbolic dimension, its signifier—the phallus—can only be con-
> ceived as an extrapolation from the real body. . . . In the psycho-
> analytic view of signification, subject processes are essentially
> phallic; that is to say, they are *subject* processes insofar as they are
> instituted in a fixed order of language—the symbolic—by the
> function of castration. Again female sexuality is negated, assimi-
> lated to the male's.[25]

Derrida comments upon this limitation of Lacanian thought in "Le
Facteur de la vérité" (*The Post Card*, 477–83) and returns in *Spurs* to the
obvious point that castration is an affair of man, not of woman, and
that one "ought to interrogate . . . the metaphorical fullblown sail of
truth's declamation, of the castration and phallocentrism, for example,
in Lacan's discourse."[26]

Trying to locate a place in which the female subject can constitute

---

lary, Derrida has prefaced and commented upon ("Fors," translated in *Georgia Review*
31 [1977], 64–116; and "Me—Psychoanalysis," *Diacritics* 9, no. 1 [1979], 4–12). See also
"My Chances/*Mes Chances*: A Rendezvous with Some Epicurean Stereophonies" in
Taking Chances: Derrida, Psychoanalysis and Literature, ed. Joseph H. Smith and William
Kerrigan (Baltimore: The Johns Hopkins University Press, 1984).

For a thorough analysis of the relation between Derrida's work and psychoanalysis,
see Sarah Kofman, *Lectures de Derrida* (Paris: Galilée, 1984), 51–114.

[24] Perhaps the best argument *for* an application of Lacanian thought to feminism remains Jacqueline Rose, "Introduction—II," in *Feminine Sexuality: Jacques Lacan and the
école freudienne*, ed. Juliet Mitchell and Jacqueline Rose (New York: Norton, 1983), 27–
57. See also Stephen Heath's "Difference," *Screen* 19, no. 3 (1978), 51–112; and Jane
Gallop, *The Daughter's Seduction: Feminism and Psychoanalysis*.

[25] *Alice Doesn't: Feminism Semiotics Cinema* (Bloomington: Indiana University Press,
1984), 23. It should be added that many feminist theorists, including de Lauretis, have
increasingly returned to Freud's texts on sexual difference, on the grounds that they are
finally richer and more open to alternative readings than Lacan's texts on the same subject.

[26] *Spurs: Nietzsche's Styles*, trans. Barbara Harlow (Chicago: University of Chicago
Press, 1979), 59–61.

herself in the movie theater and elsewhere, some feminists have fruit-
fully returned to the idea of a pre-Oedipal psychic space, in effect refusing to go along with Freud in seeing femininity as a debased or
inherently incomplete version of masculinity. Others have been led to
ask, for example, why little boys and little girls do not perceive the
structural difference of the symbolic as a function of having/not having
breasts rather than having/not having a penis. This can be considered
a deconstructive strategy for the effect is to reverse the hierarchical
opposition male/female in which the first term is privileged. Here the
penis becomes that which makes the male different from (and thus, by
implication, inferior to) the female, who becomes the norm.[27] Of
course a simple overturning of a hierarchy is only one part of a deconstructive move; lest a new hierarchy be installed, the "new," "principle" category (breasts) must be problematized to subvert the operation
of the hierarchical system. The work of French theorist Luce Irigaray
is perhaps the most striking example of a feminist use or adaptation of
Derridean practice. She displaces the phallus/clitoris relation by positing the labia as the "basis" of female sexuality—but not just the lips of
the genitalia, for the very point about the lips is that they set up a
structure of duality that becomes plurality as it is doubled and repeated
throughout the body. This gesture thus rewrites a masculine logic of
singularity by valorizing the plural, the indirect, the diffuse, and so
on.[28] Given the interest shown in Derrida's work by French feminist
theorists, it is surprising that his name has not been more frequently
invoked by feminist film theory.

This neglect is symptomatic of the extent to which Derridean
thought has been elided from film theory in general, in spite of the fact
that literary criticism—which has generally led developments in film
criticism, at least until recently—has increasingly turned to decon-

---

[27] See especially *New French Feminisms*, ed. Elaine Marks and Isabelle Courtivron
(Amherst: University of Massachusetts Press, 1980) for a discussion of feminist theorists
who privilege the female infant's pre-Oedipal relation with the mother. See also *The
(M)Other Tongue: Essays in Feminist Psychoanalytic Interpretation*, ed. Shirley Nelson Garner, Claire Kahane, and Madelon Sprengnether (Ithaca: Cornell University Press, 1985).
In the specific area of film studies, see Gaylyn Studlar's "Masochism and the Perverse
Pleasures of the Cinema," reprinted in *Movies and Methods Volume II*, 602–21. Studlar
argues provocatively for differentiating masochism, which, following Gilles Deleuze,
she sees as representing a pre-Oedipal desire for reunion with the mother, from sadism,
which is Oedipal.

[28] See especially Luce Irigaray, *This Sex Which Is Not One*, trans. Catherine Porter
with Carolyn Burke (Ithaca: Cornell University Press, 1985). For a discussion of the
general impact of Derrida on feminist theory, see Alice Jardine, *Gynesis: Configurations
of Woman and Modernity* (Ithaca: Cornell University Press, 1985).

structive strategies over the last fifteen years or so. The reasons for this
state of affairs are related to the supposed apolitical and ahistorical nature of deconstruction. For one thing, most film criticism that has
sought to move beyond the level of film "appreciation" or formalist
interpretation has, unlike literary criticism, been overtly political in
nature.[29] This makes sense considering the close relationship between
film and certain economic realities, especially as embodied by Hollywood, as well as the obvious sociological questions film raises as one
of the mass media. In this regard, post-structuralist film theory has
always been quite explicit in its use of the discourse of liberation of one
variety or another. Another reason for the relative absence of Derrida
in film studies is that the crucial mediators between French and American film theorists were critics writing for the English journal *Screen*
during the seventies, most of whom came from a strong Marxist tradition and who took it as their task from the beginning to reconcile
politically progressive thinking with the kind of advanced psychoanalytic conceptualizations being worked out by Lacan. And rightly or
wrongly, and in spite of Michael Ryan's attempt to bring politics and
deconstruction together in his *Marxism and Deconstruction*,[30] most political film critics distrust what they consider the conservative streak of
the Yale School of J. Hillis Miller, Geoffrey Hartman, and the late Paul
de Man.[31] In our view the stumbling block that will always remain for
Marxists is that deconstruction does not allow *any* text to remove itself
from the play of difference, including even those political texts that
may "use" deconstructive techniques to analyze culture but that then
characteristically want to privilege their own discourse. What decon-

[29] In this sense, of course, film theory might easily be said to have led literary theory.
We do not have the space here to develop the complex history of the emergence of film
studies and film theory as academic disciplines. It seems possible to say, though, that
many literary theorists continue to regard film theory as a derivative branch of their own
discipline and remain unaware of the extent of the work done in the areas we are discussing. We would certainly not wish to encourage such condescension.

[30] (Baltimore: The Johns Hopkins University Press, 1982).

[31] The discovery of Paul de Man's wartime anti-Semitic journalism was made public
when this book was substantially complete. Given the complexity of the issue and the
fact that even as this book goes to press the pertinent information for a proper historical
judgment remains incomplete, we have decided that it would be inappropriate for us to
comment on this subject in the present context. We want to insist, however, that if Paul
de Man's work is seldom mentioned in this book it is not because we feel that his ideas
on deconstruction have been compromised by his wartime activities. Rather, it is because our book is meant primarily to be a study of a possible relation between Derrida
and film theory and because de Man's literary criticism seems to us, finally, less specifically or less immediately applicable to film theory than Derrida's more generalized theoretical explorations.

structionists have always insisted upon, to the understandable dismay of some, is that political texts as well are written in language and not in some unmediated metalanguage far above the fray. Furthermore, as Miller has pointed out in a discussion of literature that seems equally relevant to film, social-minded critics who want to take language for granted will always have to come back to it, simply because things and ideas will always have to be represented in words:

> The most resolute attempts to . . . . shift from the study of rela-tions of word with word to the study of relations of words with things or with subjectivities, will only lead back in the end to the study of language. . . . Any conceivable representation of the re-lations of words to things, powers, persons, modes of production and exchange, juridical or political systems (or whatever name the presumably non-linguistic may be given) will turn out to be one or another figure of speech. As such, it will require a rhetorical interpretation.[32]

Ryan has discussed in some detail how a deconstructionist reading of Marx might operate, developing the Althusserian idea of a hetero-geneous text, and has also provided some background to Derrida's po-sition on Marx. Perhaps too conscious of his readership, he wants to reconstruct a Derrida who goes through the experiences of 1968 to emerge as a self-confessed Marxist of some sort (44–46), but he has rightly pointed out that there is a strong materialist basis to Derridean thinking as well as an anti-monolithic, if not deconstructive, impulse in Marx.

In the interview in *Positions* (37–96) that is the traditional source for situating Derrida's politics[33]—an emphasis that unfortunately avoids engaging the detailed politics of his textual practice—it becomes clear that what his detractors object to is not only, or not so much, his rel-ative silence on the texts of Marx but his putative "rejection of history" (60). It is history that supposedly exists on the outside of discourse, as

---

[32] "The Search for Grounds in Literary Study," in *Rhetoric and Form: Deconstruction at Yale*, ed. Robert Con Davis and Ronald Schleifer (Norman: University of Oklahoma Press, 1985), 31.

[33] Some less well known but equally explicit remarks by Derrida are reported in *Les Fins de l'homme*, 526–27. He explains his "silence on Marxism" in terms of not wanting to participate in a concerted anti-Marxist current that existed in France at that time, in spite of his objections to a certain theoretical naivete and his distrust of the notion of revolution as a metaphysical concept. This deference, in our view, is in itself a political gesture. Derrida also discusses politics and his relation to Marxism at length in the in-terviews entitled "Entre crochets," *Digraphe*, no. 8 (April 1976), 97–114; and "Ja, ou le faux-bond," *Digraphe*, no. 11 (April 1977), 83–121.

the guarantor of the political, as that which should serve to bring to an end the indeterminacy of the signifier. Yet Derrida maintains that what he rejects, along with Althusser, is simply the idea of "one single history" (57–58): "I very *often* use the word 'history' in order to reinscribe its force and in order to produce another concept or conceptual chain of 'history': in effect a 'monumental, stratified, contradictory' history; a history that also implies a new logic of *repetition* and the *trace*, for it is difficult to see how there could be history without it" (57). Thus history is reinscribed rather than rejected in Derrida, for just as such a concept cannot be left unproblematized, neither can it be simply struck from the record. In the interview the word "history" becomes the basis of Derrida's reaffirmation of the double strategy of his critique (59–60).

It seems to us that whatever domestication of Derrida's work has taken place in America is due not so much (or not only) to a weakening of its political perspective but to the assumption that the complexity of his logic can be imported into a homogeneous form of discursivity that represses the more difficult side of his undertaking. But we do not expect that the exploitation of a more bifid form of deconstruction would be of any comfort to critics troubled by its supposed apoliticism, if the visceral comments of one like Terry Eagleton are anything to go by.[34] A close reading of such objections might disclose that it is not in fact apoliticism that is rankling here so much as a type of political thought that does not easily fit in with any of the reigning orthodoxies.

Thus we do not accept the view that deconstruction is unable to provide its own kind of political analysis. The example of recent texts by Derrida makes increasingly explicit what was always part of his critique, namely the ways in which authority and power constitute themselves through logocentric, oppositional hierarchies that a deconstructive strategy may then seek to reverse and displace. As long as politics has anything to do with structures of power and the workings of economies, Derrida's work has been addressing political questions. And increasingly, as we have suggested, Derrida has turned his attention toward the institutional and political ramifications of such founding concepts as reason. For example, in a provocative essay entitled "The Principle of Reason: The University in the Eyes of its Pupils"[35] Derrida's political analysis of the role of the university in so-called

---

[34] See, for example, Terry Eagleton, *Walter Benjamin, or, Towards a Revolutionary Criticism* (London: Verso, 1981), 131–42.

[35] *Diacritics* 13, no. 3 (Fall 1983), 3–20.

"pure" (versus "applied") research demonstrates that in the modern university the two categories have been collapsed, such that "never before has so-called basic scientific research been so deeply committed to aims that are at the same time military aims" (12). Even semioticians, literary critics, and philosophers can now be co-opted for "ideological warfare": "At the service of war, of national and international security, research programs have to encompass the entire field of information, the workings and thus also the essence of language and of all semiotic systems. . . . From now on, so long as it has the means, a military budget can invest in anything at all, in view of deferred profits: 'basic' scientific theory, the humanities, literary theory and philosophy" (13). For Derrida this situation has come about because even what has traditionally been considered "pure" research is itself unquestioningly committed to the "principle of reason," which is itself always a "principle of grounding, foundation or institution" (11) and which, as Heidegger has shown, is always intimately related to questions of science and technology. Furthermore it is Derrida's view that the metaphysical itself, from Aristotle onward, is complicit with the technical, and nowhere is this clearer than in the arena of information, usually taken to be neutral and value free. As Heidegger demonstrates, according to Derrida, "information does not inform merely by delivering an information content, it gives form, 'in-formiert' . . . it installs man in a form that permits him to ensure his mastery on earth and beyond. All this has to be pondered as the effect of the principle of reason . . ." (14).

What then should be the response to this co-optation of the humanities by the utilitarian aims of the social, political, military, and industrial powers that the university serves? Derrida implies that those who attempt to analyze "the structures of the simulacrum or of literary fiction," who investigate "the effects of undecidability" or "a poetic rather than an informative value of language"—in short, those who practice "deconstruction" (though he never uses the word[36])—have an important role to play:

> Those analysts . . . are interested in possibilities that arise at the outer limits of the authority and the power of the principle of reason. On that basis they may attempt to define new responsibilities in the face of the university's total subjection to the technologies of informatization. Not so as to refuse them; not so as to counter

---

[36] Except in a footnote, quoting the National Endowment for the Humanities Chairman as one of two highly placed representatives of institutions who perceive it as so much of a threat that they resort to "ignorance and irrationality" in order to defend the university as locus of knowledge and rationality (15). We take up this matter below.

with some obscurantist irrationalism (and irrationalism, like nihilism, is a posture that is completely symmetrical to, thus dependent on, the principle of reason). (14–15)

There will of course always be those who are opposed to "these new
modes of questioning that are also a new relation to language and tradition" and that Derrida does not hesitate to call "a new *affirmation*,
and new ways of taking responsibility" (15).

The comments Derrida makes in this regard highlight the ill-informed perception of deconstruction within a certain segment of literary studies. Derrida argues that "obscurantist irrationalism" and "nihilism," the sort of epithets often attributed to deconstruction, more
clearly belong to those ardent defenders of the institutional status quo
who are willing to drop their dearly held principles to "heap insults
and say whatever comes into their heads" (15) in response to the perceived threat of something like deconstruction. The radicality of deconstruction thus lies not in its irresponsibility but rather in its very
pertinent insistence on interrogating the grounding of its own discourse and that of the institution in general.

In reaffirming the need for a well-developed set of strategies in order
to practice this mode of questioning and in order to take this new responsibility—new not because it has never been done before (indirect
models cited later are Kant, Nietzsche, and Heidegger) but because it
resists an orthodoxy—Derrida returns to the idea of a "double gesture," an idea we have tried to emphasize:

> They [deconstructionists] may continue to assume *within* the uni-
> versity, along with its memory and tradition, the imperative of
> professional rigor and competence. There is a double gesture
> here, a double postulation: to ensure professional competence and
> the most serious tradition of the university even while going as
> far as possible, theoretically and practically, in the most directly
> underground thinking about the abyss beneath the university.[37]
> . . . "Thought" requires *both* the principle of reason *and* what is
> beyond the principle of reason, the *arkhe* and an-archy. Between
> the two, the difference of a breath or an accent, only the *enactment*
> of this "thought" can decide. That decision is always risky, it al-
> ways risks the worst. (17, 18–19)

Since the university is itself in a supplementary position to a society
that wants to keep it outside itself and yet remain in complete control

[37] Derrida refers throughout the essay to the location and topography of the Cornell
campus where he is delivering this address as professor-at-large.

of it, and since through this supplementarity the university is said somehow to "reflect" society, Derrida proposes exploiting the double sense of *reflection*—following the logic of the supplement—both to take advantage of the freedom of contemplation and to analyze the modes of seeing involved.

Derrida's emphasis on the political importance of deconstruction in the context of institutionalized thinking, especially that of the university, is repeated in other texts of the last few years. In his essay in the "Nuclear Criticism" issue of *Diacritics*[38] he comes back to the role of the humanities within the military-industrial complex and their particular relation to nuclear war in terms of the representation of fictions. Derrida has also been actively involved in what might be considered the more practical consequences of his position as a state-employed professor of philosophy. For example, he was an active participant during the 1970s in a group called "Groupe de recherches sur l'enseignement philosophique" (GREPH), a response to the Haby reform in France by which the Minister of Education sought to restrict the teaching of philosophy in secondary schools. Derrida's later participation in the *Etats généraux de la philosophie*,[39] a national meeting of philosophers convened to resist the so-called reforms, comes out of this. In his very practical and specific remarks included in the collective text he is particularly aware of the power of the media. He complains that if the capacity for critical thinking is weakened and marginalized by restrictions on the teaching of philosophy—not that the teaching of philosophy has itself always addressed that concern—manipulation and control will be easier than ever thanks to the power of the telecommunicational media: "In short, the more that philosophical training is curtailed in this country, the less critical competence there will be outside of the educational institution" (41; our translation). Yet it is this very competence that can serve as "an arm of resistance (for example against all violations of human rights, abuse of police power, and injustice)" (41). Just as Derrida pointed to the complementarity of institutional powers and those who resort to a type of nihilism in rejecting deconstruction as an interrogation of that power, so here he finds a similar collusion between the "most immobile, most uptight" kind of academic teaching of philosophy and the new popularizers, neither of whom would find the philosophy class to be the appropriate place to discuss official education policy or telecommunicational apparatuses.

[38] "No Apocalypse, Not Now (full speed ahead, seven missiles, seven missives)," *Diacritics* 14, no. 2 (Summer 1984), 20–31.

[39] (Paris: Flammarion, 1979).

As a final reference to Derrida's explicit political interventions in the name of deconstruction we should mention the exchange concerning apartheid that took place in the pages of *Critical Inquiry* during 1985 and 1986. In a lyrical, even moving piece called "Racism's Last Word" Derrida discusses the relation between language and a brutal political reality. He points out that "no tongue has ever translated this name [*apartheid*]—as if all the languages of the world were defending themselves, shutting their mouths against a sinister incorporation of the thing by means of the word . . ." (292). This comparison between apartheid as political practice and certain operations of language becomes the basis of Derrida's article, a contribution to the catalogue of an international exhibition of art dedicated to a free South Africa (and destined to travel the globe in exile until it can be donated to such a place). Insisting that "there's no racism without a language" (292), he explains that this in no way means violence only takes place in words but that violence is a function of man as a talking animal, one capable of naming, dividing, inscribing, prescribing, marking off space, and closing borders. And taking the sense of the word (meaning "separateness," the word itself has been kept separate) he shows apartheid to be a reflection of the contradictions upon which Western culture in general is constructed. The relation between deconstructive thinking and political realities could not be clearer here, and when two writers reply with the familiar charges of apoliticism, claiming that at best Derrida is failing to recognize the relation between language and history and at worst advocating a laissez-faire attitude toward apartheid, Derrida reacts more strongly than ever, uncovering yet another collusion between conservatives and so-called militants:

> On one side and the other, people get impatient when they see that deconstructive practices are also and first of all political and institutional practices. They get impatient when they see that these practices are perhaps more radical and certainly less stereotyped than others, less easy to decipher, less in keeping with well-used models whose wear and tear ends up by letting one see the abstraction, the conventionalism, the academism, and everything that separates, as you would say, words and history. On one side and the other . . . there is an interest in believing, in pretending to believe, or simply in making others believe that the "text" which concerns "deconstructionists" . . . can be found neatly in its place on some library shelves . . . in order to act (!) in the area of *real* politics, in history (!), these poor "deconstructionists"

should go *"beyond* the text," into the field, to the front! As you do I suppose. ("But Beyond," 168–69)

The suggestion that deconstruction is being made the victim of a form of intellectual apartheid is expanded upon as the language gets less and less amicable in the final paragraphs.[40]

If all of the above is not political thinking, political engagement, whether in a traditional sense or not, it is difficult to know what is. Of course, as we have already suggested, even if the political force of Derrida's work is admitted, detractors of deconstruction will claim that this force is completely vitiated in the work of his American followers. Yet the work that Paul de Man was engaged upon at the time of his death sought to understand ideology, through the tradition of philosophical aesthetics—he had already written on Hegel's *Aesthetics* and Kant's *Third Critique*—by means of the insights that the latter could provide about epistemology and thus about the way we conceptualize politics.[41] Similarly, Barbara Johnson in her recent book, *A World of Difference*, expressly considers "the possible political functions of undecidability," pointing out that the left's attacks on deconstruction have been welcomed by the right because "nothing could be more comforting to the established order than the requirement that everything be assigned a clear meaning or stand."[42] Furthermore, Johnson argues, deconstruction can be more attentive to historically marginalized voices (for example to the voices of the black women writers to whom part of her book is devoted), because it preserves the otherness in what is written. She asks: "Isn't each radical theoretical revolution . . . a reinvention of what reading is, such that the formerly unvoiced speaks and is heard?" (31). In a provocative concluding essay on abortion and the figure of apostrophe in poetry, Johnson points out: "It is often said, in literary-theoretical circles, that to focus on undecidability is apolitical. Everything I have read about the abortion controversy in

[40] For a more recent and more dispassionate intervention on the question of apartheid, see Derrida's "The Laws of Reflection: Nelson Mandela, in Admiration," in *For Nelson Mandela*, ed. Jacques Derrida and Mustapha Tleli (New York: Seaver Books/Henry Holt and Co., 1987), 13–42.

[41] See for example "Hegel on the Sublime," in *Displacement: Derrida and After*, ed. Mark Krupnick (Bloomington: Indiana University Press, 1983). There de Man makes the claim that "aesthetic theory [in Kant] is critical philosophy to the second degree, the critique of the critiques. It critically examines the possibility and modalities of political discourse and political action, the inescapable burden of any linkage between discourse and action. The treatment of the aesthetic in Kant is certainly far from conclusive, but one thing is clear: it is epistemological as well as political through and through" (140).

[42] *A World of Difference* (Baltimore: The Johns Hopkins University Press, 1987), 30–31.

its present form in the United States leads me to suspect that, on the contrary, the undecidable *is* the political. There is politics precisely because there is undecidability" (193–94).

It is clear, then, that both Derrida and many of his Anglo-American counterparts deeply consider the political in their work. But even more important, perhaps, is the new perspective on the nature of history and ideology, which is without doubt central to a politically informed film theory, that deconstructive thinking can provide. An important starting place in this regard is a recent book by Australian literary theorist John Frow called *Marxism and Literary History*.[43] Though he claims at one point that the politics of many deconstructionists "tends to be a version of Nietzschean romanticism" (31) (and one might argue that his formulation is a contradiction in terms), Frow makes clear that the theoretical and by extension the political potential of deconstruction is great. Thus he criticizes Fredric Jameson's insistence in *The Political Unconscious*[44] on preserving a notion of a "real world" always prior to textuality (thus claiming history is *not* a text), while admitting that we can only get to history through a process of textualization. As Frow points out, "This is surely a case of having one's referent and eating it too" (38). His larger point then becomes:

> If history is accessible only through discursive or epistemological categories, is there not a real sense in which it therefore only has discursive existence? In which its very otherness, its excess over the textual, is still a textual construct? But the really important question, I think, is why there should be any *necessity* for Marxism to ground its politics in an appeal to a transcendental realm prior to any mediation. . . . (38)

According to Frow, Terry Eagleton, like Jameson, continues to make "nostalgic references to the referent" and wants to ground "Marxist politics in a category of History which would be external to its discursive mediations" (46). For Frow, this seeking after an extrasemiotic, ontological ground for political structures of power inhibits our understanding of the workings of power through discursive systems; rather, Eagleton and other Marxist theorists must accept the challenge offered by various post-structuralists, including Derrida, "to rethink the status of the dialectic and to build a semiotic politics on the ruins of a metaphysics" (50).

[43] (Cambridge: Harvard University Press, 1986).
[44] *The Political Unconscious: Narrative as a Socially Symbolic Act* (Ithaca: Cornell University Press, 1980).

A certain anxiety about what such a semiotic politics might be seems to emerge from an article by Philip Rosen representing one of the rare cases in which a film theorist deals directly with Derridean thinking.[45] Though generally sympathetic with a theoretical critique of the sign, Rosen is concerned that "For political analysis and evaluation of the sign to be possible, there must be something regulating the play of difference that is accessible in our discourse and allows a conception of the determinations of that play in its textual specificities. To conceptualize the politics of the sign, we seem to need a conception of an 'outside' at work 'inside' signs" (10). Rosen discusses two discursive practices as potentially permitting that sort of regulation of the play of difference. The first is Barthes's notion (from *Writing Degree Zero*) of a mode of writing that "represents a specific relation between creation and society" (Rosen, 15); the second concerns psychoanalytic theories of subject positioning "inseparable from the larger question of conceptualizing human agency in history" (19). In each case, society and history stand, as for Jameson and Eagleton, as the referents of final recourse, the undefined and unproblematized outsides that can only be made to function within the sign through some sort of surreptitious metaphysical intervention. For Rosen, "writing cannot be divorced from the sociality of its situation" (17), but what he forgets is that the "sociality" of the situation of writing is itself, always already *written*, constituted differentially, forever implicated in a mediated textuality.

What actually constitutes the political in Rosen's terms can only be guessed at. But a closer reading of Derrida's textual practice might have recognized that Derrida's politics is as explicit as Barthes's in advocating that "to struggle on the level of modes of writing is to struggle on the level of institutionalization" (Rosen, 17). Of course that becomes unavoidably clear in the more recent texts we have just discussed, but it is something that informs just as powerfully the terms of Derrida's first critique of the sign.

To return to Frow, the semiotic politics he advocates involves rethinking the very nature of ideology. Even in revised Marxist thinking ideology is often seen as error or false consciousness, but, as Frow

---

[45] "The Politics of the Sign and Film Theory," *October*, no. 17 (Summer 1981), 2–21. Interestingly, Rosen notes that "though his work is not very often explicitly cited in film theory, Derrida's arguments, or something like them, are evident in the work of those more commonly cited as theorists of the sign, such as Kristeva and Barthes" (6–7). And later: "Given the ideological and institutional role of the cinematic apparatus . . . as an imprinting machine, it may be that the cinema provides an especially productive site for exploring the ideological dispositions of the metaphysics of presence deconstructed by Derrida" (8). That is precisely the position we develop in later chapters.

points out, this view necessitates a position of authority, a position always complicitous with power. The conventional view of ideology also divides phenomena into the real and the symbolic; Frow wants rather to see the real as "a texture of symbolic systems," following a post-structuralist view of textuality, and, conversely, to regard the symbolic as something having real effects.[46]

Finally, in spelling out his requirements for a "working theory of ideology," it is clear how compatible Frow's thinking is with a deconstructive theory of textuality:

> First, that it not assert a relationship of truth to falsity (and so to its own mastery over error) but concern rather the production and the conditions of production of categories and entities within the field of discourse. Second, that it not deduce the ideological from the structure of economic forces or, directly, from the class positions of real subjects of utterance; that it theorize the category of subject not as origin of utterance but as its effect. Third, that it not be an ontology of discourse deriving effects of meaning from formal structure, but rather theorize the multiple and variable limits within which relations of power and knowledge are produced. (61)

The implications of this kind of conceptualization for film theory, especially the sort that concerns itself with questions of politics and ideology, seem to us to be very large indeed. Currently too many leftists seem to combat the absolute presences of oppressive systems with other absolute presences that are really only their symmetrical opposites and are therefore involved in the same constricting economy. Deconstruction demonstrates that specific interventions in political struggles must go hand in hand with attempts to rethink the ways in which political problems themselves are conceived. Michael Ryan, in an il-

---

[46] Frow also criticizes the idea of a fixed subject that is inherent in conventional views of ideology: "What is assumed in the thesis of ideology as a representation of an alienated reality is, first of all, preconstituted subjects who represent to themselves an objectivity which presents meaning directly to them; and second, that there is a necessary congruence between the subjects' position in the production process and their ideological position" (56). Along with Althusser, he sees ideology as "a product of social determinations" but goes further in considering it "discontinuous with the structure of production. It is not the expression or the transformation of a concealed deep structure (the structure of production which would be its secret truth). Rather, it represents the intrication of relatively self-contained semiotic systems in the field of antagonistic class relations rooted in relations of production" (56). For another discussion concerning Marx's representation of ideology, matters of cinema, and a deconstructive analysis of rhetorical operations see Sarah Kofman, *Camera obscura: De l'idéologie.*

luminating chapter of *Marxism and Deconstruction* called "The Metaphysics of Everyday Life," states that "the deconstruction of metaphysics can be integrated with the critique of ideology because
metaphysics is the infrastructure of ideology" (117). As Ryan describes
it, capitalist ideology cannot function without such "natural" oppositions as mental/manual, public/private (both of which depend, like so
much else, on the opposition of inside/outside, an opposition we shall
consider in more detail in later chapters), nor without such undiffer-
entiated, supposedly homogeneous presences as "the people," or "the
Third World," which deconstruction can help us to dismantle.[47] Feminists like those already mentioned have used deconstructive strategies
to understand the "internal" differences *within* the concepts "male" and
"female" rather than passively accepting differences *between* these supposedly stable entities. What is there of the male in the female and vice
versa? How might the so-called marginal areas of hermaphrodism and
homosexuality challenge this division even further? One must be in-
tent on altering power relations, in other words, but these relations can
never be altered if we continue to view the elements within them as
hierarchically dependent according to a logocentric model of reasoning, no matter which term of the opposition is privileged.

We have devoted so much time in this chapter to a discussion of the
political potential of deconstruction because we are convinced that it is
especially the misunderstanding of this potential that has made deconstruction so unpalatable to many film theorists. In the following chapter we turn our attention more specifically to a discussion of Derrida's
ideas in relation to film studies as presently constituted.

[47] For further discussion see also Michael Ryan, "Deconstruction and Social Theory,"
in *Displacement: Derrida and After*, 154–68.

CHAPTER TWO

DERRIDA
AND CONTEMPORARY FILM
STUDIES

Having considered Derrida's ideas from the more general point of view of politics and, to some extent, psychoanalysis, we now want to look more specifically at the various ways in which a deconstructive perspective on film studies may alter the terrain of that discipline. We shall consider questions directly pertaining to cinematic representation and such obviously cinematic notions as the image and the frame in later chapters, but here we want to take up those assumptions and prior formulations that currently ground film theory and criticism in general. It is not our intention, in what must remain a cursory analysis, to "correct," let alone dismiss, what is a large body of diverse work within a growing discipline. We seek rather to outline some general questions that remain unanswered (or unposed) in both traditional approaches to the study of film—histories and genre studies, for example—and those informed by a more theoretical approach; questions upon which the work of Derrida has shed light.

Surveying the field, one quickly discovers that much serious writing about film is based upon a constant, enabling assumption concerning the possibility of accurately describing different kinds of *totalities*. In other words, film history and film interpretation, especially, rely on the assumption that both the body of films to be classified historically and the individual films to be interpreted are in some way comprehensible wholes, complete unto themselves. It is understood, of course, that the goal of a "complete" description will always remain virtual, never truly attainable; yet the assumption that such a description is at least theoretically possible provides the motivating force for much work in film studies. The description of these entities thus always at least aims to be all inclusive and is underwritten by a teleology providing the completion and closure that any specific study must always admit to lack in absolute terms.[1]

[1] Derrida takes up this matter in his analysis of Lévi-Strauss (*Writing and Difference*,

33

Thus in film criticism, as in literary criticism, the understanding or interpretation of a text taken to be the best is usually the one that manages to explain the greatest number of particular textual details.[2] Similarly, when abstract, generalized theories about how we watch films or how we make sense of them come to be articulated, it is usually assumed that the theorist is trying to make rules or principles that apply to all films, or to all the films within a specifically demarcated category. Accompanying this constant assumption of totalization is the force of a certain epistemological violence. Paradoxically, totalization is, after all, only another word for finding an essence, or "discovering" a truth, through the suppression of elements deemed to be "inessential" and thus irrelevant to truth. This operation usually takes the form of a marginalization of the "unimportant" or, as Derrida shows in "Signature Event Context," his analysis of Austin's *How to Do Things with Words*, the "non-serious." In the case of individual texts, moreover, it is usually forgotten that even to speak of "textual elements" that can or cannot be readily accommodated to an interpretation or a theory is already to presuppose a great deal, for these elements are not simply lying around in the text waiting to be picked up. In fact, such details often come to be individuated in the process of looking for evidence to prove a point; what one is looking for often determines what is found. If, as we shall see later on, even the integrity of individual texts and the boundaries between them are not as fixed as we might like, since inside and outside can never be definitively established, the very existence of the entity under study is called into question.

Let us now look at some particular instances of these totalizing assumptions. Most immediately, such strategies can be recognized in the writing of film history. In the last few decades, we have come to un-

---

278–93), where he argues that the realization of the impossibility of totalization can be construed in two different ways. First it can be regarded as "the empirical endeavor of a finite subject or discourse panting after an infinite richness that it can never master" (289; English translation marred by a number of omissions on this page, translation modified. Cf. *L'Ecriture et la différence* [Paris: Seuil, 1967], 423). Alternatively, the failure of totalization can be attributed not to an infinite field under examination by a finite discourse but to the fact that the field itself is one "of infinite substitutions" within a finite ensemble lacking "a center which arrests and grounds the play of substitutions" (289). For Derrida, these are only variations on a theme, important though their differences might be, for both dream of and assume a resolution of nontotalization, either by transcendence to totality or by reduction to a centralized stability.

[2] Obviously we are not arguing against the collection of textual data, or details as such, as a basis for any commentary. Rather we would hold that there is no minimal basis any more than there is a maximal basis for a reading and that there are ways of treating or processing textual data other than in terms of the totalizing gesture referred to here. What some of these ways are should become clear in the rest of our discussion.

derstand more clearly that film history, like any other history, is also always a narrative, and thus both "distorted" (not that a truly "pure" history would ever be possible, either) and enabled by the constraints of narrative structure and technique. As Hayden White has pointed out in his recent book *The Content of the Form*, "narrative is not merely a neutral discursive form that may or may not be used to represent real events in their aspect as developmental processes but rather entails ontological and epistemic choices with distinct ideological and even specifically political implications."[3] Furthermore, in all historical narratives historians quite willingly, even happily, seek out heroes and villains or, perhaps more likely in historical narratives concerning the arts, creative geniuses and commerce-minded hacks, in order to propel their readers through what can only be called these "stories." (Interestingly, the word "story" is more negatively charged and thus perhaps more revealing than the more neutral term "narrative."[4]) These narratives are also nearly always marked by versions of Freytag's triangle, causing the historian to impose upon the often disparate and random particulars of the past familiar literary patterns of exposition, rising action, climax, and denouement. The excuse offered is that this is the only way to "make sense" of history and its countless particulars, but it is likely that what makes for a good story is not always what makes for the most convincing truth claim, the claim that one has captured the "most important features" (that is, the essence) of an age, period, government, country, and so on—in other words, the way things "really were" and what those things "really meant." Furthermore, history writing is often directed by a covert teleological project: the fact that we know the outcome of history has a powerful impact on the way the story is told. For example, the triumph of Renaissance humanism now seems to have been inevitable, although at the time it was merely one within a complex network of disparate historical forces. History is usually portrayed as the result of a series of events that were in some inexplicable, almost mysterious way preordained; rarely is it conceived of dynamically, as a combination of various historical and political forces that did not prevail naturally.

Besides its recourse to narrative, history, including film history (and film theory and interpretation, for that matter) also relies on certain

[3] Hayden White, *The Content of the Form* (Baltimore: The Johns Hopkins University Press, 1987), ix. See also Roland Barthes, "The Discourse of History," trans. Stephen Bann, in *Comparative Criticism: A Yearbook*, vol.3, ed. E.S. Schaffer (Cambridge: Cambridge University Press, 1981), 3–20.

[4] Note that the Romance languages preserve the Latin (*historia*), which unites both concepts within the same word.

unrecognized rhetorical operations such as synecdoche and metonymy. These come into play, for example, when certain films are taken as being "representative" or "typical" of the thirties, the eighties, German expressionism, the Western, and so on. (The same thing occurs in formalist interpretation when certain frames, shots, or sequences are individuated and cited as being representative of the text as a whole, as being central to its meaning.[5]) The very nature of this typicality is problematic, of course, and is closely related to the complicated status of the "example" itself. In what way can a part legitimately stand for a whole? What about other elements of the example—there is always a surplus—that remain as a kind of residue? If this independent entity (the example)—whether it be a phrase, a passage, or a "work"—is always constituted in its uniqueness as a singular event, how can it be essentialized in order to stand for something else? As Derrida asks in *Signsponge*, how does one "cite a text, an example in a demonstration, if every text is unique, the example of nothing other ever . . . ?"[6]

In film history the inchoate mass of details of nearly a century of filmmaking, including thousands upon thousands of films, are reduced and fitted to the Procrustean bed of historical narrative. Certain recurring themes, motifs, patterns, or structures are found to run through the gross, random particulars of the last hundred years in ways that "make sense" of these particulars. Those films and those events in filmmaking finally deemed important are those exemplifying the same patterns and their underlying structures.

The same essentializing gesture, or repression of difference, reappears in the use to which periodization is put in film history, for the periods thus created can never be more than virtual sites utilized for convenience. According to Barbara Johnson in *The Critical Difference*, deconstruction reveals that in the Western tradition differences *within* are inevitably recast as differences *between*,[7] and this is nowhere more true than in our description of "1930s film" or of such self-identical "movements" as Soviet montage or French New Wave. For example, critics have spent much time in fruitless argument trying to fix chronological, formal, stylistic, and political borders between movements and periods. Endless pages have been devoted, especially in Italy, to various ill-fated attempts to decide once and for all when neorealism

[5] Again, we do not suggest that citation is avoidable but argue (and in much more detail later) for a radicalization of citation and representativeness that subverts the will to centrality.

[6] *Signéponge/Signsponge*, trans. Richard Rand (New York: Columbia University Press, 1984), 20.

[7] *The Critical Difference*, x–xi.

really began (with Rossellini's *Open City* [1945] or *Paisan* [1946], Visconti's *Ossessione* [1942], or even earlier?) and when it really ended (with De Sica's *Umberto D.* [1952] or his *Il Tetto* [1956], or is it still alive today in filmmakers like Olmi?). "Within" the period, Roy Armes has even gone so far as to call one of the episodes of Rossellini's *Paisan* a "remove from true neo-realist practice"[8] because it contains a flashback sequence, which, according to him, excludes it from the category. Similarly, most Italian critics have wanted to see Rossellini as a realist and, having to deal with such "artificial," brooding, heavily stylized films as *Una voce umana*, *La macchina ammazzacattivi*, and certain of the Bergman era films (films that can hardly be considered realist), have dismissed them as unimportant failures because they do not fit the paradigm.[9]

An examination of various general histories of film is also instructive in this regard. David Cook's *A History of Narrative Film*, John L. Fell's *A History of Film*, David Robinson's *The History of World Cinema*, and Jack C. Ellis's *A History of Film*[10] all repeat almost exactly the same historical categories as those referred to earlier. Now it is hardly possible that the same groupings could be found over and over, empirically, from the raw cinematic material of the tens of thousands of films that have been made since 1895. Within these categories themselves the same sort of essentializing operation is repeated, always under the rubric of "general characteristics." Thus, Ellis has this to say in his discussion of German expressionism: "Looking at these German films of 1919–25 as a body, film historians have identified three prominent types and themes that make most evident most of the major German contributions. First were . . ." (87). A curiously circular logic is at work. For one thing, it is clear that no one has ever actually looked at all the German films produced between 1919 and 1925 "as a body"; rather, various critics have looked at all or most of the films that have over the course of the decades been instituted into the canon of "German expressionism." But why have these films been included? Besides those films that entered the canon out of sheer historical and economic accident, most were probably included because they exemplify certain traits of the German films of this period that have come, for a host of

[8] *Patterns of Realism* (Totowa, N.J.: A. S. Barnes, 1971), 77.

[9] For a discussion of the "neorealism" of Rossellini see Peter Brunette, *Roberto Rossellini* (New York: Oxford University Press, 1987), 41–106.

[10] David Cook, *A History of Narrative Film* (New York: Norton, 1981); John L. Fell, *A History of Film* (New York: Holt, Rinehart and Winston, 1979); David Robinson, *The History of World Cinema* (New York: Stein and Day, 1981); and Jack C. Ellis, *A History of Film*, 2nd ed. (Englewood Cliffs, N.J.: Prentice-Hall, 1985).

cultural, social, historical, and political reasons not necessarily related to the films themselves, to seem significant. When such films are examined by subsequent historians, they not surprisingly comprise "three prominent types" and so on, which is why they were included in the first place.[11]

Aside from the question of periodization, these histories openly work to essentialize a category known as mainstream narrative film. Cook, for example, excludes documentary, animation, and experimental film because "the language common to the international cinema from the last decade of the nineteenth century through the present has been narrative in both aspiration and structural form" (xix), without considering that the cinematic modes he excludes are almost always themselves also narrative. These forms are surely part of our historical experience of film as well—can one conceive of the origins and early history of film without giving thought to the "documentary" films of the Lumière brothers? But in order that a coherent historical narrative be constructed, all "non-narrative" films must be marginalized, implicitly or explicitly confined to the category of the unimportant and placed outside of history. They form the "other" that retrospectively is then used to constitute mainstream narrative film as some kind of distinguishable entity held up as a totality ready for description.

In addition, hierarchical distinctions between such impossible to specify categories as realism vs. expressionism, open vs. closed form, and montage vs. long take are invariably relied upon in such histories (and even more so in the interpretation of individual films) to make sense of things. But when examined more closely, especially in the context of specific films, the integrity of these categories disintegrates. Louis D. Giannetti, for example, relies upon a distinction between open and closed form in his widely used textbook *Understanding Movies*,[12] but anyone who has ever used his text in a class knows how many

[11] A more sophisticated attempt to deal with the problem of periodization is made in David Bordwell, Janet Staiger, and Kristin Thompson, *The Classical Hollywood Cinema: Film Style and Mode of Production to 1960* (New York: Columbia University Press, 1985). In Bordwell's introduction he admits that "historical analysis demands a concept of periodization" (9). However, he will not assume regular historical periods like the forties or post–World War II; instead he bases analyses on an idea of prevailing "norms, yes; but also the film industry, the most proximate and pertinent institution for creating, regulating, and maintaining these norms" (9). It is our contention, expanded upon below, that even a more complicated effort to periodize such as this is inevitably founded upon arbitrary exclusions, marginalizations, and so on.

[12] *Understanding Movies*, 3rd ed. (Englewood Cliffs, N.J.: Prentice-Hall, 1982). Giannetti claims on the one hand that "there are no movies that are completely open or closed

films students can find—Chaplin's *The Gold Rush*, for example—whose elements (often the *same* elements) can be described as either open or closed. Using a similar strategy, Ellis at one point tries to distinguish sharply between German expressionism and American realism—a commonsense distinction, of course—but to today's average spectators, 1930s American films, with their phony sets, artificial lighting, and highly literate, polished dialogue delivered with unnatural diction, look as expressionist as their German counterparts. What then anchors such classifications so as to make them valid distinguishing categories throughout the course of history? Apparently, very little.

It is important to keep in mind that these historians are not making some sort of mistake that better historiography could rectify, nor are they unaware of the pitfalls facing them. John L. Fell, in *A History of Film*, rhetorically asks "What, in fact, is the 'history' of a commercial art like the movies? It depends on the historian" (vii) but then proceeds to duplicate the most common historical categories. David Robinson, in *The History of World Cinema*, admits: "I can only hope that most of the time I have found some sort of logic to the story. Not that there is invariably logic in history. It is every historian's ambition to capture the sweep of history. Unfortunately, history is inclined to leap, hobble, double back, repeat itself, stop still, and indeed do anything in the world but sweep" (xv). Again, though, this does not keep Robinson from trying in turn to rewrite history's discontinuous leaps and hobbles as a smooth sweep in his own book. Ellis stresses that no two histories can be the same—"this is *a* history of film. . . . The indefinite article should indicate that this is only one kind of film history. . . . There are many valid and illuminating ways to approach the subject" (xi)—yet he goes on to produce the same tired categories in his table of contents. He at least attempts a justification of sorts for the reproduction of these categories:

> Among film scholars and critics it is generally agreed that for brief periods certain countries made seminal contributions to the evolution of film form and content. Of course, there are brilliant individual film makers who exist outside the construct, and coun-

---

in form, only works that tend toward these polarities" and that these concepts "should be applied only when [they] are relevant and helpful in understanding what actually exists in a movie"; in the next paragraph, however, he goes on to say that "Realist filmmakers tend to employ open forms, while Expressionists veer toward closed" (75). The oppositions open/closed and realist/expressionist, in other words, are used to prop each other up, and whenever one opposition is questioned, the other can fill in the gap.

tries whose achievements are parallel. Even admitting the
Procrustean limitations of any kind of history scheme, this one
has proven serviceable and does permit variation and amendment
with relative ease. (xii)

Notice first Ellis's appeal—one that is commonly heard—to a notion
of the "evolution of film form and content," which evokes, once again,
a teleological trope of organic growth and development that may have
nothing to do with the historical particulars of the medium. But just
as importantly, what does it mean for a scheme to be "serviceable?"
Doesn't any history inevitably make a truth claim that this is the way
it happened, this is what is important, these are the patterns worth
noticing? To fall back on a notion of serviceability, however intellectually honest it might be, also ends up calling the historian's entire
project into question. Finally, the ease with which such a scheme permits "variation and amendment" is irrelevant, for the addition of any
new historical particulars is unlikely to have the slightest effect on the
static categories that will always necessarily determine the ways in
which these particulars are incorporated into film history.

In spite of the comments of these film historians concerning the obvious relativity of historical periodization, their practice discloses the
assumption that somewhere behind it all the total history already exists
and waits to be revealed. While various written forms of film history
may, in principle, differ (though in actuality they rarely do), the "history" itself, as a kind of totality of all the films ever made, is seen as a
consistent, self-contained entity available for some form of description, no matter how incomplete and flawed. For example, Ellis is concerned with articulating film history's "parts in relation to its whole"
(xii). As we have said, however, no one has even begun to approach a
true empirical study of the whole body of films and, especially since
over half of the 21,000 American films made before 1951, for example,
have, by Ellis's own count, already been destroyed (6), no one ever
will. Are these missing films also a part of film history? Furthermore,
of the thousands of films that remain, only a small percentage are chosen for discussion or even mention. But on what basis? That of quality,
however it might be measured? As any festival goer knows, each year
hundreds of excellent films are produced around the world that, for
one reason or another (usually economic), will not be purchased for
international distribution, thus effectively eliminating them from film
history.

The same operation of relegation seems to be at work in *The Classical Hollywood Cinema*, by David Bordwell, Kristin Thompson, and

Janet Staiger. As is indicated in the title, "Hollywood" as a category is essentialized from the very beginning, for it is assumed that Hollywood films have sufficient common characteristics to warrant recognition as such. Now that makes obvious sense in terms of the economic means of production or the geographical location of studios for a certain period of American cinema, but the authors go further, insisting on regarding "Hollywood filmmaking from 1917–60 as a unified mode of film practice" produced within "a coherent system whereby aesthetic norms and the mode of film production reinforced one another." For them, "this argument is the basis of this book" (xiv), and although these factors may change through time, "certain fundamental aspects will remain constant" (xiv). Recourse to the idea of a self-identical, coherent system is frequent, along with a concomitant desire for totalization: "The Hollywood mode of film practice constitutes an integral system, including persons and groups but also rules, films, machinery, documents, institutions, work processes, and theoretical concepts. It is this totality that we shall study" (xiii). Furthermore, in order to back up the claim that the Hollywood film constitutes a system, Bordwell (who signs this introduction) repeats the standard categories of the film histories discussed above, appealing to the idea of a "group style" and specifically naming German expressionism, Soviet montage, and the French New Wave as examples. Later, in order to preserve the integrity of the category, elaborate arguments must be adduced to reintegrate the obvious "deviants" of *film noir* and Hollywood auteurist cinema (77ff.).

In attempting to reconstruct the "norm" of the Hollywood classical cinema and thereby establish its boundaries, the authors will presumably have recourse to an empirical investigation. But a strange logic soon sets in. Though their argument "makes use of a great deal of empirical data about filmmaking" (xv), their description of Hollywood film practice, they claim, is not arrived at simply by looking at films and documents: "For rhetorical purposes, our argument is cast chronologically, but the idea of a 'classical Hollywood cinema' is ultimately a theoretical construct and as such must be judged by criteria of logical rigor and instrumental value. The book thus stands out not only as a history of the Hollywood cinema but also as an attempt to articulate a theoretical approach to film history" (xv). "Theoretical" seems here to mean nonempirical, but then we are led to ask what descriptive value their work may justly claim. Is this a description of what Hollywood films were actually like or is it just a theoretical construct, a model? On the following page, then, Bordwell states that while a historical argument for a Hollywood style will be made later, "at this point, a prima facie case for a 'classical Hollywood style' depends upon critically examining a body of films" (3)—back to an empirical study, in other words. A curious economy has thus developed between empiricism on the one hand and theory on the other. Though Bordwell seems to accept their interdependence, he never confronts the contradictions that this entails and continues to give priority to one over the other as it suits his argument. What is only partially masked here is a recurring crisis in logocentrism, described time and again by Derrida in its multiple forms. Whatever is posited as the basis for a thesis finds itself before long in need of supplementary support, but the category called upon as a supplement threatens the integrity of the first ground. Thus Bordwell et al. must introduce a notion of the theoretical ("the theoretical concepts introduced in this chapter are indispensable to grasping the classical style's systematic quality" [xv]) in order to "supplement" an empiricism that, as we shall see, inevitably fails when it stands alone.

Which films, then, will make up this body of films to be examined empirically? Bordwell insists that they will concentrate on the "typical work," the "quietly conformist film," rather than the "masterworks and innovations [that] rise monumentally out of a hazy terrain whose contours remain unknown" (10). This sounds like a laudable goal, one that will at least obviate the circular problem described above. Yet what has already been introduced is the problematic, discussed briefly earlier, of typicality and what it means for a film, or anything, to be representative. Will not the typical work, like the masterwork, be similarly situated within "a hazy terrain whose contours remain unknown?" Indeed, does not the definition of the typical work rely upon its opposition to the masterwork that is, by admission, only hazily defined? Bordwell informs us that some 15,000 films were made between 1915 and 1960, and out of these 100 were chosen for close study: "To construct a model of the ordinary film, we have selected *in an unbiased fashion,* 100 films from this period" (10; our emphasis).[13] He claims that though this method is "unprecedented . . . we believe it to be a sound way to determine historical norms" (10).

When the interested reader checks the appendix, however, he or she discovers that the random method employed by the authors actually

---

[13] Another sample referred to throughout the book contains 200 films deemed to be "quality" or historically important films, in contradistinction to the 100 more "typical" films, yet the integrity of the two samples is seriously compromised when Bordwell admits that many of the films in the larger sample were in fact as "undistinguished" as the films in the "unbiased" sample.

yielded 841 films, of which only 100 could be found in various collections and archives. They then admit—in the appendix—that:

> This was not, strictly speaking, a random sample. Every film made in American studios did not have an equal chance to be viewed, since not every film has survived. None the less, our selection procedures represent the closest a researcher can come to random sampling when dealing with historical artifacts. The point remains that our choices were not biased by personal preferences or conceptions of influential or masterful films. (388)

No doubt this is the closest a researcher can come to "random sampling," but that does not make it random sampling. The authors claim that their choices have been unbiased, but clearly the bias has merely been displaced elsewhere. Films that show up in collections and archives, in other words, tend to be films that have been valorized or singled out in some way at least once during the course of their histories, often because they were deemed to be "influential or masterful films" or for a variety of other reasons, good and bad. While few archives nowadays would turn down *any* film for conservation, this was not always the case (and certainly not with studios), and thus films remaining from earlier periods have most often been preselected on some explicit basis or another. Even today decisions are constantly made by archives the world over (for example, at the Library of Congress) concerning which films to transfer to safety stock from nitrate, and these decisions in fact dictate which films will be available for viewing by scholars. Clearly, such decisions are not made on a random basis, and it is those decisions that will inevitably determine the raw data out of which "film history" in general, and the contours of the "classic Hollywood cinema" in particular, may be constructed. In any case, the objection still remains that the researchers could not know that they were operating without the bias of "conceptions of influential or masterful films" unless they had a conception of what such films were, and such a conception automatically implies some sort of bias. The process, then, belies the claim that the sample can ever truly be random and thus ever be truly "typical" of that totality "film history" that remains forever out of reach. For it is not finally faulty empiricism that we are arguing about here but the will to totalization necessitating such empiricism, and along the way necessitating that it attempt to cover its shortcomings.

This tendency toward epistemological violence, which inevitably accompanies the writing of all histories, film and otherwise, will also function at the level of an authorial corpus—and even of individual

text, sequence, shot, and frame—that must be read for the most part
univocally in order to support the essentializing demands of film history's narrative, as well as normal critical and interpretive practice. In
"empirical" terms, clearly, every unit or entity that can be individuated
for study, including authors, invariably contains within it disparate elements that insist on going their own way. This is also the case within
individual film narratives, despite the influence of what Bordwell,
Staiger, and Thompson, following the Russian Formalists, call the
"dominant."[14] This appeal to a concept of dominance seems to us to
rely, once again, on the finding of an essence that imposes order on
recalcitrant particulars. Another version of the hermeneutic circle is
operative here, for the element found to be dominant is always the
element or pattern deemed significant in the light of certain desired or
preconceived thematic or structural outcomes.[15] Any counter elements
risk being repressed in the drive to construct a unified, master narrative
of organic relations, part-whole configurations, and self-evident patterns of domination. Similarly, a director's films that perversely resist
a teleological ordering—usually a narrative in which the auteur is seen
as making unimportant films until he "finds" his true style, which "develops," even through the occasional relapse—will be pushed into line.
In this operation, critics invariably look at a director's earlier films and
judge them to be good or bad (usually bad, because such critics are
also unconsciously following a model provided by the psychology of
human development) in terms of the criteria for unity and excellence
provided by the later films. For example, two recent critical studies—
Robert Kolker's *Bernardo Bertolucci*[16] and Seymour Chatman's *Antonioni; Or, the Surface of the World*[17]—persistently discuss their subjects'
earlier films in the light of a narrative trajectory imposed on their ca-

---

[14] Cf. Roman Jakobson, "The Dominant," in *Readings in Russian Poetics: Formalist and
Structuralist Views*, ed. Ladislav Matejka and Krystyna Pomorska (Cambridge: MIT
Press, 1971), 82–87: "The dominant may be defined as the focusing component of a
work of art: it rules, determines, and transforms the remaining components. It is the
dominant which guarantees the integrity of the structure" (82).

[15] The hermeneutic circle is, of course, a mainstay of phenomenological interpretation. Rodolphe Gasché interestingly compares its use by Heidegger with Derrida's strategic use of a logocentric discourse for deconstructive ends: "Thus the circularity of
logocentrism and deconstruction may well be akin to Heidegger's hermeneutic circle,
which, far from being a *circulus vitiosus*, to be avoided at all costs, is a circle into which
one has to come in the right way if one wants to think *at all*" (Rodolphe Gasché, *The
Tain of the Mirror: Derrida and the Philosophy of Reflection* [Cambridge: Harvard University
Press, 1986], 164). Cf. also *The Truth in Painting*, 32, for Derrida's discussion of this
Heideggerean strategy of encirclement in *The Origin of the Work of Art*.

[16] (New York: Oxford University Press, 1985).

[17] (Berkeley: University of California Press, 1985).

reers in the form of an analepsis based always on their later, more fa-mous films. In studies like these, criticism always constructs and de-pends upon an exciting narrative of the artist unconsciously seeking his true self, already there but hidden. Chatman's opening chapters, for example, detail Antonioni's attempt to cast off the inessential and get to "his mature style and preoccupations" (39).[18] Similarly, Kolker speaks on the first page of his book of Bertolucci struggling in his early films "to discover his own style."

Let us reiterate that the operations described above are not "errors" in the sense of avoidable mistakes that better critics would not have committed. Indeed, the sorts of pitfalls just mentioned, which are a particular feature of single author studies, are inevitable unless they take cognizance of the theoretical debate that has surrounded the no-tion of the author for some time now; and in this sense our critique here is not new.[19] In the end such gestures are simply the paradoxes that both allow and prevent film history. It is only through them that the narratives of film history can be written at all, yet they also keep it from ever fulfilling its goals.

Apart from film history another particularly important notion for film studies, historically at least, is the concept of genre. As a means of categorization it raises the question of relations between inside and outside, a question of increasing importance to our discussion. It can be said from the outset that from a deconstructive point of view the concept of genre is, strictly speaking, untenable, relying as it does on exclusions and valorizations that are logically indefensible. Derrida di-rectly addresses the issue in his essay "The Law of Genre": "As soon as the word 'genre' is sounded, as soon as it is heard, as soon as one attempts to conceive it, a limit is drawn. And when a limit is estab-lished norms and interdictions are not far behind."[20] Derrida maintains that a certain notion of "purity" is always understood in connection

[18] Other random examples of Chatman's teleological narrative of artistic develop-ment: "Antonioni had to learn to avoid the constraints of formula . . . before the true beauties of his long-take style could emerge" (21); "*I vinti* and *Tentato suicidio* are so different from Antonioni's films of the sixties and seventies that we may wonder how the same man could have made them" (28); "he had only to figure a way out of the impasse of story" (28).

[19] See for instance, *Theories of Authorship*, ed. J. Caughie (London and New York: Routledge & Kegan Paul, 1981).

[20] *Glyph 7* (Baltimore: The Johns Hopkins University Press, 1980), 203.

with genre, even when genres are "mixed," since the very notion of mixing seems to confirm "the essential purity of their identity" (204). But, on the contrary, Derrida asks: "What if there were, lodged within the heart of the law itself, a law of impurity or principle of contamination? And suppose the condition for the possibility of the law were the *a priori* of a counter-law, an axiom of impossibility that would confound its sense, order and reason?" (204). In other words, it might be said that the law of genre, which underwrites the attempt to establish categories with supposed clear lines of demarcation between them, is in fact always motivated by its opposite, that is, the impossibility of there ever being any such self-identical unity. For every *mark* or *trait* will always already be divided and lacking the wholeness that could generate whole categories or genres.

All texts are always part of a genre but are also subject to the operation of what Derrida thus calls "the law of the law of genre": "It is precisely a principle of contamination, a law of impurity, a *parasitical* economy. In the code of set theories. . . . I would speak of a sort of *participation without belonging—a taking part in without being part of.* The trait that marks membership inevitably divides, the boundary of the set comes to form, by invagination, an internal pocket larger than the whole" (206). To understand what Derrida means here we must make a short digression to discuss the idea of invagination. It is one of the terms he has adopted as a strategy for deconstructing the fundamental division between inside and outside.[21] Briefly, invagination destroys the notion of a clearly identifiable and intact inside easily distinguishable from an outside, since the vagina (or the mouth or the anus or the ear, for that matter) can be seen in a sense as exterior tissue that has been folded inside, and thus as exterior and interior at the same time. This internalized pocket of externality can in fact even be larger than the exterior that is said to enclose it.[22] The concept can be applied to film by considering that genre distinctions are usually seen as existing *outside* or drawing their definition from *outside* the individual film, but are actually always *inside* it at the same time through citation and reference and through each text's individual semiotic functioning, which must always apply to a code that exists without. All of the traits constituting a given genre and that are of course larger than the individual

[21] For further discussion by Derrida of invagination, see "Living On: Border Lines," in *Deconstruction and Criticism*, ed. Harold Bloom et al. (New York: Seabury Press, 1979), 97–103.

[22] Looked at from the perspective of fractal geometry, for example, the "inner" surface of the human lungs is said to be larger than the surface of a tennis court. Cf. James Gleick, *Chaos: Making a New Science* (New York: Viking, 1987), 81–118.

text are paradoxically folded into the text, creating an internal pocket through the process of invagination that is larger than the text's boundaries. (The reverse is also true in that the individual particulars of a text are always "larger" than any external categorization of the text can contain.) Thus the very nature of generic boundaries is called into question.

Derrida is speaking principally of literary genres here, which differ in important ways from film genres. Nevertheless, he does not hesitate to generalize,[23] for the basic principle of classification, which operates by means of inclusions, exclusions, and the integrity of borders, clearly separable insides and outsides, remains the same whatever the field. (In addition, the whole question of "exemplarity" is raised once again, for when we attach a genre label to a work we are always in effect saying that it is an "example" of that genre.) According to Derrida, to participate in a genre, what is necessary is "the identifiable recurrence of a common trait by which one recognizes, or should recognize, a membership in a class. There should be a trait upon which one could rely in order to decide that a given textual event, a given 'work,' corresponds to a given class" (210–11). However, once a *recurrence* is necessary to constitute a genre trait, we are inevitably in the problematic field of repetition (which implies an "original"—self-identical and fully present to itself—that is repeated), a notion that we see Derrida questioning time and time again. Not only does this mean that a "single" occurrence of a trait in a single work would not be sufficient to constitute a genre classification, but that the trait, or mark itself, as single occurrence, is, as we have insisted, unable to be constituted in its original fullness. A mark, like a trace or a footprint, is a kind of paradoxical present that marks, or signifies, something no longer there, something absent. And as such it is always already what Derrida calls a "re-mark," since a distinct origin, which would entail a moment of complete self-presence, is by definition an impossibility.

However, that is not the main paradox of genre itself, rather it is a fact of every mark. As Derrida goes on to show, this re-mark is necessary, even constitutive, for any work of art, because a work that did not have any of the genre traits recognizable as literary would not be literature, and the same could be said for films as opposed to news-

---

[23] In fact this generalization goes well beyond the question of genre strictly speaking, which is of course not a strict question, since it concerns the very matter of how categories are circumscribed: "The question of the literary genre is not a formal one: it covers the motif of the law in general, of generation in the natural and symbolic senses, of birth in the natural and symbolic senses, of the generation difference, sexual difference . . ." (221).

reels, home movies, x-rays, and so on. Yet the paradox is that "this supplementary and distinctive trait, a mark of belonging or inclusion, does not properly pertain to any genre or class. The re-mark of belonging does not belong. It belongs without belonging, and the 'without' . . . which relates belonging to non-belonging appears only in the timeless time of the blink of an eye" (212). The blink of an eye is that moment "without" sight, of nonsight or absence, which allows sight to take place. Thus the process itself by which a genre trait works to establish a genre can only operate by means of a contradictory movement of inclusion and exclusion.

Derrida's example here is the novel: the designation "novel" (and that is only the most obvious and explicit of any number of other formal traits that could be mentioned—prose form, narrative techniques, pagination, etc.), even when it appears physically on the title page of a novel, is never itself novelistic yet is part of the text in which it is found and acts to direct the text's meaning.[24] What is constituted is a unique "non-place" that, once again, calls into question notions of inside and outside, of borders. (The idea of the frame functions similarly in the visual arts, as later discussion will show.) Applying Derrida's insight to film, we can say that the designations "Western" or "thriller" or "melodrama," even though they mark given texts as part of a genre, are not *themselves* part of the genre. Similarly, the presence of six-guns, cowboys, and a Western locale may be marks of the genre "Western" but will, unlike the texts in which they appear, themselves never belong to the genre of the Western. They also "belong," respectively, to a historical practice of law enforcement or law breaking, a sociological category, and a geographical region, all of which, larger than the text in which they appear, come to inhabit it. That is to say, a specific text containing these marks of genre will never simply belong to a genre because these marks refer to a system of difference outside any given genre. Summarizing, Derrida adds: "Every text *participates* in one or several genres, there is no genreless text; there is always a genre and genres, yet such participation never amounts to belonging. And not because of an abundant overflowing or a free, anarchic and unclassifiable productivity, but because of the *trait* of participation itself, because of the effect of the code and of the generic mark" (212). The word "trait" that Derrida uses, in its usual (although figurative) meaning in French, refers to a characteristic that is assumed to belong intrinsically;

---

[24] The text that Derrida treats in this essay is *La Folie du jour* by Maurice Blanchot, which ends with the question "Un récit?" (Fr. "story") and which is also the title of another piece by Blanchot. However, in different citations within the review in which it appears Blanchot's title retains or drops the question mark. Thus the word (questioning a genre) that appears within one text is the title (in question) encompassing another text.

but more simply it means the stroke of a pen or brush, a written line—such as one uses to strike something out, a "purely graphic element," a piece of writing, a mark of "pure" exteriority. Thus a genre trait will be, like speech, similarly divided between inside and outside, it will be *différant* and thus always constituted by its opposite. This division always allows a kind of otherness, an indefinite openness or incompleteness, to exist at the very heart of the concept of genre. Genre is thus always indispensable and impossible at the same time, and what designates it disqualifies it.

To return to the specific case of film genre, it can be seen that the term is marked by an ambiguity that explicitly ensures what Derrida calls its "formless form" from the outset. In cinema the term "genre" refers not to a series of forms such as those operating in literature—poem, novel, play—but to a series of subsets of standard narrative film, what is often referred to as Hollywood "formula" film. Although there is some variation of form[25]—songs in musicals, farcical situations in comedies—all of the traditional generic categories remain within a standard conception of narrative film. A more viable series of genres, in terms of the comparison with literature, might be Hollywood narrative vs. documentary, sound vs. silent film, adaptations vs. "new" scenarios, and so on. Yet these genre divisions will always be found to be equally problematic. (For example, silent film was here always accompanied by music and in Japan had live commentators, and was thus never silent.) None of these oppositions, in other words, can ever be kept pure.

The problem of cinematic genres relates no doubt to a more complicated question, that of the opposition between genre criticism and auteur criticism. Such an opposition is common to a number of attempts at formulating, if not theorizing, the question: for instance, Jim Kitses's *Horizons West*,[26] Andrew Tudor's *Theories of Film*,[27] and Thomas Schatz's *Hollywood Genres*.[28] For the notion of the auteur as imported into Anglo-American film scholarship relied on rescuing from the mass of genre films, or Hollywood studio formula films, those which, it was argued, bore the signature of an author. Thus the notion of the auteur, which by definition implied the possibility of the director's creating a genre film outside of the genre system, acted as an invaginated category within that system.

---

[25] Not only does the definition of genre become irredeemably problematic here but also the form/content distinction. Is the singing of a song within a film that nevertheless preserves narrative conventions a matter of form or content?

[26] (Bloomington: Indiana University Press, 1969).

[27] (New York: Viking Press, 1973).

[28] (New York: Random House, 1981).

Schatz attempts to avoid the dilemma of the auteur/genre opposition by concentrating instead on the contrast between genre and non-genre films in this way:

> In general, the commercial cinema is identifiable by formal and narrative elements common to virtually all its products. . . . The genre film, however, is identified not only by its use of these general filmic devices to create an imaginary world; it is also significant that this world is predetermined and essentially intact. . . . [its] significance is based on *the viewer's familiarity with the "world" of the genre itself rather than on his or her own world.* (10; our emphasis)

Yet Schatz's example (of a gunfight in a Western) merely serves to open up the enormous problem of referentiality itself. For the viewer does not recognize "the characters' dress, demeanor, and weapons" (10) as belonging to the Western without also recognizing in them a whole range of historical, cultural, and technological concerns that remain part of "his or her own world." Thus is repeated the sort of necessary contamination or invagination Derrida describes in "The Law of Genre."

A final alternative then, is to appeal to the idea of repetition, fraught with the difficulties we have already discussed: "A genre's evolution involves both internal (formal) and external (cultural, thematic) factors. The subject matter of any film is derived from certain 'real-world' characters, conflicts, settings and so on. But once the story is repeated and refined into a formula, its basis in experience gradually gives way to its own internal narrative logic" (36). In fact this recourse to repetition does not hold even for Schatz, for each repetition is admitted to be a repetition with a difference—"[filmmakers] must continually vary and reinvent the generic formula" (36).

In the final analysis the genre problem is symptomatic of a larger difficulty that also emerges in structuralist semiotics of film, and indeed it is to Metz that Schatz refers in developing his idea of variation and invention within the generic formula. Although the concept of genre is not important to Metz's analysis of the language of cinema, he introduces a discussion of the Western as an evolving genre in a section of *Language and Cinema* entitled "Textuality and Generality." There he develops the idea of genre as a problematic notion on the edge of a structuralist approach to cinema, better described in terms of Kristeva's "intertextuality" or Genette's "palimpsest."[29] Outlining how the

[29] See Christian Metz, *Language and Cinema* (The Hague: Mouton, 1974), 151. The article by Genette that Metz refers to here is in fact a much earlier essay than that in

Western has passed through parody and contestation to deconstruction and concluding "Such is the infinite text of what one calls a *genre*" (152), Metz nevertheless maintains throughout that all of the variations he has cited remain "Westerns." In other words, for us Metz is introducing an operation of the supplement when he admits that "the ensemble of films made constitutes an immense text, which always opens onto its own (more or less disruptive) *prolongation*" (151; translation modified), for he finally sees this prolongation as less rather than more disruptive of the integrity of a category such as the Western. Although of course he does not present it in these terms, the implication is that there is an original Western from which later parodies and remakes developed; there is always, within this schema, a notion of structure defined without contamination.

The matter of structure, like that of genre or of history, involves drawing limits, and as Derrida notes, once one draws limits one is inevitably involved also in norms and prohibitions.[30] For the structuralist enterprise to succeed, uncontaminated categories must be assumed, as well as hierarchical relations between them. Hence Metz, in his structuralist mode,[31] would establish categories of the filmic and cinematic, of specific and nonspecific codes, and then discuss the complex interactions of those categories, where Derrida would question from the beginning the self-constitution of such categories. And by the same token, the hierarchies and exclusions practiced in order to arrive at those categories—narrative mainstream film vs. "marginal" film, the *grande syntagmatique*, and the idea of a fixed textual system or series thereof—are remarkably close to those adduced by the film historians discussed earlier.

---

which Genette develops his idea of the palimpsest. Metz's discussion of the Western is based on André Bazin, "The Evolution of the Western," in *What Is Cinema?*, trans. Hugh Gray (Berkeley: University of California Press, 1971), 2:149–57.

[30] Dudley Andrew, referring to remarks by Stephen Heath, accentuates the political aspect of the question of genre by situating it in the context of the shift in film studies from a "first structuralism" to a critique of the ideological underpinnings of cinema. In this later development of film theory, genre comes to represent the normative operations of the Hollywood industry, "ensur[ing] the production of meaning by regulating the viewer's relation to the images and narratives constructed for him or her" (*Concepts in Film Theory* [New York: Oxford University Press, 1984], 110).

[31] It must be noted that the formulations of the Metzian semiology of film, at one point described as "a stuttering discipline" (*Essais sur la signification au cinéma* [Paris: Klincksieck, 1972], 2:206), are under constant revision. See for instance the footnotes to later editions of the *Film Language* essays (trans. Michael Taylor [New York: Oxford University Press, 1974]); the discussion with Bellour in *Essais*, vol. 2; the softening emphasis on the *grande syntagmatique* in *Language and Cinema*; and the move away from certain positions of that text in *The Imaginary Signifier* (Bloomington: Indiana University Press, 1982), 28–29. We return to this matter in a later discussion.

It may be that the prominence of structuralism in film studies relates to a wider problem stemming from the particular cultural and historical background of Western cinema. Film theory up to and including the first wave of semiotics was underwritten by a desire for artistic and cultural legitimacy. In that context it was important first of all to borrow one's discourse on film from other art forms and then to assert the specificity of film, to adapt forms of analysis so that they became particularly cinematic. Metz's *grande syntagmatique*, based on a linguistic model, is an obvious example of this second phase, which is of course not to say that intervening in the normal forms of reception of film in order to subject it to formalist analysis was not an important strategic move. (Following this it might be said that the later and extensive application of psychoanalysis, accompanied as it was by so much discussion of its relevance, was part of the same movement to co-opt a discourse that could then be used to buttress film against claims that it was intellectually lightweight or academically inferior.) For although we are not suggesting that these moves were conscious, and although a major breakthrough made by semiology was its ability to investigate cultural manifestations of various types in order to effect a necessary and revolutionary demystification of the processes of culturation, one can read in the discourse of these film theories a certain will to integrality, a desire for a new discipline with all that that implies.

The problem of a structuralism that functions as what Derrida has called a kind of "totalitarianism," reducing textual phenomena to a formula that would govern them totally, is characteristic of the whole project of narratological analysis that has been so important for film studies. An example of this tendency is Seymour Chatman's *Story and Discourse*, a book that aspires to nothing less than a total explanation of narrative structure in fiction and film.[32] Reliance upon the structuralist distinction between story and discourse provides a schema that allows Chatman to construct an all-inclusive "Diagram of Narrative Structure" (267), a tree diagram whose multiple branches are designed to accommodate every possible narrational alternative. What a structuralist like Chatman or, for that matter, any formalist generally wants to do is to elide the text's heterogeneity, materialized by its extension in space and time, preferring instead what Derrida in "Force and Signification" calls a "theological simultaneity," which would have the text all *there*, all present, at any given present moment: "Th[e] history of the work is not only its *past* . . . but is also the impossibility of its ever being *present*, of its ever being summarized by some absolute simulta-

---

[32] *Story and Discourse: Narrative Structure in Fiction and Film* (Ithaca: Cornell University Press, 1978).

neity or instantaneousness" (*Writing and Difference*, 14). (Note the complaint of pre-theoretical critics who feel condemned to "break up" a text when they write about it, appealing once again to a myth of totalization, forgetting that the text is already broken up.) This desire for the totalization of simultaneity is even more evident in film, given its insistent temporality and the unstoppable onrush of images and sounds that the very continuity of standard narrative film seeks to reduce to a kind of simultaneity. The idea of structure is in these terms an attempt to construct metaphorically a simultaneous spatialized version of what is in fact a sequential, temporal phenomenon.

The soft structuralism of *The Classical Hollywood Cinema* takes a similar totalizing turn. Closely following the Russian formalists, its authors appeal to a notion of "plot," defined as "the totality of formal and stylistic materials in the film. . . . The plot is, in effect, the film before us" (12). This term is immediately distinguished from "story," which is "our mental construct, a structure of inferences we make on the basis of selected aspects of the plot" (12). This distinction seems to us to be closely related to the classic idealist one, repeated in various forms and deconstructed by Derrida, between the sensible and intelligible or between the materiality of the signifier and the conceptuality of the signified. It is as if the totality they imagine to exist as "plot" were being guaranteed by a doubling at the conceptual level, that of story. For if these categories are of different orders, how does one negotiate the gap, cover the distance between the material level and the mental or transcendent level except by recourse to some metaphysical operation? However much one might promote a dynamic conception of that relation—and we can recall Saussure's model of two sides of a piece of paper that an operation of language cuts through like a pair of scissors[33]—Derrida will insist that such distinctions are always founded on the possibility of absolute difference and hence of a transcendental resolution of that difference (*Of Grammatology*, 20).[34]

A structure cannot define its limits and preserve its integrity unless it be assigned the same by a similarly delimited and integral subject. Thus one encounters hand in hand with formalisms in general the (usually unexpressed) notion of a transcendent subject, an undivided

[33] Ferdinand de Saussure, *Course in General Linguistics*, trans. Wade Baskin (New York: McGraw Hill, 1966), 113.

[34] For a critique of structuralism in film studies made from a strictly materialist perspective but not without parallel with some of our comments, see Brian Henderson, *A Critique of Film Theory* (New York: E.P. Dutton, 1980), ch. 9, especially pp. 215–17.

subject equipped with a self-identical consciousness untroubled even by the dividing effects of the unconscious. The assumption of the opening theoretical section of *The Classical Hollywood Cinema*, for example, an assumption so basic that it is not even signaled or addressed, is of a unitary "spectator" who performs "activities," who *"participates in creating the illusion"* (7; Bordwell's emphasis). Anxious to attack the continental model of the conventional spectator as someone who, given the nature of the film apparatus, is always passive and manipulated, the authors rely heavily throughout the book on a notion of cognitive strategies based on the premise of a unitary spectator who operates those strategies. Agreeing with Gombrich's views, Bordwell portrays the spectator as one who "riffles through the alternatives" and claims that "in describing the classical system we are describing a set of operations that the viewer is expected to perform" (8). Bordwell insists upon the notion of a dynamic, active spectator who, even when completely absorbed in a film, is doing "hypothesis-checking that requires the viewer to meet the film halfway" (9).

The short space in which Bordwell describes the spectator is an indication of the extent to which he considers the category to be an unproblematic given. More surprising is his claim that a "comprehensive theory of film viewing has yet to be constructed" (7), in view of the large body of work done in this area beginning with Metz's *Imaginary Signifier* and including the whole domain of feminist theories of spectating. The question to be asked, however, is whether this body of work does not itself continue to rely on ideas of a transcendental subject, in spite of its obvious move away from the positions of structuralism. Laura Oswald suggests as much in a recent paper, arguing that in spite of Metz's rewriting of the "ontology of cinema based on the spectator's relation to the film," he "perpetuates a phenomenological understanding of the subject as origin rather than function of discourse by granting primary status to the spectator's inscription in the film image."[35] She continues: "Though the notion that there exist two moments of identification in cinema reveals the original division of the subject in the imaginary/symbolic realm, Metz' phenomenological account privileges the moment in which this division is healed by means of narrative strategies for guaranteeing identification in film discourse" (327). Oswald's argument follows a deconstructive mode by exploiting what seems to be a contradiction between the spectator that Metz describes and the cinema that the spectator watches. It is clear that

[35] "Semiotics and/or deconstruction: In quest of cinema," *Semiotica* 60, nos. 3/4 (1986), 324–25.

Metz's psychoanalysis of the spectator begins from the premise of a divided subject on the Lacanian model, and second that when he describes the spectator identifying with himself "as a pure act of perception . . . as the condition of possibility of the perceived and hence as a kind of transcendental subject, which comes before every *there is*" (*Imaginary Signifier*, 49), he is describing the unitary subject that dominant narrative cinema strives to create and position, thereby making an implicit critique of such positioning. Nevertheless, as Oswald sees it, Metz allows the positioning of the subject as prescribed by dominant cinema to constitute itself as *the* model of spectating, somewhat in the way that narrative cinema became the model for semiological analysis in the earlier Metz.[36] "The classical narrative cinema, a system of codes for producing closure, unity, and plenitude in the spectator's experience of film, prolongs, on the level of discourse, the theological return to the source, to the transcendental subject and signified as origins, initiated on the level of the image" (327). Metz would thus perpetuate the Bazinian gesture of ascribing an ontological essence to cinema, positing an ideologically and economically produced narrative cinema as "a kind of origin from which alternative cinemas would derive" (327).

Though there is rigor to Oswald's logic, a certain glibness creeps in when she extends her critique, within the space of a parenthesis, to "an entire tradition of film theory, including the work of Bazin, Heath and Oudart" (327). For her, because of the link between a transcendental subject and normative cinema, theorists from formalism to post-structuralism participate in a system that "posits division, noise and feminine desire as perversions of an original phallic unity" (327). Now (as we saw in the last chapter) inasmuch as psychoanalytic theory follows Lacan, it is susceptible to the critiques made by Derrida in "Le Facteur de la vérité" regarding the assumption of a central truth, that of the phallus. But Oswald tends to ignore, on the other hand, the extent to which Metz's work opened the possibility of the investigations undertaken by Heath and others, which have in turn been responsible for the

[36] Oswald, drawing on Benveniste regarding the involvement of the subject in enunciation, also objects that Metz's detailed discussion of metaphor and metonymy in the second half of *The Imaginary Signifer* avoids connecting such textual operations with the production of the subject discussed in the first half of the book: "It is as if, having argued . . . for the transcendental subject and the mirror stage as origins from which theories of film discourse derive, Metz had obviated further discussion of the subject with regard to specific film figuration" (325). She notes elsewhere, however, that these essays by Metz have been rather neglected by critics ("The Subject in question: New Directions in semiotics and cinema," *Semiotica* 48, nos. 3/4 [1984], 306).

elaborate critique of the ideological effects of the cinematic apparatus, including its privileging of masculine desire.

Perhaps the strength of Oswald's analysis is its identification of a problematic whose nodal "progressions" constitute the pivots upon which film theory continues to turn. In the recent formulation of the feminist perspective made by de Lauretis, for instance, a questionable distinction or articulation arises between "woman" as "fictional construct, a distillate from diverse but congruent discourses dominant in Western cultures," and *women*, "the real historical beings who cannot as yet be defined outside of those discursive formations, but whose material existence is nevertheless certain" (*Alice Doesn't*, 5). Given that de Lauretis's theoretical position prevents her from reading women outside of discursive formations and that her investment is really in favor of a rewriting of the current constructions of "woman," it is difficult to conceive of the function women fulfills here as anything other than the promise of, or nostalgia for, a transcendent subject existing before the fall into discourse—or for a real that can exist independent of representation, for structures uncontaminated by difference.[37]

Moving from questions of the subject to questions of the constitution of meaning in cinema, we might look more closely at the concept of figuration, whose importance for Metz Oswald has already signaled and that is the subject of a chapter of Dudley Andrew's *Concepts in Film Theory*. Andrew argues for increased attention to this area, echoing, perhaps unwittingly, the deconstructive view that we must "pass from the logical clarity of linguistics to the murkier discipline of rhetoric. Henceforth the study of *figures*, not codes, must be paramount in an examination of cultural artifacts" (161). However, Andrew's definition of figure as "a direct representation of meaning, nearly a visual representation . . . something that presses to be expressed" (158) seems again to fall prey to an idealist definition of the sign and the relation between signifier and signified. It avoids any thought of mediation in favor of directness; such a formulation of necessity obliterates the complexities always attending representation. Andrew's conception of figuration is developed in contrast to both classical rhetoric and psychoanalysis: "In both cases figures operate as detours from, and substitutions for, a more direct formulation that the author cannot or will not provide. Thus in both cases the figural nature of a text is a transitional stage through which, as critics, we may try to pass on our

---

[37] For a more lengthy treatment of this problematic in de Lauretis see "A V," in Alec McHoul and David Wills, *Writing Pynchon: Strategies in Fictional Analysis* (London: Macmillan Press, 1989).

way to the recovery of total sense (meaning) or total energy (the drives)" (163). Yet if rhetoric and psychoanalysis conceive of figures as detours that always imply a return, as shifting signifiers guaranteed by a signified that never moved—as Derrida analyzes metaphor in "White Mythology"[38]—Andrew on the other hand promotes an even more mystical idea, akin to religious "insight": "Figures are thus more than shortcuts by way of association and substitution; they have the power to disrupt the relation of context to sign and reorient not only the discursive event but the system itself which will never be the same afterwards" (170). This "system which will never be the same afterwards" is however one which does not seem to have moved very far from Romanticism. For in spite of the fact that in the course of his discussion Andrew unconsciously raises the possibility of a radical rearrangement of the system à la Derrida, he opts instead for a return to an almost precritical notion of interpretation that ignores the whole impetus of critical rhetoric—Barthes, Genette, and De Man—let alone the immense Derridean work on reading.

For though he seems to celebrate the fact that figures "complicate and derail structure" (158), Andrew forgets that figures, as functions of the displacement that is language, can also complicate and derail any coherent meaning—for example, by working against each other or by refusing to be co-opted and homogenized in order to allow a univocal reading or any consistent "organic" meaning, such as that accessible to "insight," to be applied to a text. Furthermore, where deconstruction would insist on the impossibility of granting primacy to either (grammatical) structure or (figural) event—maintaining that trying to decide which came first would be to remain trapped in the myth of pure origins—Andrew's view is finally that "the system was born and exists only as a residue of such events of figuration" (170). For one thing, to oppose figure and structure, and to favor the former over the latter, is to continue to operate within the same economy of a hierarchy of opposites—for the terms have merely been reversed and not displaced. Moreover, "residue" is here a telltale word, but one symptomatic of a difficulty in the argument as a whole. First, as Andrew suggests, it always marks that which is "left over" in representation, which cannot be accounted for in structural terms. But second, since the very idea of a residue contradicts any thought of a system, it could hardly give birth to a system, either. And finally, the idea of residue will always contradict any notion of meaning as direct and fully present, such as

---

[38] *Margins of Philosophy*, 207–71.

obtains in Andrew's concept of figuration, for this excess will always remain to resist the will to a unitary meaning.

Ultimately, Andrew's anti-structuralist position is taken in order to return to a phenomenological, quasi-religious perspective, updated by recourse to Ricoeurean hermeneutics. His figures, as we began by saying, always point to a place beyond the materiality and mediacy of the signifier and, as he claims, beyond the intentional force described by psychoanalysis, to a place granted to a transcendent artistic insight. But figures also have a forceful alogicality of their own that will always derail the ostensibly regulating strictures of authorial intentionality. Given the dislocations and internal divisions to which representation is heir, it seems clear that neither the structural analysis Andrew wants to dethrone nor the analysis of figures he offers to replace it will ever be able to tell us, in his phrase, "what was meant" (170).

Finally, then, the greatest impact of a Derridean point of view on film studies—beyond the questions of film history, genre, and various theoretical models—may very well be in the area of interpretation itself. Clearly, many of the arguments we have been developing would also be applicable to the interpretive process. This is something that we have already touched upon and that we shall continue to develop, but we would prefer to organize the discussion more in terms of *reading* than interpretation. However, in the context of the ideas that have shaped our discussion in this chapter, we can say that the will to totality or integrality, the inevitable essentialization, categorization, and repression of elements that "don't fit" that marks much film history and theory continues to be a dominant factor in practices of reading as well. We are generalizing here, of course, and it must be admitted that recent criticism has come a long way toward treating film as an interplay of presence and absence, of the seen and not seen, in relations not reducible to either totalization or transcendence. The work of the *Cahiers* critics inspired by Althusser broke important ground here, and feminist theory, aided by psychoanalysis, has continued in that vein: "The symptomatic reading of films as filmic texts has worked against closure, seeking out the invisible subtext made of the gaps and excess in the narrative or visual texture of a film, and finding there, concurrent with the repression of the female's look, the signs of her elision from the text" (*Alice Doesn't*, 57). The risk is—and we do not suggest that feminist film criticism reduces to this, although such a risk may represent one current within it—that these readings aim simply to reintegrate what has been elided, to reinstate what has been repressed, thereby aligning criticism once again with a totalizing gesture that elides or represses its own theoretical consequences.

A deconstructionist criticism, based on the Derridean example rather than on what is regarded as the American version, would seek a more adventurous marrying of theory to reading practice. It would see the gaps of a text not so much, or not only, as signs of elision but as aporias representing important points of articulation between its inside and outside. It would accept that although such aporias might be productive of further readings, there can be no simple reduction of them and thus no simple way in which one reading could "correct" another—thus no way out of reading itself. Before proceeding further upon the road of deconstructive reading practices, however, we need to return to the Derridean concepts that provide their framework and bring them to bear more closely on the matter of film.

CHAPTER THREE

FILM AS WRITING:
FROM ANALOGY TO ANAGRAM

Throughout the two previous chapters we have occasionally referred to Derridian "concepts," but strictly speaking this is a misnomer. The words that Derrida throws into a constantly mutating chain of signification, or the words that he revives within that chain, cannot properly be called concepts, nor can they easily be applied to textual systems other than those he discusses, such as literature, painting, or philosophy—for example, a textual system such as cinema. Yet the various domains in which these terms were first employed also may not exercise proprietary claim over them, hence leaving them open to adaptation.

Derrida himself has recognized that a certain sliding is "permissible," indeed inevitable, among the various terms he has employed throughout his writings: "The word 'deconstruction,' like all the others, has value only in terms of its inscription in a chain of possible substitutions. . . . It is only of interest within a certain context in which it replaces and comes to be determined by so many other words, for example, 'writing,' 'trace,' '*différance*,' 'supplement,' 'hymen,' '*pharmakon*,' 'margin,' '*entame*,' 'parergon,' etc. By definition, the list can never be closed" ("Lettre à un ami japonais," in *Psyché*, 392; our translation). The reader should understand that what is being evoked and encouraged in our text is the *strategy* for which such terms are the shorthand, rather than any glib borrowing of a ready-made theory, complete with jargon. Despite what a certain, probably inevitable vulgarization has reduced it to, Derridean thinking is anything but that. Having made these qualifications, we can say that what we want to do in this chapter is to attempt to reread certain Derridean "concepts" in the context of cinema, especially his notion of writing and, later on, of "hymen," taken from his discussion of Mallarmé's *Mimique* in "The Double Session" (*Dissemination*, 172–286).

We have already summarized, in chapter 1, the position that writing occupies vis-à-vis speech in the Derridean elaboration of the history of Western thought. For our purposes the most important characteristic of writing, one that is germane to all language, is the question of distancing, which brings with it the idea of mediation. This is most obvious in the case of the written, that form of language by definition enacted in the expectation of a certain absence. That is, the act of writing assumes (at least structurally) that writer and reader are involved in a *rendez-vous manqué*: they will not both be present at the same time, now or in the future, or there would be no need for writing. By extension, writing comes to cover all forms of reproducible language, including those that leave traces, like a voice on a tape. As we have seen, though, even spoken language is constituted by the possibility of repeatable units, phonemes, words, syntaxes, and therefore the spoken must also be defined as "written."[1]

The same can be said of film: to the extent that it is a language, it is to be considered as a type of writing. Traditionally, of course, film is held to be natural and direct, much as speech, throughout the history of the West, has been held to be natural and direct in opposition to the supposedly obvious artificiality of writing. We now know, however, from the many semiological studies initiated more than twenty years ago by Christian Metz and others, studies that have considered narrative cinema as industry and institution, as system of representation, and as subject effect, that cinema can never be directly "spoken." We would merely add that this is because it is always *written*. Cinema, like all other forms of writing, leaves something behind, something involving material effects that cannot be hidden if the operation is to continue to function, like printed letters and words or reels of celluloid.[2] This is of course the way all language functions, for spoken words only seem to disappear after they enter the ear of their listeners, but they are very much there[3]—accessible, transferable, and negotiable—the moment those listeners in turn open their mouths to speak. By definition, these words can never be unique occurrences, nor is a new or private language ever a logical possibility.

In the case of cinema, its "writtenness" simply seems less obvious because it is received as still more natural and direct than speech. Ver-

---

[1] See "Signature Event Context," in *Margins*, 314–18.

[2] For Marie-Claire Ropars it is montage that is most explicit in permitting cinema to be inscribed within the general perspective of writing. See *Le Texte divisé*, 35–36. We return to her discussion of montage in chapter 4.

[3] They are also "not there," for a function of writing is always that it inscribes an absence, as we mentioned above. The spoken traces we refer to here are not full presences but the very marks of those paradoxical functions of writing; as Derrida insists, writing is never reducible to the sensible presence of the graphic, because this would only serve to make it a new ground (Cf. *Positions*, 65).

bal expression, for one thing, obviously manifests itself in many different registers, as well as different languages, and does seem to require at least a modicum of "effort," whereas watching a film seems to require no effort at all. From this point of view, the visual occupies a position of primacy with respect to the verbal similar to that which speech occupies with respect to the written. Yet by simply requiring an "apparatus," no matter how rudimentary or sophisticated, cinema fulfills the definition of writing as easily as does the word. Whether that apparatus be the camera itself, or, at the other end of the spectrum, the system by which the spectator puts desire into effect, the same structural result is achieved. In its offering of a certain appearance of fullness of vision, however, cinemato-graphy wants to forget that it is always written.

If it can be agreed that the Derridean concept of writing applies also to film, it then becomes a matter of the strategy implied by such an application. For us, it is strategically important on two counts: first, it inscribes film (or cinema—the distinction does not mean the same for us as it does for semiotics, as we shall suggest below)[4] within the domain of the *textual*; and second, it can perhaps provide new insights into the ancient problematic of the relation between image and referent.

As regards textuality, the concept of writing is important because the text in Derrida takes on a radicality that far exceeds its treatment by semiotics. It is within this concept of textuality that the consequences of the refutation of the origin as controlling center of meaning and coherence are exploited to the fullest.

While it is true that film studies has been for some time engaged in profoundly and systematically analyzing the ways in which an image or a film, with the collaboration of the spectator, works to produce a contrived coherence, we wish to argue that the text is *fundamentally* incoherent. In saying this we do not mean that the text is a nonsense but rather that since it is a structural impossibility for it to have been constituted or even conceived as a fullness, one is forced to treat it as a graft, a series of omissions, an accident. From a deconstructive standpoint, analysis would no longer seek the supposed center of meaning but instead turn its attention to the margins, where the supports of meaning are disclosed, to reading in and out of the text, examining the other texts onto which it opens itself out or from which it closes itself off.

---

[4] Metz usefully distinguished between film and cinema, the one being the text itself, the other referring to all the institutional support (sociological, technological, political, and economic) that enabled it. Even if this distinction is productive, we would want to say that, nevertheless, *both* are forms of writing (Cf. *Language and Cinema*, 9–49).

A certain material disunity is immediately apparent in the textuality of a film, a disunity perhaps most evident between the image and sound tracks. For Marie-Claire Ropars, it is thus that cinema reveals the rupture constituting all language: "Image and sound introduce a rupture at the heart of the enunciation that mobilizes both of them simultaneously; or, more precisely, they reveal within enunciation a breach that purely linguistic usage ordinarily occludes" (*Le Texte divisé*, 159; our translation). Like spoken language, conventional cinema, through the careful suturing of sound and image, offers an illusory wholeness. The potential for rupture that this suturing implies has been fully exploited by a filmmaker like Marguerite Duras, with the result that a certain anxiety pervades her films, the constant threat that a part of the film will simply take leave of another part, diverge beyond retrieval. This is the case with the female voices who comment in the first part of *India Song* (1974) and who suddenly reveal their desire for each other, a desire that subsequently intrudes upon the film, threatening to break it apart, to make it other. And indeed the threat is carried out, not in this film nor in this manner but by the production of another film, *Son nom de Venise dans Calcutta désert* (1976), which utilizes the same sound track as the earlier film but whose image track is in many ways the ruins of the image track of *India Song*.[5] It is important to recognize, however, that such a threat of disunity is apparent not only in what might be called "experimental" films such as Duras's but also in more conventional, mainstream films. For example, a technique that has actually become rather common—beginning the sound track from a subsequent scene while the image track still shows the previous scene—always opens at least a small breach, a breach (which when the technique first appeared must have seemed even greater) sutured by means of the visual cut, leaving little but the memory of a momentary *frisson* of uncertainty. We return in a later discussion to the question of how such a disunity might be read but simply emphasize here that this disunity must be recognized as a constitutive structure of any sound film.

The decentered text and the sense of unlimited context that that decentering provokes, two qualities defining a film considered as "writing," derive their impetus to a great extent from the notion of "adestination," whose elaboration underwrites Derrida's extensive discussion of Lacan and psychoanalysis.[6] Though we shall consider this concept in detail in chapter 6, it may be useful to indicate here that

[5] See *Le Texte divisé*, 140–41.

[6] See especially "Envois" and "Le Facteur de la vérité," in *The Post Card*.

it is a function of the rewriting of the author or origin, of the author as origin, an awareness that intention can no longer determine the itinerary of sense and meaning in a text. Historically, it is intentionality that has acted as a kind of ground for or bridge between a theory of the text and a theory of reading. But simply because a message has been addressed somewhere (by the inscribed intention of its author, for instance), this is no guarantee that it will arrive safely at that address. And Derrida insists that a message's going astray or being stolen, interfered with, or diverted in some fashion is not simply an unfortunate accident that can befall sense along the way. On the contrary, those possibilities are always present at the very point and in the very event of the message's formation. Hence the formula *a letter can not arrive* becomes *a letter cannot arrive*. If and when it arrives—and of course it very often does—this is a matter of arrival and not a function of its being a letter, since there is nothing in the constitution of the letter that guarantees its arrival.

The division of meaning implied by adestination is also formulated in terms of dissemination, that is, the tendency of textual "meaning effects" to move outward in all directions at once, resisting closure, always in process, always being written and rewritten. Derrida uses this term in contrast to "polysemy" to suggest a much more multiple and indefinite sowing of the seeds of sense and also to suggest by means of the prefix "dis-" that there is something in the operation opposing a unitary meaning. Dissemination is to be distinguished from polysemy in that "it does not give rise to a hermeneutic deciphering, to the decoding of a meaning or truth" (*Margins*, 329). Since the notion of artistic intentionality has historically been crucial for establishing more or less stable meanings in texts, film, as a necessarily collaborative and thus inherently disseminative medium is an important place to study the problems of intentionality sometimes obscured in literary study. It seems no accident, in other words, that film was not taken seriously until auteurs, in whatever guise (as directors, producers, screenwriters, stars, or even studios), were found. A general anxiety about representation and signification seems to be a factor here. Unless someone or even some group can be seen to be initiating and thus directing and controlling meaning through the imposition of consciousness, the disseminative possibilities inherent in any text come to the fore and can be regarded as threatening. (From our point of view, the auteur is a construction that can only be located provisionally at the "head" of a series of shifting marks; it is a series of texts that retrospectively creates an auteur, rather than an auteur who creates texts.) The notoriously unconvincing attempts to avoid this problem of dispersed intentionality in film by relocating the missing single consciousness in the collective consciousness of an epoch or a nation (as, for example, Kracauer's *From Caligari to Hitler*[7]) might be considered a further symptom of this anxiety. In any case, there seems always to be a desire to posit a centering consciousness *somewhere*, and if this consciousness is removed from the agency of a human author (or a national culture), it becomes difficult to resist investing it instead in a kind of intentionality ascribed to the work itself.

It is important to note, however, that Derrida does not wish to do away with the concept of intentionality altogether, nor does he subscribe completely to the structuralist and semiotic description of the "death of the author," in Barthes's phrase, in favor of "the birth of the reader." Rather, what he calls an "intention effect" can often become the genesis of a deconstructive reading of a given text. Characteristically reversing terms and sequence, and thus standard oppositional hierarchies, Derrida considers intention not something "prior" to a text but one important organizing strand *constructed* in any given reading. As Jonathan Culler has put it, "For Derrida . . . intention may be viewed as a particular textual product or effect, distilled by critical readings but always exceeded by the text" (*On Deconstruction*, 218). In his reading of Plato, for example, Derrida makes the point this way:

> The word *pharmakon* is caught in a chain of significations. The play of that chain seems systematic. But the system here is not, simply, that of the intentions of an author who goes by the name of Plato. The system is not primarily that of what someone *meant-to-say* [*un vouloir-dire*]. Finely regulated communications are established, through the play of language, among diverse functions of the word and, within it, among diverse strata or regions of culture. These communications or corridors of meaning can sometimes be declared or clarified by Plato when he plays upon them "voluntarily." . . . Then again, in other cases, Plato can *not* see the links, can leave them in the shadow or break them up. And yet these links go on working of themselves. In spite of him? thanks to him? in *his* text? *outside* his text? but then where? between his text and the language? for what reader? at what moment? (*Dissemination*, 95–96; quoted in Culler, 218–19)

Thus, intentionality is rewritten in Derrida rather than done away with. It becomes, once again, a matter of a certain kind of reading, an

[7] Siegfried Kracauer, *From Caligari to Hitler* (Princeton: Princeton University Press, 1971).

active but always rigorously logical play with the elements of the text. This particular brand of play—at least insofar as it is directly related to questions of intentionality—has become increasingly centered in the last fifteen years in Derrida's work in the concept of the "signature effect," a complex dynamic involving questions of the frame, concerning, for example, whether the author's (painter's, filmmaker's) "signature" is inside or outside the work. If it is outside, how can it have an effect on the text? If it is inside, what prevents it from being considered another textual element, with its own effects and its own consequences for an "interpretation" of that text? Also involved are questions of the status of the proper name and its relation to common nouns, a problematic Derrida has been exploring at least since *Of Grammatology*. The signature effect, as Derrida points out in *Signsponge*, "is not inconsistent with that death or omission of the author of which, as is certainly the case, too much of a case has been made" (22). We will discuss the signature at length in the next chapter, where it can be more fully examined as part of the inside/outside dynamic of the frame.

Once the hold of a presumed intentionality is broken, little remains to anchor or legitimate traditional reading strategies, and texts open up to the possibility of what might be called "radical reading." It is in this light that Barthes examines cinematic excess in his essay "The Third Meaning."[8] For Barthes, the third meaning, also referred to as the "obtuse" meaning, concerns the operations of the signifier and goes beyond the two "obvious" meanings of communication and signification. Here Barthes comes close to a deconstructive perspective, as when he describes the "supplementary" structure of the third meaning and likens it to the signatory anagrams that Saussure found in Latin poetry. (It is also remarkably similar to what he will call the *punctum* of a photograph in his last work, *Camera Lucida*,[9] which we shall discuss in the following chapter.) For Barthes, this meaning is that which goes beyond language, even a language of symbols, provoking a "dissociation" which "has a de-naturing or at least a distancing effect with

---

[8] In *Image—Music—Text*, trans. Stephen Heath (New York: Hill and Wang, 1977), 44–68. See also Kristin Thompson, "The Concept of Cinematic Excess," in *Narrative, Apparatus, Ideology: A Film Theory Reader*, 130–42. It should be clear that ours is not the first attempt to account for what escapes signification in the image. Julia Kristeva's notion of *significance* and paragrammatic space, as well as Jean-François Lyotard's concept of libidinal economy, for example, are obviously highly relevant to this discussion. For a useful summary, see Maureen Cheryn Turim, *Abstractions in Avant-Garde Films* (Ann Arbor: UMI Research Press, 1985), 7–22.

[9] Roland Barthes, *Camera Lucida: Reflections on Photography*, trans. Richard Howard (New York: Hill and Wang, 1981).

regard to the referent" (61). Perhaps most interestingly, though, he links the third meaning to a politics of subverting rather than destroying narrative, seeing in it "an imperishable signature" of the artist (in this case, Eisenstein). For Barthes, it is also the possible location for the beginnings of what he calls the "filmic," which is "the *passage* from language to *signifiance* [the realm of the signifier]." Where Barthes differs from a deconstructive perspective is in seeing the filmic, this realm of the obtuse, third meaning as "rare (a few flashes in [Eisenstein], perhaps elsewhere?) so much so that it could be said that as yet the film does not exist" (65). More radically, we see the disseminative potential that Barthes describes as a necessary constituent of all images, all texts.[10]

The most adventurous example of this treatment of the text in Derrida's own writings is no doubt *Glas*, a text that appeared in French in 1974.[11] As Gregory Ulmer explains: "*Glas* teaches dissemination, a theory of writing, by means of its namesake in botany. . . . The whole process by which certain plants conceive . . . emblematized in the explosion of the pod and the scattering of seed, is offered as an analogy for an intellectual conception generated in the process of writing—the flowers of rhetoric" (*Applied Grammatology*, 25). This brief description outlines both the complexity of a decentered textuality and the wide-ranging productiveness of its effects. For, as Ulmer emphasizes, and we shall return to his discussion, the aim of Derrida's technique here is to point the way toward new or different kinds of conceptualization, paradigm shifts such as have occurred in other disciplines at other times, most recently perhaps in physics or geometry. Specifically regarding the subject of our inquiry, it is clear that film has emerged as the first of what we call the mass media, whose functioning seriously and irreparably disrupts and redefines our conception of artistic creation. It is our contention that despite the historically close relation between literary studies and film studies, film should be more closely aligned with modern music, television, video, and the information sciences than with literature. Yet, except for recent and welcome forays

[10] Expanding on the notion of excess as a function of writing in Derrida's sense, we might go so far as to suggest that just as certain gender stereotyping and positioning dominates in narrative cinema and is reinforced and perhaps determined by the sexualized positioning involved in the viewing process, so too the excesses of various types that have come to dominate the content of much cinema—excesses of violence or sexuality or the excess represented by fantasy of any type—should be considered as functions of the excess that is cinema in its conception.

[11] Actually, any of a number of other texts by Derrida—"Envois" in *The Post Card*, *Spurs*, and *Signsponge*—might appear equally adventurous. *Glas* can perhaps be called the most monumental.

into the world of television, film theory has not really developed as media theory, giving that domain wholly over to the reductive empirical discourse of communications science on the one hand and to the sort of journalism that used to pass for film studies on the other. Since cinema participates in a new conceptualization of art and communications, one still to a great extent lacking in a theory, it seems well placed to provide a new context for the development of that theory.

Thus far we have been discussing the widened sense of textuality that results from regarding film as a form of writing, and we intend to develop this perspective as our discussion proceeds. The other basis for the relevance of this idea to film concerns the relation between image and referent. If one recalls the most explicit realist position propounded by André Bazin, for example, in which he claims that the photographic image is a kind of "fingerprint" or "imprint" of reality, just as the holy shroud of Turin was supposed, until very recently, to bear the imprint of Christ's body,[12] we have both a striking example of the logocentric position and the possibility of its deconstruction, given the explicit references to the idea of a trace. This deconstruction also provides the possibility of shifting the debate away from the circular terms in which it has always been argued.

For as reality imprints itself upon the image, it must always necessarily imprint itself as difference from itself. The image is not reality, of course, but it appears as even "less" reality, and in more striking a fashion, precisely by virtue of its being so close—in terms of the reigning conception of resemblance—to that reality. What an argument taken from Derrida contributes here is not the ability to identify the exact type of resemblance constituting the image but rather the possibility of showing how the notion of resemblance itself, with its assumed priority over the manifold and incessant workings of difference, relies on an operation of elision to connect it with the proper, the original, the intact, and so to conceal the fact that it will belong, always, to the family of differences.

Resemblance, for one thing, usually depends upon the figure of analogy, a figure that occupies a traditional place in film theory but whose lineage is much more ancient. In its larger sense analogy is the repetition with a difference from which all rhetoric, perhaps all discourse, departs. It is the awkward shape given to the uncontrollable set of possibilities through which the same concedes the functioning of its

[12] "The Ontology of the Photographic Image," in *What Is Cinema?*, trans. Hugh Gray (Berkeley: University of California Press, 1967), 1:14–15. Bazin uses the phrase "true imprint of reality" in *What Is Cinema?*, 2:98.

other, through which the *logos*, in the course of its delivery, comes to be written as a series of deferrals. Analogy is also a trope by which discourse adorns and embellishes itself (puts on its make-up?). In fact, a certain operation of analogy, a form of resemblance, is at the basis of the speculative or contemplative exercise the moment it becomes language. As Derrida has said in the "Exergue" to "White Mythology," "the link of the signifier to the signified has had both to be and to remain a link of natural necessity, of analogical participation, of resemblance" (*Margins*, 215).

More commonly in film theory, though, analogy refers to the question of mimesis, to the relation between the photographic image and its referent. That relation takes a variety of forms, from Bazin's "representation" to Metz's "absence of double articulation" and Barthes's contrast with the digital operations of the arbitrary signifier,[13] or more generally to the notion of the impression of reality. But as long as that relation is described as one of analogy, it must either be considered a tautology or admit its difference. Instead of fixing image and referent in a close relationship, the figure of analogy effects a type of *mise en abyme* of the referential play of the signifier, so that the image has its own difference mirrored within itself. Any representation, like analogy or cinema, whose claim to privilege relies on the idea of its being a faithful copy is caught in such a bind. If it is a repetition of the model, it can have no value in itself; but if it is not a simple repetition, it is not a faithful copy. If the cinematic image merely reproduces reality, it is a type of pure excess. On the other hand, if recourse to the notion of analogy is the mark of its difference, it is precisely difference and not similarity that should be insisted upon as constituting its ontology. By referring to sameness as the basis of its referential status, the image imports the paradox just referred to into its own signifying space.

The result of a representation caught in the bind of tautology on the one hand—a sort of degree zero of representation—and superfluous excess on the other is reflected throughout Bazin's realist discourse in a kind of repeating mirror effect that bears closer examination. In each case, one finds posited a certain self-evidence, a discovered specificity like the ontology of the image, which is subsequently, and seemingly unnecessarily, complicated by a doubling that brings about the *mise en abyme* of that self-evidence.

Such a doubling occurs first of all with respect to Bazin's most im-

[13] André Bazin, "The Ontology of the Photographic Image"; Christian Metz, "Problems of Denotation in the Fiction Film," in *Film Language*; Roland Barthes, "Rhetoric of the Image," in *Image—Music—Text*.

portant realist principle, referred to above, the matter of the image as
imprint of reality. This fundamental tenet is inscribed with truth value
as an innovation that functions beyond the human: "For the first time,
between the originating object and its reproduction there intervenes
only the instrumentality of a nonliving agent. For the first time an
image of the world is formed automatically, without the creative intervention of man" ("Ontology," 13). All the realist prescriptions for
a cinema that duplicates faithfully, for styles that are "self-effacing"[14]
and show an ethical "concern for truth," depend on the idea of the
imprint alone. Yet Bazin's realism refers often to a second principle,
that of the impression of reality.[15] And this second principle, while
perhaps reinforcing the first in phenomenological terms also threatens
to render it superfluous. Clearly, in order for the impression of reality
to function an exact duplication of the real (whatever that could be) is
not required. Undoubtedly, a whole set of approximations exists that
would have the same effect, as is demonstrated by the well-known
shock induced by such a rudimentary film as the Lumières' *Arrivée d'un
train en gare de la Ciotat*. The fact that nothing human is interposed
between the object and its representation is superfluous to the contention that the spectator perceives the cinematic image as if he or she
were perceiving reality.

The second doubling occurs through the much vaunted term "ambiguity" that, according to Bazin, mise en scène and deep focus are
supposed to allow. First of all, one could object that this staging of
mise en scène forgets that it is also a framing, as if the disposition of
objects in space and the choice of a certain focal length had no relation
to the limits of the space enclosed within the frame. And by definition
if reality is framed, it cannot be complete.[16] Let us accept for convenience that this ambiguity is that of the real transferred to the image,
an ambiguity that can be distinguished, for instance, from that manip-

---

[14] For instance, Bazin praises De Sica's *Bicycle Thieves* as "one of the first examples of
pure cinema. No more actors, no more story, no more sets, which is to say that in
the perfect aesthetic illusion of reality there is no more cinema" (2:60). Elsewhere he
maintains that "the structure which Rossellini has created allows the viewer to see nothing but the event itself" (2:101).

[15] Bazin's terms are "aesthetic realism" and "psychological realism," or "true realism"
and "pseudorealism" (See "Ontology," 12). For an example of Bazin's elaboration of the
contradictions involved in his promotion of the two realist principles—photographic
reproduction and spectator's impression—see *What Is Cinema?*, 2:26–27.

[16] Bazin does not ignore this contradiction any more than that mentioned above. His
discussion of the advantages of mise en scène and deep focus also becomes an exposition
of the contradictions they imply (Cf. "Ontology," 34–37, and *What Is Cinema?*, 2:64–
68).

ulated by the filmmaker who shows a close-up of a doorknob in a suspense film so that the spectator knows the murderer is entering but
does not know who that murderer is. Bazin's ambiguity is that which
supposedly occurs within the total picture, but as soon as it is introduced it cannot help but problematize to the point of contradiction the
idea of a total picture. Ambiguity, presumably by definition, is an effect of *occultation*, as when two senses of a word fail to give each other
sufficient space or clarity, or when one object within an image is obscured by another or lacks definition. Ambiguity, in other words, is
the very denial of the total picture. No doubt the "total picture," which
is not Bazin's term but our shorthand,[17] always existed for him as transcendent principle, even before its formulation, but that is not the
point here. Nor is it that cinema can only tend toward that totality but
remain unable ever to reach it. This ambiguity is not the result of a
falling short; on the contrary, Bazin would have it that as realist cinema
tends toward revelation, it also tends toward mystery. His ambiguity
is thus doubled by its own self-contradiction.

Finally, the tendency to revelation, which might be called the asymptote effect of realist cinema, falls prey to its own doubling. For if
reality equals truth, what need is there for cinema? Reality thus doubles with truth to exclude cinema, whereas the whole point of realism
was to tie reality to cinema in simple material effect. This paradox is
made explicit in a recent essay by Joël Magny. Speaking of "the maxi-
mum respect for the immanent structures of the real,"[18] which must
always remain relative in cinema, as an ideal toward which it aspires,
he concludes: "But at the same time, this limit for cinema, its omega
point, is it not a matter of reaching the ambiguity of the real in the
sense that it is always objective and subjective, immanent and transcendent? Truth, as the identification of the subject with the world, is really
the asymptote of cinema, unattainable, but that toward which it never
ceases to tend, whose realization would mean its abolition" (50). Thus
we have the equation: cinema $\approx$ reality $\approx$ truth, in which it is cinema
that is introduced as the third term, the other two continuing to function in tautological fashion despite it. For since cinema will never attain
either—and if it did it would cease to exist—its very necessity makes it
the fly in the ointment preventing reality from being isomorphic with
truth. As long as cinema remains in the equation, the approximation
remains. If the approximation were to resolve into the exact equiva-

[17] For "total cinema" ("Ontology," 17); "transference of reality" (14); "virginal purity" (15); "natural image" (15).
[18] Joël Magny, "Epiphanie du réel: André Bazin et le cinéma," *CinémAction*, no. 20
(1982), 50. Our translation.

lence toward which realist cinema aspires, cinema would have to drop out (on the realists' admission), leaving truth equal to reality.

The quandary realism makes for itself can be seen as the function of a more fundamental "will to analogy" thanks to Jean-Louis Baudry's analysis of the apparatus as subject effect.[19] Baudry's recourse to the Platonic myth of the cave, as "prehistoric" example of the desire for a form of representation analogous to the cinema also provides an interesting connection between psychoanalysis and Derridean theory.

On the surface, the cinema, which Baudry finds to be motivated by a desire to reproduce the human perceptive faculty, exists at the other end of the scale from the Derridean practice of deconstruction. The latter is thought to be as far as possible from perception of the physical, the pure reflection of a philosophical discourse. Yet etymologically speaking the theoretical and the scopic are similar,[20] both being systems of *auto-reflection*. And conceptually speaking, a more pertinent similarity is found in the myth of the cave. Plato's myth of the cave, after all, not only provides the common ground Baudry finds between a theory of perception and a desire for representation but also raises the whole problematic opened by philosophical enquiry: namely, that there is perhaps no structural distinction between the simplest speculation concerning the nature of the physical world—or the discourse of truth—and the rhetoric of sophistry. What falls between the two, or rather what exists always already as constitutive of the smallest operation of sense making, is representation, some of the mechanics of which lead to the allegory of the cave and so evoke cinema. It is the same mechanism of representation that operates, in different forms, in media as far apart as dialectical reasoning or rhetoric on the one hand and photographic reproduction or computerized abstraction on the other.

Philosophical speculation resorts very quickly, as Plato's cave demonstrates, to analogy. Analogy introduces difference while retaining a close resemblance to that which it represents. Thus there are good and bad analogies according to whether the resemblance is preserved or difference asserts itself as rupture. What at first was necessary then becomes an imitation threatening to replace or distort its model. Cinema, as we have seen, is caught in such a paradox. A discourse such as realism, which rests on the image's analogical relation to reality, leads straight to questions of close or distant analogy, and close or distant quickly becomes a matter of good or bad. Psychoanalytic film theory

[19] "The Apparatus: Metapsychological Approaches to the Impression of Reality in Cinema," in *Narrative, Apparatus, Ideology*, 299–318.

[20] Gk. *theorein*, to view.

develops from Metz's rationalization of the differences between spectating and dreaming, or spectating and the mirror stage, to Baudry's elaboration of what might be loosely called an *analogicization* effected by the desiring subject. Cinema becomes then not so much a system of representation marked by a distinct and privileged relation to the real; rather it is a function of the articulation by desire of difference, an example of the peculiar economy serving both to resolve and preserve difference. Within that economy it seems impossible to determine whether cinema is analogous before it becomes cinematic or whether analogy is libidinal before it comes to underwrite cinema.

Let us now look more closely at the status of this "reality" in cinematic representation. As we have seen, in the realist argument the photographic image is a supplement to reality somehow deriving its superiority over other forms of representation by its own effacement. It claims to be only slightly different from reality when compared with other forms of representation, more a deferral than a difference. But the effect of such a priority based on proximity to a supposed original is to undermine the integrity of that original and so to throw off the whole basis of comparison. The problem, of course, is that the closer the copy seems to be to the original and the more the idea of difference that the copy demonstrates and conceals is suspected to reside within the original itself, the more one comes to conceive of the original as composed of an interminable series of minute differences or deferrals. Hence if the original reality is not the intact notion that it was thought to be, if the work of representation that one normally recognizes in the copy can be "located" so close to the original, one might reasonably assume that representation and the difference it represents are at work within the very conception of reality thought to be the starting point.[21]

---

[21] Various theorists have already correctly pointed out, of course, that the "reality" that film is said to copy, to imitate, or to record is itself already an ideologically determined *representation* enabling it to appear to be coherent in different ways to members of different societies in different eras (Cf., for example, Peter L. Berger and Thomas Luckmann, *The Social Construction of Reality* [New York: Doubleday, 1966]; and Bill Nichols, *Ideology and the Image* [Bloomington: Indiana University Press, 1981]).

Similarly, any idea of a direct perception of reality is itself also called into question. Note, for example, the following remark made by Derrida in the discussion period after his paper "Structure, Sign, and Play in the Discourse of the Human Sciences," delivered at the Johns Hopkins University in 1966:

I don't know what perception is and I don't believe that anything like perception exists. Perception is precisely a concept, a concept of an intuition or of a given

As Derrida asks in *Of Grammatology*, "Is that imitative [mimetic] supplement not dangerous to the integrity of what is represented and to the original purity of nature?" (203).

Bazin is led to a similar conclusion in his defense of Italian neorealism. For him, the principle characteristic of neorealism is that it is able to represent the "essence" of the reality appearing on the screen and, by extension, the essence of reality itself. By definition, however, in this logocentric model the essence of reality can never be part of the "inessential" material details actually shown, and thus the essence is a kind of supplement coming from the outside, from elsewhere. Bazin, perhaps recognizing the danger, complains that the "necessary illusion of film . . . quickly induces a loss of awareness of the reality itself, which becomes identified in the mind of the spectator with its cinematographic equivalent" (*What Is Cinema?* 2:27).[22]

The hierarchy between original and copy, usually assumed to involve the temporal primacy of the former over the latter, can be deconstructed from another point of view. Indeed, in any operation that involves copying, for example photocopying, one never uses the word "original" until there is a copy, which retrospectively creates the "originalness" of the original. There can never be an original until there is a copy of it. In a sense, then, the original can be said to be constituted by the copy, just as cause and effect, as Nietzsche pointed out, can be reversed, from a temporal perspective, once we realize that it is always the effect that comes first, causing us to look for its cause.[23] In film, this can perhaps be seen most clearly in the context of documentaries, which usually offer themselves as more or less objective depictions of certain aspects of reality. Yet it is equally clear that such documentaries individuate new areas to be explored, new problems to be solved, and so on in such a way as to "create" a new reality. They institute borders and construct frames around an inchoate reality, thereby making it meaningful, but always in a way that intends to be perfectly natural and that claims to follow the contours of reality itself.

---

originating from the thing itself, present itself in its meaning, independently from language, from the system of reference. And I believe that perception is interdependent with the concept of origin and of center and consequently whatever strikes at the metaphysics of which I have spoken strikes also at the very concept of perception" (*The Structuralist Controversy*, ed. Richard Macksey and Eugenio Donato [Baltimore: The Johns Hopkins University Press, 1972], 272).

[22] For a fuller discussion of Bazin and neorealism, from a deconstructive point of view, see Peter Brunette, *Roberto Rossellini*, 53–60.

[23] Cf. Culler's discussion in *On Deconstruction*, 86–88.

In a parallel gesture, the original so created is always essentialized and those aspects deemed inessential are omitted.[24]

We do not want to say, however, that the copy only and always creates the original; this would be merely to reverse the hierarchy. Rather, the relation between reality and, say, a documentary on it, would be displaced and redefined such that the two terms came to be seen as mutually constituting each other. The relation between them would thus be an intertextual one.

In cinema it has always been the very ability, first of the photograph and then of the motion picture, to claim priority for themselves by virtue of their realism that has to a great extent made cinema such a monolithic structure whose various forms are measured in terms of how they stand with respect to the dominant model of narrative film. Yet if Bazin were to be taken more at his word when he evokes the traces of reality that can be found in the film, if the word "trace" were to be exploited in a Derridean sense, in order to extract the image from the oculocentrism that so determines the uses to which it is put, one could perhaps begin radically to displace the conventional terms of discussion concerning the relations between image and referent.

If the image-referent relation were to be conceived in terms of writing, questions of iconicity, which still inform much discourse on film theory,[25] would open onto the wider context of rhetorical relations. The image would have to be conceived of as issuing from an absent or "dead" reality, much in the same way that writing is held, at least structurally speaking, to issue from a dead author.[26] The image is conceived, in these terms, within the perspective of reality's absence; it is meant to be received, and is allowed to circulate, without that reality. It is subject then to the same vagaries (and they are not so much vagaries, mere accidents, as structural necessities) as the letter. If the image is a trace, it is the mark of an absence, and if there is something privileged about it in comparison to other representations, its privilege is to show more clearly than those other forms how systematically in our

[24] For example the television network news, and the media in general, are continually discovering new problems on which to produce documentaries and thus to construct reality after the fact. Examples might be the current representation of "the drug problem" or the suddenly pressing national "problem" of child abduction some time back.

[25] Cf. de Lauretis, *Alice Doesn't*, 40–45.

[26] Cf. "Signature Event Context": "For the written to be written, it must continue to 'act' and to be legible even if what is called the author of the writing no longer answers for what he has written, for what he seems to have signed, whether he is provisionally absent, or if he is dead . . ." (*Margins*, 316). In view of our previous comments, and indeed in the context of Derrida's article, this "death" of the author must be understood to remain "signed."

culture, whenever absence comes into relation with presence, by some trick of magic the latter always asserts itself at the expense of the former.

We should emphasize here that our desire to read film as writing in Derrida's sense is not an argument for fewer narrative films; nor for more nonrealist images (for it is by no means clear what that might mean, since the nonrealist representation may well be in the same relationship as the realist copy with respect to its "original"); nor for less cinema and more video. As Marie-Claire Ropars emphasizes in her discussion of Duras's *India Song*, any simple opposition between an originary realism and a form of modernism that is a departure from realism hides the fact that that departure or spacing is precisely what constitutes the very process of representation and that "realist codification is merely one formula among others, seeking to reduce or counteract the extent of that spacing" (*Le Texte divisé*, 158; our translation). Hence we seek rather to shift the basis of discussion so that the relations between different forms are compared in new ways, without recourse, either implicit or explicit, to a hierarchy that was never really as well founded as it claimed to be. Indeed, it is not only the realist/nonrealist opposition that might need to be rewritten but also the various oppositions that supposedly obtain between film image, video image, and computerized synthetic image. In the domain of the trace there might be more to be gained from comparing the film image and the telex or satellite information transfer, say, since both can be seen as short-circuit representations, conveying copious amounts of information within a restricted time frame, or between film and some other form by virtue of its reproducibility.

Cinema, as we began this chapter by saying, is a medium whose line of communication, because of its immense technical apparatus, is particularly indirect and complicated. Once the critique turns to the wider context of the apparatus of cinema, any remaining hint of ideas of directness and immediacy, such as obtain in the image-referent relation, is dispelled by the complex system of production and reception. Here we refer not only to the obvious technical and economic complexities of production itself and to the arbitrariness of the distribution process but also to the structures of spectating uncovered by psychoanalytic film theory. The complicity between textual operations and the operations of the viewing experience that feminist psychoanalytic theorists have delineated, the so-called complicity of the looks comprising cinema and their repetition through various mechanisms of the apparatus,[27] as well as the unique type of mirror that the screen comes to

---

[27] For a recent summary of such studies, see de Lauretis, *Alice Doesn't*, 37–69.

represent in such discussions—all these matters can be read as pointing to the structure of differential repetition that underwrites cinema as writing.

But there is another point to be made regarding the special materiality of film, which argues for further work on rewriting the relation between text and apparatus. Film, by virtue of the editing process, produces leftovers of enormous proportions. If one compares it with the medium of literature, it becomes apparent how much the final product of cinema emerges from a process of discard. Books, of course, are composed out of notes and mental jottings that may or may not find their way into the wastepaper basket or become subject to a "delete" command, and also out of prior readings whose materiality usually gets reduced to a simple mention in a bibliography. Film, however, requires a particularly explicit act of material overproduction (a shooting ratio, it is assumed, will never be 1:1), followed by one of selection and excision. And the construction of the film through montage is paradoxically rendered possible only by that operation of discard. What is demonstrated again is that both apparently opposed gestures participate in the same structure, that of the supplement, and that in the film's construction the materiality of the signifier is constantly elided, providing the lure yet inscribing the impossibility of an intact origin.

Furthermore, a particularly strange set of contradictions comes into play in the materialization of "reality" that the film operates. Writing (in the usual sense), for example, begins with the blank page, like the unexposed celluloid. But unlike the blank page, unexposed celluloid can have no sense with respect to the system of sense, namely the visual, that the film medium brings into play.[28] Unexposed film cannot be seen, because the medium in its "original" form is not just the vehicle for but the very contradiction of the light that will come to constitute it. This contradiction represents only the first in a series of negative/positive relations leading through exposure, developing, printing, editing, screening, and perception. For example, the editing process involves the cutting and montage to which we have referred; the screening of a film relies on a play of the presence and absence of light—the white screen has to be blackened in order to light up with

---

[28] Paradoxically, of course, the "opposition" between film and writing being developed here is designed to promote film as writing in the Derridean sense. However, the limitations of the analogy should not be obscured. On the one hand, in contrast to manual composition and editing, writing by word processor would seem to have a structural progression somewhat analogous to cinema as "writing"; on the other hand, the play of blank page and black letters can also be compared to the articulation of light and dark on the screen.

images; and the images themselves, like words on a page, can only come into existence through the same differential play of light. Finally, the perception of the film mirrors the exposure of celluloid with which the process began, as successive images are imprinted on the retina. Thus it is as if the paradoxical structure of absence and presence that we have maintained, following Derrida, to be constitutive of any utterance, is deployed in a kind of syntagmatic chain of contradictions that produce cinema's "reality," with each material step along the path of cinematic enunciation being in effect a negation of the previous step.

The idea of a teleological evolution of reality's representation of itself, like the idea of instant reproduction, can therefore be seen to be a metaphysical overlay rather than an accurate description of the process of cinematic mediation. The distancing effect that undermines notions of immediacy in cinematic representation is matched by this string of contradictory supplements required for the so-called image of the real to appear on the screen.

Doubtless, film's claim to priority as realist representation, which amounts to a claim for truth ("the camera never lies"), derives from the status given to light and the visible in Western metaphysics, discussed at length by Derrida in "White Mythology." In the chain of supplements described above it is the white screen that represents the central material support for the differential play of the image. As such, the screen seems to us to take its place within another set of Derridean terms developing out of the series including *différance*, trace, supplement, and writing. Being physical marks on a page as well as abstract notions that can lead all the way to the literary, "writing" stands between a concrete reference and an abstract concept and thus serves to demonstrate how Derrida's use of these terms resists the hard and fast distinction between abstract and concrete. *Différance*, to take another example, has its difference from "difference" registered in the written form but not the spoken and so comments concretely on the relation between the two. It is homonymic in its effect. But there is another such series—pharmakon, tympan, hymen, parergon—exploited by Derrida to develop further his effort at reconceptualization. These work, like "writing," from their reference to objects to form the basis of "ideas" that would not then rely on the idealization implied in the normal emergence of concepts. It is this series that invites comparison with the screen. A further shift in Derrida's choice of models leads him to such figures (for they perform what we must still call, short of another vocabulary, "rhetorical functions") as the umbrella, postcard, and matchbox, "whose functioning he interrogates as modelling the most complex or abstract levels of thought" (*Applied Grammatology*, xii). These we will refer to in a later discussion.

If the cinema, as we have argued, is no longer to be considered as the means by which a privileged visual medium controls and guarantees reality's "fall" into language or representation, with minimal loss of its original integrity, but rather as the series of deferrals and play of ruptures and differences constituting any language and any utterance, the screen becomes not the site of the consecration of that former metaphysically oriented or motivated operation but rather its marginal or liminal support. Its supposed diaphanous quality then results not so much from its being an imperfect window upon the world but from its functioning as membrane, locus of relay and articulation, as well as system of protection involving its own abolition. In other words, the screen must both be present and obscured, or absent, for its effect to be realized.

There are two such membranes evoked in Derrida's writings, namely the tympan and the hymen. Both have additional senses besides the physiological ones immediately called to mind: notably "marriage" in the case of hymen and "a type of support chassis in a printing press" in the case of the tympan. Although the tympan is obviously important in any discussion of a system such as cinema—which because of its reliance on orality/aurality preserves its privilege by means of a notion of proximity through the supposed limited circulation of sense or meaning—we have no need to emphasize further what we have already said in that regard. In any case, it is clear that the tympan performs contradictory functions, both separating and transmitting, functions that destroy any self-evident sense of inside and outside.[29] On the other hand, the hymen, whose sense is developed especially in the seminar published as "The Double Session," is useful to us in elaborating the particular function of the screen in the cinematic apparatus. That it is a sexed object/concept/metaphor is of course not to be overlooked, and as such its strategic importance demands all the more that we treat of it.

Now, as tempting as a simple and literal application of the sense of hymen to the cinematic screen might be, that tack cannot be adopted here. The least reason is the very complex sense of the word, as of any of Derrida's terms, which develops from the context in which he discusses it—that of the work of Mallarmé but also of Mallarmé in the

[29] "Tympan," in *Margins*, ix–xxix.

context of Plato, thematic and idealist literary criticism, and the work of contemporary French writer Philippe Sollers. In fact, to produce the sense of hymen as a notion applicable to cinema, one needs to read "The Double Session" in somewhat the same way that Derrida reads the relation of Plato to Mallarmé on the question of mimesis in the first part of that essay.

In juxtaposing a fragment of Socratic dialogue (*Philebus*) and a piece of text by Mallarmé (*Mimique*) discussing a mime performance (or at least an account or the "libretto" of that performance), Derrida sets out to undo an idealist reading of Mallarmé. According to that idealist reading the statement "the scene illustrates but the idea, not any actual action" (175) would repeat, in contradicting it, Socrates' distinction between true and false thoughts and statements, and by extension the concept of mimesis. "One would then say: of course, the mime does not imitate any actual thing or action, any reality that is already given in the world, existing before and outside his own sphere; he doesn't have to conform, with an eye toward verisimilitude, to some real or external model. . . . But the relation of imitation and the value of adequation remain intact since it is still necessary to imitate, represent, or 'illustrate' the idea" (194). Derrida's aim is to read the text otherwise, and in order to do so he fastens upon the word "hymen," which occurs in the next part of Mallarmé's sentence quoted above: "The scene illustrates but the idea, not any actual action, in a hymen (out of which flows Dream), tainted with vice yet sacred, between desire and fulfillment . . ." (175). This word, generally meaning marriage, is common enough in Mallarmé's writings and, in fact, in the history of mime and the *commedia dell'arte* as well. What is interesting about it, however, and what makes it function in the same manner as Derrida's other key words, is that if it brings two things together, it also separates them. The hymen is that which occurs between two things, like a marriage, and which signals their collapse into one, but it also stands *between* these things like a membrane, creating an inside and an outside. As Derrida defines it in *Positions*, "the hymen is neither confusion nor distinction, neither identity nor difference, neither consummation nor virginity, neither the veil nor unveiling, neither the inside nor the outside" (43). Investigating the dynamics of the double sense of this word, Derrida suggests that a hymen exists between Plato and Mallarmé, described as that between literature and truth. However, as the discussion progresses and centers upon Mallarmé's text and on the instance of the word "hymen" in that text, its sense is conflated with and doubled by the word *entre* (between, enter), according to the logic of the syntax. For Mallarmé refers to a "marriage (*hymen*) . . . between (*entre*) desire and its fulfillment," but as Derrida points out by evoking the series of revisions that the text underwent and by paying close attention to the punctuation, Mallarmé's text has introduced progressively more ambiguity at this point of its enunciation (and no one was more conscious of the ambiguities of syntax than Mallarmé), so that in the final version "hymen" reads in apposition to *entre*, whose homonymic double sense (*antre*) repeats to a great extent the senses of the former word (209–12).[30]

One could go into more detail concerning Derrida's discussion, but let us attempt to outline the operation at work here. First, there is a typically Derridean shift of attention from the main clause of the sentence (which tends more "naturally" to the idealist reading) to the rest of the same sentence, and a corresponding shift from what seems to be the central explicit idea to the finer points of punctuation and the indirect functionings of sense. Derrida maintains finally that the sense of the syntax exceeds and, as it were, supersedes the semantic references.[31] The process could stop here, for in many ways the whole Der-

---

[30] Derrida quotes the French dictionary *Littré*, according to which "antre," meaning a cave or a grotto, comes from the Sanskrit *antara*, meaning "interval," and so relates to Latin "inter," which in French is "entre" (212). In a later discussion of this passage, Derrida also takes up the question of intentionality in an interesting way:

This reading is possible. It is "normal" both from the syntactic and from the semantic point of view. But what a laborious artifice! Do you really believe, goes the objection, that Mallarmé consciously parceled out his sentence so that it could be read two different ways, with each object capable of changing into a subject and vice versa, without our being able to arrest this movement? . . . Whatever might have been going on in Mallarmé's head, in his consciousness or unconscious, does not matter to us here; the reader should now know why. (225)

Despite the above disclaimer, however, Derrida goes on to offer an elaborate proof of his reading "for those who are interested in Stéphane Mallarmé and would like to know what he was thinking and meant to do by writing in this way." After showing that the ambiguity has been introduced only in the third printed version of this passage, Derrida then neatly turns the tables on those who always want to link sense to the centering intentionality of the author: "Perhaps he didn't know what he was doing? Perhaps he wasn't conscious of it? Perhaps, then, he wasn't completely the author of what was being written?" (225–26).

[31] It is important to signal the extent to which Derrida insists on ascribing the resonance these terms carry to syntax rather than to semantics:

What counts here is not the lexical richness, the semantic infiniteness of a word or concept, its depth or breadth, the sedimentation that has produced inside it two contradictory layers of signification. . . . What holds for "hymen" also holds, *mutatis mutandis*, for all other signs which, like *pharmakon, supplement, différance,* and others, have a double, contradictory, undecidable value that always derives from their syntax, whether the latter is in a sense "internal," articulating and combining

ridean enterprise is encapsulated in these small but crucial shifts. We would however like to pursue the extent to which writing (in Derrida's terms), and Derrida's writing specifically, in a complex fashion shows and tells in the same movement. For it is this idea, finally, that we want to bring to bear upon film theory.

Derrida concentrates on the ways in which a word in Mallarmé's sentence begins to exceed the normal operations of sense, to underline its own semantic and etymological resources, and to put into effect the operation of "literature," the operation that is writing and as a result of which idealism cannot so easily assert its claims and its will to truth. A certain shift occurs that brings about a suspension, or vice versa (the paradoxical play of time in mimesis is discussed in both Plato's and Mallarmé's texts), all of which is subsumed, without being contained, by the notion of the hymen. For since what counts is the displacement of and for which the hymen is the site, it has of itself no centralizing force.[32] Indeed, a further important wordplay that Derrida uses to indicate the shift just described is that from *centre* to *entre*. The removal of the "c" from *centre* refers back to comments at the beginning of his essay concerning his resistance to assigning a title or headword (or letter) to it (177–78).

Derrida's reading thus relies on the possibility of interventions with respect to the materiality of the signifier provided by anagrammatical and etymological play. It should be noted, however, that Derrida's usage of such play, particularly in this essay, is in fact very judicious. Part of the reason for such a strategy is to confound sameness with unnoticed difference—as with the homonyms *différence/différance* or, in this essay, *entre/antre*, where speech does not distinguish between written differences. The ambiguity of the word *hymen* is suggested by Mallarmé's use of it, and its relation to *hymne* has some etymological justification (which Derrida takes pains to spell out [213]). What is achieved then by this technique may be likened to a type of poetic condensation, analogous to that effected by Mallarmé, bringing the sorts of shifts that Derrida finds within the development of an idea or

---

under the same yoke, *huph'hen*, two incompatible meanings, or "external," dependent on the code in which the word is made to function. But the syntactical composition and decomposition of a sign rends this alternative between internal and external inoperative. (220–21)

[32] In the ultimate shift, Derrida points out that "We have indeed been making believe that everything could be traced to the word *hymen*. But the irreplaceable character of this signifier, which everything seemed to grant it, was laid out like a trap. This word, this syllepsis, is not indispensable; philology and etymology interest us only secondarily, and the loss of the 'hymen' would not be irreparable for *Mimique*" (220).

throughout a work to reside within the limited space of a single word. As such, it can then also be seen as part of a larger strategy calling into question the traditional distinction between criticism and literature or between discursive and "creative" writing.

Thus what the hymen means is a series of shifts and a certain undecidability (and Derrida makes reference to Gödel's theorem [219]), an undecidability of reference and of representation: "The Mime mimes reference. He is not an imitator; he mimes imitation. The hymen interposes itself between mimicry and *mimesis* or rather between *mimesis* and *mimesis*" (219). In the end what must be recognized is the breaking down of the separation (although no rupture of a classic type shows) between the traditionally conceived content of a text and the formal practice which that text engages. The hymen, with its connotations of veil, of whiteness, and of suspension, relates to a whole thematic in the poet's work that Mallarmé scholars have extensively discussed. But Mallarmé's texts do not merely speak of the hymen, they in fact "hymenize," if such a word could exist. They put into effect their own suspension. Then, in the final analysis, so do Derrida's texts, and Rousseau's, and Plato's, and so on. For none of these names can be credited with discovering this practice, even if in Mallarmé's case it seems to lie so close to the surface (though generations of commentators apparently failed to notice it), and even if Derrida has analyzed it more systematically than his predecessors. What is at work here is nothing other than a fact of language, the fact of its double effect, its simultaneous will to coherence and the overstepping of its own boundaries; the mime of its sameness—always with a difference—and the pirouettes of its performance.

Let us now operate our own shift in sites of representation, from mime and writing to film. There occurs in Derrida's essay the following sentence: "[The Mime] is both read and reading, written and writing, between the two, in the suspense of the hymen, at once screen and mirror" (224). This mention of "screen and mirror" is a fortuitous event like the anagrams and etymological chances Derrida exploits, but, as with the word "hymen" in Derrida's analysis of Mallarmé, it is by no means a necessary pretext for our shift. The scene of cinema is already explicitly set by the simple fact of the discussion's being centered on matters of realist and idealist representation. One could also note, by the way, since the reference is made in "The Double Session," Mallarmé's allusion to an incipient cinema in answer to an enquiry concerning the advantages of illustrating texts: "I am for—no illustration; everything a book evokes should happen in the reader's mind: but, if you replace photography, why not go straight to cinematography, whose successive unrolling will replace, in both pictures and text, many a volume, advantageously" (quoted by Derrida, 208). Following Derrida's lead we shall read that suggestion by Mallarmé not as another idealist preference for a more putatively direct, less mediated means of representation but as the invitation to include cinema within the structure of the book, within the space we are calling writing.

In the extract from *Philebus* discussed in "The Double Session" Socrates explains how a speaker, ruminating in the absence of an interlocutor, makes use of an "internal scribe" since "the conjunction of memory with sensations . . . may be said as it were to write words within our souls." But there is also someone else at work there, a "painter who comes after the writer and paints in the soul pictures of these assertions that we make." This painter also performs the converse task of providing for the mind the image of reality once the immediacy of actual vision no longer operates; it is a mnemonic device. The role of this mental "painter," this representative of the visual, is to fill in for a lack of speech in the silent speaker, to compensate for the fullness that "opinions and assertions" together with "the act of sight" (175) would otherwise provide. Both painter and writer share the same space in this construction, that of mimesis, which is governed by the relation to speech. The book of the mind or memory is a silent dialogue. The painting of the mind therefore is, one could say without too much exaggeration, a silent film, a series of images without the sound track that is speech. And since mimesis underwrites these operations ("imitate" has the same root as "image," as Derrida points out [188]), it is the possibility of visual representation that is the guarantee of truth.

Although the truth or falsity of what is recorded by these processes remains by Socrates' admission a separate issue from the matter of representation itself, the operation of mimesis has, as Derrida mentions (186–87), a particularly ambiguous status in Plato's writings. Sometimes it is condemned as a process of duplication having of itself no value, but at other times it is disqualified because of the falsity of its model, the mimetic operation itself being considered, in this case, neutral. Yet this ambiguity derives quite simply from the paradox of any representation, particularly that which, like the cinematic image, claims to be most faithful to its model: simply by doubling its referent, like a mirror, it exposes both its pure supplementarity and its profound difference, its potential deformation of that referent.

Mallarmé's mime operates, as it were, at the extreme or outside edge of that ambiguity: "That is how the Mime operates," the poet says, "whose act is confined to a perpetual allusion without breaking the ice or the mirror [*la glace*]: he thus sets up a medium, a pure medium, of

fiction" (quoted by Derrida, 175). Mime could be that faithful representation of the model required when the voice (of truth) is lacking,
but it becomes instead, in Mallarmé's terms, a "pure medium," the
space of representation itself, and as a consequence a medium of fiction. A certain mirror effect is preserved, with mimesis continuing to
subsume the exercise, but the plane of the mirror is lined with the
marks of writing, a "perpetual allusion" (note that Mallarmé's word is
not *illusion* but *allusion*). What is involved then is a type of quotation,
an operation that by definition, because of the displacement it implies,
cannot but be indirect speech, unfaithful translation.

We want to insist, in the context of this opacity occurring between
Plato and Mallarmé, this marriage or joining of Plato and Mallarmé,
that cinema can be read as the locus of such a transfer and of such
play—a marriage even—with the sense of mimesis. In fact, we shall
not hesitate to call cinema the deconstruction of the mimetic operation
rather than the confirmation of it, and it is in this sense that the screen
can be called a hymen. In the space of the hymen/screen/mirror, a site
that marks the inside of the apparatus from its outside, one encounters
the limit to which realist representation can extend itself and the frail
support for an operation that traverses it without rending it. But it is
also at that point or through that structure—we would not want the
operation to be governed by teleological overtones—that realist representation is required to engage its other. This other is—as we mentioned earlier—on the one hand, the spectator, an engagement implying a radicalization of the context of the image through film's
involvement in the various processes that psychoanalysis has detailed
as well as the image's inscription in any number of discursive processes—syntagmatic, historical, social, and so on—that a film brings
into play. On the other hand, realist representation must confront the
"other(s)" of realism and mimesis and thus be regarded, as in Plato, as
either a type of monumental superfluity, or as an "error" that is the
logical consequence of the operation of mimesis.

Depending as it does on the idea of visual resemblance, which involves, after all, the promise or the assumption of an originary perception, mimesis must always refer to a model that is itself an image, as
we saw in our earlier discussion, "before" its operation comes to be
defined as the (imperfect) visual copying of that model. The "origin"
is thus itself always mimetic, and the imaging process is always already
at work in the very conception of the reality whose wholeness mimesis
is asked to preserve and blamed for undoing.

The hymen must therefore also stand for the unseen of cinematic
representation, for the support of a visuality that would otherwise be

random play of light. And to return to a point made earlier, the hymen must stand for the marriage or rupture between sound and image, for if the sound track were to take leave of the strict context that is the screen, the plane of representation, then the overwhelming majority of films would reveal characters mouthing words, "a pure medium, of fiction," not so much charade as pure representationality. They would be miming reference, miming imitation.[33] Finally the hymen must stand for a different relation between critical discourse and its cinematic object. Such a discourse can remain transfixed by the apparent immediacy of the images on the screen and their incontrovertible explicitness, or it can reinvest that medium with what might be called a rhetoric of anagrammaticality whose terms we shall develop in the pages that follow.

In order to understand the intricate logic of anagrammaticality, it is necessary to examine in more detail the notion of iterability that Derrida discusses in his debate with Searle. Iterability or repeatability[34] is that to which difference as the founding principle of language gives rise. Unless language is composed of units that can be used over and over, it cannot function as a means of communication; rather, it becomes a proliferation of private languages with no hope of mutual comprehension. But even repetition is the mark of difference. Two of the same can never be the same as one alone. Thus the supposed absolute difference founding language in terms of the distinction between sensible and intelligible, and that Derrida deconstructs, is here compounded by a difference identified where it is not normally, that

[33] Sound does and does not "appear" on screen: the dialogue "appears" in the mouths of the characters, except in films like those of Duras, but it is heard "off"; conversely, music does not normally "appear," except in a film like Godard's *First Name Carmen*. Cf. Mary Ann Doane, "The Voice in the Cinema: The Articulation of Body and Space," in *Narrative, Apparatus, Ideology*:

> The hierarchical placement of the visible above the audible, according to Christian Metz, ["Le perçu et le nommé," in *Essais sémiotiques* (Paris: Klincksieck, 1977), 129–161] is not specific to the cinema but a more general cultural production. And the term voice-off merely acts as a reconfirmation of that hierarchy. For it only appears to describe a sound—what it really refers to is the visibility (or lack of visibility) of the source of the sound. Metz argues that sound is never "off." While a visual element specified as "off" actually lacks visibility, a "sound-off" is always audible. (338–39)

[34] Derrida uses the word "iterability" (Latin *iter*, again) because its root is supposed to be the Sanskrit word *itara*, meaning "other" (*Margins*, 315).

is, within the process of repetition itself. Repetition is the certainty of its own demise, for repetition cannot be simply repetition. Iterability, the basis of language, rather than ensuring the coherence of language, introduces the possibility of irreducible difference (because repetition always carries difference along with it) and the undermining of language as simple act of communication, as the conveying of a message from sender to addressee.

More generally in Derrida's texts the type of iterability within which the possibility of anagrammaticality falls is referred to as "citationality." Citationality is here synonymous with iterability in terms of the capacity that any utterance has of being repeated out of the context of its "original" constitution. Hence, in the extreme, an idea of reversibility is implied. It must be made clear that all this remains a structural necessity as long as the utterance is to function in language. Established first as a principle of written language—a type of language designed to function in the absence of its originator—Derrida extends the principle to all linguistic utterance by proving the structural similarity between writing and speech. As a consequence, since language necessitates the use of utterances out of the context of their imagined original conception, it can be said to be constituted by citation. Speaking and writing, for all their capacity to be acts, are thus equivalent to quoting, and all elements of discourse must submit to being marked by quotation marks. Speech marks surround any speech act; language is prefaced by the scratches of writing that speech omits.

Derrida compares the action of language to a type of grafting,[35] and in "The Double Session" he already calls for a typology of graft techniques to describe the ways various parts of a text—especially footnotes, titles, epigraphs, and prefaces—relate to one another (*Dissemination*, 202, as well as "Living On," in *Deconstruction and Criticism*, 80–81). In "Signature Event Context" this leads him to make his now oft-quoted remark:

> This is the possibility on which I wish to insist: the possibility of extraction and of citational grafting which belongs to the structure of every mark, spoken or written, and which constitutes every mark as writing even before and outside of every horizon of semiolinguistic communication. . . . every sign . . . can break with every given context, and engender infinitely new contexts, in an absolutely nonsaturable fashion. (*Margins*, 320)

[35] "Graft" (Fr. *greffe*) and "graph" in fact have a common etymology in the Greek *graphion*, a stylus.

As Culler points out, when Derrida argues for a relationship between words "present" and other words in the signifying system, "he is denying that there are principles by which signifying possibilities can be excluded in advance" (*On Deconstruction*, 219). Anagrammatical interventions within a word can be justified, on one level, on the grounds that one cannot finally decide between what is original context and distorted or derived context, what is "proper" and improper, what is serious or not serious, or what is correct and what is a gimmick. In any case, any use of anagrams by Derrida is always part of a close reading but a reading without the guidance of what De Man has called "the teleology of controlled meaning." The anagram is never completely arbitrary in its manipulation of the sign. An anagrammatical variant of a word preserves its signs of grafting by recalling the context of the first word and introducing another; it is in these terms, perhaps, that its connection with iterability and citationality can best be understood. Anagram is a kind of literality against the grain, underwritten not by the notion of an intact original sense but by the possibility of a "nonsaturable" context. From this point of view it can be said that *cinema is an anagram of the real*.

The notion of anagrammaticality is perhaps most useful as a counterpoint to analogicality. Although the prefix is the same, like so many prefixes, Greek or otherwise, like any unit of language capable of being recontextualized, the "ana-" means different things in the context of each word: "back" or "against the grain" when attached to *gramma*, or the written, "again" or "anew" (both harboring and suppressing the sense of "against the grain") in the case of *logos* or spoken truth. As we have seen earlier in this chapter, analogy is the figure of visual resemblance, the figure of the cinema as traditionally conceived, and the basis for the entire rhetoric of realism, as well as the metaphysics of idealism. Were that collaboration of the visual with the controlling force of truth as self-presence to be deconstructed, analogy could no longer be used to describe the operations at play in the apparatus that is cinema. Hence our recourse to anagram as a figure for a cinema to be read as writing, as figural traces, for which a rhetoric remains to be formulated. To move from ana*logy* to ana*gram* is to begin, at least, to move from logocentrism to writing.

We do not mean by the terms "grafting" and "anagrammaticality" to return to a naive conception of images as somehow equivalent to words nor to propose a taxonomy of rhetorical figures for the cinema. On the other hand, one might investigate such examples as the intertextual graft produced by the appearance of an actor in different films and its attendant effects on meaning. What we have just called a rhetoric of anagrammaticality calls for emphasis on any material effects of film's inscription as writing, its participation in the structures of writing such as we have been delineating. Its excess, in short, however that might be defined. Anagram is the outer limit of the relation between speech and writing, the figure of excess, the hymen of mimesis with radical shift or difference.

It is clear that such a shift will seriously dislocate conventional critical practices. Thus, in *Le Texte divisé*, Marie-Claire Ropars employs interpretive strategies that implicitly challenge current notions of "propriety" in film analysis. Though she insists that her reading of Duras's *India Song* has not been undertaken to "study the film for its own sake" (128), a discussion of a specific text is always in some sense an interpretation of it as well. The question then becomes: in the context of deconstructive reading, is it ever possible or desirable to establish criteria for interpretations? Or must *every* interpretation be considered equally valid? Are there any criteria that would allow us to say what in a reading is useful or productive and what is just plain silly?

In one place in *Le Texte divisé*, Ropars resorts to anagrammatic "evidence" to support her theoretical reading of Duras's film in terms of its tension between the progression of the narrative and the disseminative play of writing:

> Repeated several times, associated with Laos, the name Savanna-khet sounds even stranger since it contains, in the center the first name *anna*, and, at either end, the initial letters of *St*retter; with these two letters gone, what is left is *retter*, the reduced mark of the double, infinitely turned in on itself. . . . Savannakhet, the hidden name of the point of origin, provides, while holding it back, the name of Anne-(Marie) St(retter), which "Bir/manie" might complete, if *r* is substituted for *n* to make *marie*. . . . *St*ein begins the same as *St*retter and also as "*st*érile"; and the beggar, "*folle*," née *là*-bas, in "*L*aos," multiplies the letters of *Lo/la*; as does the network of *l*'s built up around Bengal ("*E*lle *les laisse, les* vend, *les* oublie") and punctuated by Ca*l*cutta.[36]

A conservative critic would of course immediately want to question whether this sort of anagrammatic play is in any way even remotely available to a spectator in what might be described as her or his immediate construction of the film; that one's immediate experience of

[36] "The Disembodied Voice (*India Song*)," *Yale French Studies*, no. 60 (1980), 260. The article this translation was based on was later incorporated into *Le Texte divisé* (cf. 150–61).

any given film has to be privileged over what can sometimes appear to be little more than the critic's own impressionistic, free-associative romp through the elements of a text. Yet such a recourse to an originary concept of "experience" can itself be deconstructed, for experience is always doubled, always constituted retrospectively, after it has "happened" and is thus forever split, internally divided between the past and the future. As Jonathan Culler has pointed out, " 'experience' is divided and deferred—already behind us as something to be recovered, yet still before us as something to be produced" (*On Deconstruction*, 82). Even though while watching a film on a movieola or a video tape on a recorder, one can run a shot or scene over and over again in order to analyze it, a temporal gap or spacing, however tiny, will always remain between the "reception" of the film's signifiers and any, inevitably retrospective, construction of their meaning.

It should also be pointed out that deconstructive analysis is not the first to raise the question of what constitutes a normal or immediate viewing experience of a film. Semiology already argued for the right to resist the process of immediate consumption that the economic apparatus of cinema determines in favor of a reading practice involving intervention in that process—repeated viewings, use of an editing table, analysis of stills, etc. Video cassettes have of course made those possibilities available to a much wider viewing public. But beyond all that, as we have maintained, one must accept that there simply is no normal viewing experience, that material conditions as simple as the number of people in the cinema or the quality of the print will always affect a viewer's perception and thus his or her reading of the film. To repeat, the radical recontextualizations that an analysis such as Ropars's amounts to exist within the structure of any linguistic utterance, and hence within the audio-visual utterance that is cinema.

Once the text is considered in the light of Derrida's radicalized notion of context, there is no way around treating its disseminative possibilities; anagrammaticality becomes a structurally necessary way of reading that dissemination. On the other hand, a theorist like Tom Conley perhaps too optimistically claims that the critic's use of anagrams in interpretation "allows us to move from a passive relation with language—it usually speaks us—to the active condition of a maker."[37] Conley seems here to confuse the possibility of readerly or anagrammatical interventions within specific textual instances with a move outside the logocentric prescriptions of language. The idea that a critic

[37] Tom Conley, "A Trace of Style," in *Displacement*, 81.

can make such a rapid move from one to the other is what Derrida's painstaking analyses resist. For the final result has the flavor of a mystical experience: "This involves painful travel to and from all kinds of repression, the uneasiness of loosening moorings and encountering vertigo and nausea, but it has the stake of bringing a reader into a world with a new symbolic reflexivity" (81). We therefore remain extremely skeptical that this critical gesture will allow, in Conley's words, "the maker, the affective subject, to pass through multiple borders that define all lived experience and, indeed, to cope with the world differently" (81). We are not at all sure that logocentrism can be so easily jettisoned by such Romantic gestures, in interpretation or elsewhere. Furthermore, it is our contention that such unconventional readings must be accompanied by a careful theorization of such a strategy; otherwise the question remains why such apparently subjective and impressionistic interpretations should be read at all. Though Derrida's work has perhaps been domesticated by much of what passes for deconstructive criticism, at least in America, surely another way of defusing its potential radical impact is to trivialize it through what risks amounting to the self-indulgent display of the critic's own free play of private associations.

In any case, it is clear that the liberation of the signifier Conley seems to call for makes no sense. As Derrida has pointed out: "the signifier is [not] fundamental or primary. The 'primacy' or 'priority' of the signifier would be an expression untenable and absurd to formulate illogically within the very logic that it would legitimately destroy. The signifier will never by rights precede the signified, in which case it would no longer be a signifier and the 'signifying' signifier would no longer have a possible signified" (*Of Grammatology*, 324). Whatever "play" the critic may allow him- or herself in reading a text—and we hazard our own such readings in a later chapter—must always follow a kind of closely argued deconstructive logic of its own. For all its exuberant unconventionality, for example, Derrida's own reading of the poetry of Francis Ponge in *Signsponge* is marked by an almost obsessive rigor. Such a reading must always conform to the specific contours of the text upon which it operates. Read within the frame or the context of her overall reading of *India Song*, the passage from Ropars quoted earlier makes its own sense according to a logic that we will explore further in the following chapter. What should be kept in mind is that a deconstructive reading will always involve a doubling, a double reading and a double writing. As Derrida puts it in "Plato's Pharmacy," the critic can "err" by being either too cautious or not cautious enough:

One must then, in a single gesture, but doubled, read and write. And that person would have understood nothing of the game who, at this, would feel himself authorized merely to add on; that is, to add any old thing. He would add nothing: the seam wouldn't hold. Reciprocally, he who through "methodological prudence," "norms of objectivity," or "safeguards of knowledge" would refrain from committing anything of himself, would not read at all. The same foolishness, the same sterility, obtains in the "not serious" as in the "serious." The reading or writing supplement must be rigorously prescribed, but by the necessities of a *game*, by the logic of *play*, signs to which the system of all textual powers must be accorded and attuned. (*Dissemination*, 64)

There are further consequences of any attempt to rewrite analogical relations as anagrammatic ones. Relations between anagrammaticality or citationality and representation provide the basis for Derrida's deconstruction, in "The Double Session," of the idealist reading of Mallarmé's *Mimique*. The important central section of Mallarmé's essay, parts of which were cited above, in fact appears in the text within quotation marks, with no attribution. However, comparison with earlier versions of *Mimique* reveals that, because of progressive modifications, this is a "false" citation, a case of Mallarmé quoting himself. Derrida uses that as a pretext for analyzing all the layers of deferral from the content of the mime itself, in which a Pierrot tickles Colombine to death—a mimicking of the sexual act and of the act of murder itself, since there is no trace of the crime—through the various other texts in which such a Pierrot is represented and through the relations of performance and libretto, which finally lead to Mallarmé's text and its discussion of the mimetic. Derrida concludes with the concentrated *mise en abyme* that is the hymen, whereby the text refers simultaneously to itself and to another text:

We are faced then with mimicry imitating nothing; faced, so to speak, with a double that doubles no simple. . . . This speculum reflects no reality; it produces mere "reality-effects." . . . In this speculum with no reality, in this mirror of a mirror, a difference or dyad does exist, since there are mimes and phantoms. But it is a difference without reference, or rather a reference without a referent. . . . (206)

Taken to its logical extreme, the structure of citationality brings about the deconstruction of representation to the extent that the referent can

no longer be found. Which is not to say that all signs become meaningless, far from it; what it means is that the concept of representation
that relies on an assumed, self-identical first unit—a referent—is called
irrevocably into question and that meaning can no longer be firmly
anchored within that system.

Could it be said of the cinematic image that it is a reference without
a referent? The analogical relation between image and referent is after
all traditionally held to be qualitatively different from the arbitrary relation between word and referent. But our argument, following Derrida, aims precisely to bring those apparent opposites, analogy and
arbitrariness, within the same structure that is citationality or iterability. The aim here is not to reduce the obvious qualitative distinction
but to call for a redefinition of the conceptual field such that one form
cannot be privileged over all the others by virtue of its unwritten recourse to a metaphysics of proximity and singularity, which is ultimately a metaphysics of presence and being.

If cinema is said to hold a privileged status—perhaps universality or
comprehensibility—among forms of representation, it is because those
ideas relate back to the metaphysical guarantees mentioned above. But
if this privilege is taken away from cinema and it comes to be regarded
as a form of representation not superior to or more true than, but
merely different from, other forms on grounds other than those of
mimetic representation—say, in terms of the relation it operates between the syntagmatic and paradigmatic, as semiology has shown, or,
in terms of the speed of the informational process (where it could be
seen as inferior to cybernetic forms)—then cinema also becomes, in
the final analysis, reference without a referent, completely removed
from the mimetic model.

One is often tempted, in speaking of cinema, to refer to the real that
it represents. And one usually feels constrained to place that reality
within quotation marks, conscious of the mediation that the "real" has
inevitably undergone. The strength of Derrida's argument is that the
slight qualification that these quotation marks signal is enough to undo
the whole coherence of the representational process. Those marks,
traces of an other than simple duplication, as any duplication must by
definition be, open a spacing that is sufficient to allow a medium as
pure as a silent mime imitating nothing with an assignable origin.
What Derrida says of *Mimique* can thus also be applied to cinema:

> The center of presence is supposed to offer itself to what is called
> perception or, generally, intuition. In *Mimique*, however, there is

no perception, no reality offering itself up, in the present, to be
perceived. The plays of facial expression and the gestural tracings
are not present in themselves since they always refer, perpetually
allude or represent. But they don't represent anything that has
ever been or can ever become present. (210)

After Mallarmé and Derrida, then, we can say that the *screen* (the word
is formed by the simple addition of an "r" to an anagram of the French
[*scène*] for "stage"—like that on which a mime is enacted) *illustrates but
the idea, not any actual action.*

As we pointed out earlier, however, it would be a grave misconcep-
tion to read anagrammaticality as promoting a so-called nonrepresentational or nonrealist cinema, whose presentation on the screen of certain forms not recognized as analogous to forms perceived in reality
does not necessarily alter the structures of reference in place. The
screen, in the present discussion, is a synecdoche for the entire apparatus of cinema, and even then only metonymic to and support for the
image that, whatever its form, continues to function within a system
ruled by idealism. One could in fact imagine a nonrepresentational cinema becoming even more idealist if it attempted to use the image as a
more "direct" perception of an idealization of a supposedly truer, more
real reality. As Derrida has stated concerning literary mimesis:

> This order will no doubt appear to be contested, even inverted, in
> the course of history, and on repeated occasions. . . . In the do-
> main of "criticism" or poetic art, it has indeed been maintained
> that art, as imitation (representation, description, expression,
> imagination, etc.) must not be "servile" . . . and that it can create
> and produce works which are worth more than what they imi-
> tate. . . . But the absolute discernability between imitated and
> imitation, and the anteriority of the former over the latter, will
> never have been displaced. . . . (218)

The shift that we are outlining here would operate throughout the apparatus and would recognize it as being *composed* of shifts or displace-
ments—not merely prey to occasional mishaps—over which the idealism supporting realism could not function as the controlling force.
The cinema would be read as that which, by coming between the act
of perception and the presence of reality, irrevocably problematizes the
relation of perception to reality. Without denying such a relation, cinema would challenge the unwritten assumptions normally governing
it. We wish to argue, therefore, for another conception of cinema

within the play of representations, for another contextualization of the image within "visual" information systems—for other strategies of reading.

One important thing remains to be discussed, as we mentioned earlier, namely that the term "hymen" always has inscribed upon it its sex, the fact of its being feminine membrane, synecdoche for woman. Thus, one might ask whether the hymen, as site of potential, and perhaps structural and institutional, violence performed on real women in the real world, was not being overlooked or obscured in the appropriation of the term for deconstruction. From the perspective of that feminist critique, the hymen would indeed be reference *with* a referent, and any theory that sought to problematize the referential function might be deemed to be obscuring this co-optation of the female body.

If the hymen as Derrida uses it stands for and necessitates the displacement whereby reference based on an idealism of a transcendental signified is deconstructed, it is nonetheless also inscribed in a play of references, in a complicated transfer of sense. Within that play and that transfer the words "violence" and "woman" have explicit mention:

> The hymen, the consummation of differends, the continuity and confusion of the coitus, merges with what it seems to be derived from: the hymen as protective screen, the jewel box of virginity, the vaginal partition, the fine, invisible veil, which, in front of the hystera, stands *between* the inside and the outside of woman. . . . It is the hymen that desire dreams of piercing, of bursting, in an act of violence that is (at the same time or somewhere between) love and murder. If either one *did* take place, there would be no hymen. . . . With all the undecidability of its meaning, the hymen only takes place when it doesn't take place, when nothing *really* happens, when there is an all-consuming consummation without violence, or violence without blows. . . . (212–13; Derrida's italics)

The argument could be made that for a male critic to use the term "hymen" is to reenact structures of mastery over if not violence to woman. On the other hand this would be first of all to accept biology as destiny and second, to ignore that the potential violence occurring across the hymen is the violence that reduces the hymen to a single sense (that of woman), for it is the violence of a clash or resolution of differences, the very opposition that the hymen in question here deconstructs. The hymen both affirms and confounds that opposition. To treat it as more than inconsequential in its protective and discriminating mode[38] would be to anchor it within the logic of virginity and the marketing of woman that such a logic supports. On the other hand, to claim that it has no part to play is to revert to the idealism of unmediated transparency or mystical union between the same and its other; it would be as if the sexual act resolved sexual difference by means of a transcendental gesture.

Thus the place of the hymen is not to take place, and in referring to violence it refers to a violence without any mark; if it can be said without too much sophistry, it is the violence that occurs within the ambit of or at the limit of play. Hence Derrida's reference to violence is not strictly speaking a reference to violence, or at least it is a reference to a violence that must appear between quotation marks. And indeed, the same must be said of woman. For although it appears here as specifically feminine, the hymen, as we saw earlier, is only one of a series of terms performing similar operations: "What holds for 'hymen' also holds, *mutatis mutandis*, for all other signs which, like *pharmakon, supplément, différance* and others, have a double, contradictory, undecidable value" (*Dissemination*, 221). Derrida returns to this question in an interview with Christie V. McDonald published as "Choreographies":

> That these words signify "in their most widely recognized sense" had, of course, not escaped me. . . . That being said, "hymen" and "invagination," at least in the context into which these words have been swept, no longer simply designate figures for the feminine body. . . . [they] cannot be abstracted from the "performativity" that concerns us here . . . the labor of reading and writing which evoked them and which they in turn evoked. One could say quite accurately that the hymen *does not exist.*[39]

A more subtle critique of the hymen as operation of deconstruction would refer then not so much to violence against woman as to a more general appropriation of the feminine. And the questions posed would be: why it is that the feminine or female is asked to bear the strategies of deconstruction, whose interests are being served by it, and why she should be asked to internalize what might be seen as the final agony of a system, namely the phallogocentric, in which she was only ever the

[38] Whether or not the hymen works that way as physiological entity, it certainly performs that function as an ideological and cultural construct.

[39] "Choreographies," *Diacritics* 12, no. 2 (Summer 1982), 74–75.

victim? That possibility is raised more explicitly and in more detail in *Spurs*, where the "style" of a Nietzschean misogyny points directly at woman as figure of truth.[40]

In the opening discussion of this chapter it was suggested that the development of the lexicon including the term "hymen" constituted the "innovative" side of the Derridean enterprise, complementing the analytical critiques. The comment is made again with reserve, for the coined terms also perform critical functions, and they are usually identified or modified within the texts under scrutiny. However, the point can still be made that what is intended is not simply a rehabilitation but a revalorization (one must try to give sense to the term without having it signify a new orthodoxy) that will point the way toward a different conceptualization process. From that point of view the feminine, via the hymen, is being recognized within the enterprise as a strategic necessity whose development is important in attempting to think against the grain of, or in addition to, a metaphysics of presence.[41] The aim of deconstruction would be not to oversee that development but to put the feminine into play beyond the reaches of any originary phallogocentrism.

Just such a possibility is brought into focus by proposing a hymen to supplement or redefine a critique of cinematic representation not only in terms of the mimetic function of the apparatus but also in terms of the relation of the spectator to the screen. The feminist critique of Lacan's concept of the mirror stage objected to the transcendental (and biological) status of the phallus as signifier and to woman's being required to submit to the symbolic order in spite of the fact that the system required her silent support as other in order to function. It was found to be woman who, hidden behind the mirror, in the unseen space of virtuality nonetheless held up the apparatus, much as she bore the gaze of the male in the diegetic structures of narrative film.

With the hymen an explicitly feminine reference is recognized as the site of the transfer of meaning and its role openly debated in extensive detail. Whether that be read as more of the same, old story, old history, or as *différance* not reducible to a difference merely (at) the *discretion* of

[40] This perspective on the implications of Derrida's work for feminism is discussed in Jardine, *Gynesis*, 181–92.

[41] Cf. Laura Oswald, "Semiotics and/or deconstruction: In quest of cinema": "By beginning a theory of cinema in the spaces between the terms of the enunciation, with those traces of nonpresence . . . we replace the masculine order of castration inherent in the ontological model itself, with the feminine order of the hymen, a figure for the continual production/deconstruction of meaning and the subject in textual writing" (329–30).

the same, is precisely the gamble envisaged here. It is a gamble under-taken on impulse, on the basis of the impulse called writing that sets language back in movement instead of leaving it in the stasis of con-trolled assignation of meaning. Our discussion seeks to reinvest with that impulse the language of movement that is cinema.

CHAPTER FOUR

THE FRAME OF THE FRAME

In the absence of anything written by Derrida on the cinema, we would like in this chapter to examine what he says about the image and the frame. But consider first of all what it means to say that Derrida has *not* written about the cinema, as opposed to his having written about the image, or philosophy, or literature. Given that everything he writes *about* a medium is precisely that, about or around it—in other words, concerned as much with the separation between inside and outside as anything else—what would he have to have written before we could say that he had written about the cinema? If he were to have written about the cinema could we envisage what he might have said? In what sense is what he has already written "about" cinema?

The discussion that follows has in mind these questions without hoping to answer them. It has in mind their pertinence and their impertinence, that is to say the uneasy way in which notions of context and relevance, of relations in general, are articulated in Derrida, and the issues raised by the very idea that we might presume to know exactly what a Derrida has or has not, will or will not, write or say. In fact, and in the light of these questions, it is clear that the image becomes a central part of Derrida's reasoning, from the question of what takes place (the matter of positions and posting that depends on and opens up the functioning of the *technē*) to his ideogrammatization of language—the hieroglyph and anagram—a field including the play of the signature.

It is our contention that what Derrida has written is of extreme relevance to film theory, hence the present project. But it is also in the nature of this project to attempt to take Derrida's ideas outside of the domain of their most explicit reference, since that would seem to be what much of his writing invites the reader to do. Before the appearance of a book like Gregory Ulmer's *Applied Grammatology*, writing on Derrida seemed mostly to remain within a descriptive mode that failed to engage his ideas in such a way as to continue and expand their program, in spite of the fact that his writing often calls for just that. As early as *Of Grammatology* the extent of Derrida's critique is made explicit: "And thus we say 'writing' for all that gives rise to an inscription in general, whether it is literal or not and even if what it distributes in space is alien to the order of the voice: *cinematography*, choreography, of course, but also pictorial, musical, sculptural 'writing' " (9; our emphasis). For our purposes a series of texts comes into particular focus once it is a question of writing about the image: *The Truth in Painting*, *The Post Card*, and the recent *Right of Inspection*.[1] Since in the latter Derrida's "polylogue" follows a type of *photo-roman*, the question of whether, and if so what, he has written about film, indeed whether he is in some way "making" a film himself, becomes all the more relevant.

The discussion that follows will draw on those texts and center around three main topics. First we shall develop further our discussion of the image in the context of the directions already taken by contemporary film theory. Second, following Gregory Ulmer's extensive examination of Derrida's program of the *pictorialization* of writing and the *grammatization* of the image, we shall attempt to focus these ideas on the film image. In our final chapter we shall consider Derrida's discussion of the matters of posting, communication, and "taking place" in general and relate it to the cinema as medium of communication.

Derrida's argument around the parergon in *The Truth in Painting* aims to subvert the coherence of the image as yet another form of self-presence in the Kantian discourse. In the Third Critique, the *Critique of Judgment*, Kant is in the process of describing what constitutes the basis of aesthetic judgment, yet he is unable to define the boundaries of the artistic object. As it happens, Derrida argues, the uneasiness expressed about what is inside and what is outside the object points to the intellectual sleight-of-hand to which Kant has resorted in importing nonpertinent criteria from other areas of judgment into his discussion of art.

As one might expect from a Derridean analysis, the idea of the parergon is not actually central to Kant's argument but rather occurs in the context of examples chosen to illustrate a central idea. However, the peripheral example is shown to encapsulate the whole problematic at issue, that being exactly the problematic of integrity and coherence, the matter of how to separate inside from outside. The parergon is thus a typically Derridean metaphor that turns out to be much more than a metaphor. It is the framework for an idea precisely concerned with framing.

[1] Marie-Françoise Plissart and Jacques Derrida, *Right of Inspection*, trans. David Wills, in *Art & Text*, no. 32 (1989), 20–97.

In Kant's *Critique of Judgment* the parergon is that which is said to be supplementary or secondary to the "essence" or *ergon* of the work of art. The parergon,[2] in other words, is that which can be dismissed as "mere ornamentation" or that which is "detachable," but it turns out that in practice these distinctions are difficult to make. The frame of a painting, for example, is usually considered expendable, but in a way it can also be seen as constituting the painting entity within by framing it. Is the frame inside or outside? (For example, when one draws a square, is the line that constitutes the square inside the square or outside it?) Is the frame part of the painting or part of the wall, what might be called the "not-painting"? A century after Kant, Seurat raised this very question in his *Sunday Afternoon on the Island of La Grande Jatte* by painting his dots on the wooden frame as well as on the painting proper. It seems, in short, that the status of the frame is completely relational—like a border between two countries whose precise location can never be *exactly* specified—in other words, that it has no status. Wood or metal, it is nevertheless only a function: it is inside, but only in terms of an outside, outside only in terms of an inside. As Derrida succinctly puts it, "*There is* framing, but the frame *does not exist*" (81; translation modified). All of art depends on the frame—a complex idea whose many senses we shall develop—as insubstantial marking of a distinction, of little or no consequence in itself; it always effaces itself "at the moment it deploys its greatest energy" (61).

Early in *The Truth in Painting* Derrida speaks of the "insistent atopia" of the parergon and shows the crucial role it plays for Kant and for all subsequent discussion of aesthetics:

> neither work (*ergon*) nor outside the work [*hors d'oeuvre*], neither inside nor outside, neither above nor below, it disconcerts any opposition but does not remain indeterminate and it *gives rise* to the work. It is no longer merely around the work. That which it puts in place—the instances of the frame, the title, the signature, the legend, etc.—does not stop disturbing the *internal* order of discourse on painting, its works, its commerce, its evaluations, its surplus-values, its speculation, its law, and its hierarchies. (9)

Even more curious is the fact that, for Kant, the parergon refers not only to the frame, which is of course held to be a mere accessory, but also to elements *within* a painting, such as drapery on human figures and columns supporting palaces. Kant then goes on to distinguish be-

---

[2] Greek *para* (beside); *ergon* (work). In French, very similar to *hors-d'oeuvre*. In English, "parergon" can mean "title of a book."

tween "good" parerga and "bad" parerga, calling the former "essential" and the latter "inessential." As Derrida points out, these distinctions inevitably double the Platonic form/matter division crucial to Western philosophy in general, a division in which an ideal form is good and the material that embodies it is bad.

For Kant, "art" serves as the supplement, because the Third Critique, *The Critique of Judgment*, is precisely the third term, the term serving explicitly to bring back together the classic philosophical oppositions, subsumed in that between the sensible and the suprasensible, that Kant had adopted in his first two critiques. Indeed, the history of philosophy has always relied upon such rigid hierarchical oppositions as spirit and nature, subject and object, inside and outside, and the problem has been how to put them back into communication with one another. Kant expressly calls the Third Critique a "bridge" meant to eliminate the abyss, the gap between the *Critique of Pure Reason* and the *Critique of Practical Reason*. As Derrida points out, "The bridge is not *an* analogy. The recourse to analogy, the concept and effect of analogy are or make *the bridge* itself. . . . The analogy of the abyss and of the bridge over the abyss is an analogy which says that there must surely be an analogy between two heterogeneous worlds, a third term to cross the abyss, to heal over the gaping wound and think the gap" (36). Both the bridge and the very idea of analogy itself, which the bridge analogy produces, in other words, are needed to supplement the lacuna that develops and to negotiate the opposing shores that mutely face one another across the abyss. It is this bridge of analogy that, as we saw earlier, brings together the "two heterogeneous worlds" of reality and cinema.

This bridging of the gap between transcendent form and mere matter is repeated in a sophisticated fashion in the work of a critic like Dudley Andrew, for example, who has entitled his most recent book *Film in the Aura of Art*.[3] Andrew discusses a group of films that "promise to affect us in unique and privileged ways, hoping to attain thereby a certain importance if not immortality" (4), films that "call for repeated viewing and privileged, serious discussion" (13), "for each stands out, has been made to stand out as extraordinary, that is, as Art" (193). In these films we respect "the authentic vision of the creator" (12), and Andrew exults in the fact that "Art is the motor of this book, for these are studies conducted in the aura of art . . ." (193). The quasi-religious, even mystical tone of Andrew's book indicates that even though spirit must these days go unnamed, and the impulse to worship

---

[3] (Princeton: Princeton University Press, 1984).

at its altar must be resisted or at least remain hidden, there is *art* to take its place. Art interpellates viewers, as it were, and it is found to have certain inexplicable effects on them, which then must somehow be accounted for. And how can these effects be explained except by recourse to a transcendent realm of spirit? Otherwise, it would only be a matter of the skillful playing with codes. The problem is still how to get the two worlds of spirit and nature together, how to make the sensible lead to the supersensible, the inessential to the essential, and the material to the nonmaterial. Two centuries after the Third Critique it is still the notion of art that serves as mediator between the two worlds. It continues to act as the invisible supplement that adds something to the dull, inert materiality of individual works and thus redeems them.

Furthermore, all philosophical discourse on art, for Derrida, has required a distinction between internal meaning and the circumstances in which the work of art finds itself, between what is "intrinsic" to the work and what is "extrinsic." Hence aesthetics is always about the limit between the inside and the outside of the art object, and hence it is always a discourse on the frame. What is "proper" to an interpretation, what is a "proper" interpretation? And what is the location and status of the critical act? Where does the analyst stand, inside or outside the work? What do we mean, for example, when we say that a critic has gotten "inside" a film? Within a work, the same relation of inside and outside is doubled in the traditional distinction between form and content:

> In order to think art in general, one thus accredits a series of oppositions (meaning/form, content/container) which, precisely, structure the traditional interpretation of works of art. One makes of art in general an object in which one claims to distinguish an inner meaning, the invariant, and a multiplicity of external variations *through* which, as through so many veils, one would try to see or restore the true, full, originary meaning. (*The Truth in Painting*, 22)

Now it is particularly significant that the term "frame" in the cinema itself encapsulates the inside/outside paradox. For what usually refers to the outside border, as in painting, here also names the *inside*, or some undefined combination of inside and outside. Since the "entity" called the "frame" can only be defined through the operation of its borders, and since the term "definition" cannot function without the idea of delimitation, the definition of the cinematic frame thus folds in upon itself from the outset. Where is the film frame's frame? Obviously, the coherence of such an "entity" can never be established as long as it is called a frame.

It is worth dwelling on what may seem to be a simple quirk of the lexicon, especially since it is repeated in other languages, for instance Italian and French. The term "frame" names, in its material explicitness, a section of celluloid whose successive repetitions (and slight variations) pass in front of the lens in order to project a motion picture. Two of the sides of that piece of celluloid are defined by preceding and successive images and the borders between them, and the other sides by the sound track and sprocket holes. In each case there is a type of otherness that works to constitute the entity called a frame. The celluloid border separating the frames is of course of the same matter as the frame itself, but more than this, it also represents, in conjunction with the action of the shutter, the moment of negation or lack of sight that permits vision to take place, to the extent that it allows for the temporal overlap between the time the image remains in front of the lamp and the time it remains imprinted upon the retina. It becomes clear once again that the familiar phenomena of persistence of vision and the phi-effect require a peculiar relation of presence to absence in order to function; paradoxically there has to be that disjunction between screen time and retinal retention in order for the illusion of motion to be produced,[4] and due to the continual opening and closing of the shutter, as Bruce Kawin points out, "for about half the time we are watching a movie, the screen is totally dark."[5] The borders constituted by the sound track and sprocket holes may be seen as referring in turn to the complicated otherness that sound represents, which we have already discussed, and that of the whole technological apparatus itself.

Yet the frame in this concrete sense is doubled—and thus its sense is divided—inasmuch as the same word refers also to the moving image as it appears projected on the screen. Here the relations between the frame's inside and outside become even more complex. In the darkened cinema the "frame" outside of or "around" the cinematic frame appears superficially to be its opposite: absence of light opposed to play of light. Yet the darkness is not in fact an absolute absence of light but rather a more subdued play of light, consisting again therefore of the same "matter" or "order" as the inside of the frame. The outside of the frame, far from being the opposite of the inside, is a differential varia-

---

[4] Some commentators have cast considerable doubt on the viability of the concept of persistence of vision; see for example, Joseph and Barbara Anderson, "Motion Perception in Motion Pictures," in *The Cinematic Apparatus*, ed. Teresa de Lauretis and Stephen Heath (New York: St. Martin's Press, 1980), 76–95.

[5] Bruce F. Kawin, *How Movies Work* (New York: Macmillan, 1987), 48.

tion of the same order. This is reinforced when one considers that the subdued play of light that creates the relative darkness that is the frame's frame is constituted by the diffused light coming from the projector, and even more so by the very light reflected from the screen.

Once one extends the strict sense of the frame, as we have above, its inside opens onto its outside in a more generalized manner. From one point of view there seems not to be any identifiable frame, at least not in the sense of a frame surrounding a painting. A painting exists in the world of visible objects and thus, in order to differentiate itself as "figure" from its "ground," it requires the explicit space of negotiation that the frame provides. The film, on the other hand, exists thanks to its creation of a "not itself," a virtual frame, an other. This other is clearly related to the Other theorized by psychoanalysis as the absent one or threat of castration that diegetic suture works to conceal. What is also the film's frame is that which we imagine and construct as the "real world" against what we see on the screen. This works on two levels: on an immediate visual level involving the whole problematic of analogical reference, and secondly on the level of realist conventions and other such cinematic codes.

For all these reasons it can be said that this is no mere lexical quirk, but that the image creates its own frame that, conversely, constructs its own inside. The outside is folded chiastically back into the inside, and what was external—real life, the mirror, consciousness, desire, film history, genre conventions, a society's culture, and so on—becomes internalized through invagination. The ambiguity of the term "film frame," then, may be read as a sign of language's unconscious understanding of the work of the trace. The division of the coherence or self-presence of the image signaled by the appellation "frame" (a word that can be added to the lexicon including "hymen" and "screen") is thus indicative of a whole network of factors that contemporary film theory has already elaborated and that describe the cinematic image as anything but a fully constituted and integral presence.

Let us now outline some of these frame effects as functions of the dynamics of the image. The first area that we might consider is the hermeneutic process itself, which inevitably calls into question easy divisions between the inside and the outside of the text. From the outset, the film text can be seen, through the workings of the supplementary chain, as a graft or citation of numerous elements from the culture and history (including the history of the medium, of genres, of art in general) within which this text has come into existence. Thus the "outside" that comes to be folded into the "inside" of the text will always be larger than that which holds it. Every critical act then brought to bear on it will depend upon the assumption of an indefinite number of boundaries and exclusions, such as those between genres, movements, periods, styles, and so on. Through invagination, the critic or analyst also places him- or herself in the text, bringing along interpretive assumptions from the "outside" (methodologies, as well as political, social, and cultural views) that the "inside" of the text is nevertheless presumed to authorize or contain. Conversely, in the act of interpretation, the critic grafts, or inscribes through citation, the already invaginated film text, with its own inexhaustible particulars, within the borders of his or her own text, which is always admitted to be smaller than that which it seeks to enfold. It is perhaps only when the critic is forced to deal with self-reflexive elements—are they part of a work or commentary on it?—that the complexity of this operation is brought to light.

The second area that we might consider concerns the initial major undertaking of the semiology of the cinema, namely the narrative analysis of the image as a function of the relation between signifier and signified. Once it could be shown that there existed serious discrepancies—of time and place—between the organization of visual data appearing on the screen and the significance of those data in terms of the diegesis, the transparent immediacy and self-evidence of the image was called into question. To point out that in a chase scene, for instance, the shots of chaser and chased are consecutive, although the actions are understood to be simultaneous, is not just a minor (re)discovery of the obvious that habit has taught us to overlook. It amounts to an inscription of the individual image within a network of relations with the images before and after it that irrevocably robs it of the self-sufficiency of sense it might be presumed to have. And more than that, it suggests that the meaning of the image can never be contained within its borders but resides on another level.

Now none of this seems so extraordinary to today's film theorist, nor even to today's student of structural linguistics. But there is something to be underlined here. On the one hand the image is seen as repeating the metaphysical operation that governs the sense of the word; both are assumed to be expendable materialities whose real meaning resides elsewhere. Before it came to be governed by principles of realism, the image operated as a symbolic representation like the word. Irrespective of the change from symbolic to realist image, however, the image always fell within the general model for meaning just described. On the other hand, the advent of monocular perspective and then of the photograph meant that these traditional symbolic relations of explicit and implicit, revealed and hidden, no longer had the same force, for here was a signifier whose signified appeared to be immediately accessible. As a result the realist image, positioned as window or veil whose transparency "almost" directly conveys self-present meaning, becomes the privileged type of signifier in a new representational hierarchy. This hierarchy goes all the way from image, through the word in normal usage, to poetic language, with its play of self-reflexive signifiers that seem to have taken leave of the relation to a signified. Yet the metaphysical operation is still in evidence. For the assumption is that even in the case of the poetic trope, as with analogy, it is a matter of a temporary detour from an underlying form of referentiality that would be there to return to no matter how far the operations of the signifier strayed from it.

Thus if the arrival of the realist visual image implies a rearrangement of the hierarchy of meaning effects, it also means that the paradox of that model of meaning becomes more readily apparent. For if the image's signified is immediately accessible, in the terms we discussed earlier with reference to analogical mimesis, then it is ultimately more like the poetic model of self-reflexivity; an image whose meaning resides within it is like a poetic word that refers to itself. But according to the hierarchy, poetic usage is situated at the opposite end of the scale from the image. What is involved, then, is a collapsing of the distinction between inside and outside in locating the site of the signified.

Within film theory, the emphasis of early semiotics on the signifier/signified question fell short of recognizing the relation of that question to the inside/outside problematic we have been describing. The emphasis of Metz's *Language and Cinema*, for example, with its careful attention to distinctions between the filmic and the cinematic, between specific and nonspecific codes, clearly evokes and depends upon that inside/outside opposition. So do those areas of theory mapped out by Metz—the sociological, economic, and industrial aspects of cinema—that were not treated because they fell "outside" the competence of his study. The point here is not that such emphases were misguided in trying to decide what is specific to cinema, or what constitutes and defines cinema or film, since any analysis necessarily divides a domain in order to study it. Rather, what is made clear by the breadth of Metz's systematization is that the codes that emerge do not simply or easily articulate between an already constituted and coherent entity called cinema and a series of phenomena or practices that are not cinema. Instead, these articulations ensure that cinema's coherence is never guaranteed. The structural frame-*work*—and it is very much the dynamic operation suggested by that word—reveals rather a network of exchanges whose effect is simultaneously to outline delimitations on the one hand and to complicate them on the other.

Metz seems to state as much early on in *The Imaginary Signifier*:[6]

> I no longer believe that each film has *a* textual system . . . nor even . . . a fixed number of quite distinct textual systems. . . . The textual system as I now see it . . . [is] this perpetual possibility of a finer, or else less apparent structuration, of a grouping of elements into a new configuration . . . which does not annul the preceding ones . . . but complements or in other cases distorts and complicates them, at any rate points in a slightly different direction, a little to one side (a little, or more than a little). (29)

From this perspective we might consider as our third frame effect the second semiology of cinema, namely that which dates from *The Imaginary Signifier* and includes the large volume of work spawned by that study, which can be seen as a development from the realization just stated, namely that structural analysis inevitably points, "a little or more than a little," elsewhere.

The system of the looks that is central to the articulation of meaning in a representative narrative film requires that the image be traversed by certain lines of force that always threaten its integrality. As we said earlier, the images become interrelated in such a way that their sense is never self-enclosed but inevitably opens onto the images surrounding them. A shot/reverse shot or point-of-view shot always implies the threat that the lines of vision might continue irredeemably outside of the frame; there is always the danger that the gap caused by the out-of-frame look will not be sutured over by the succeeding shot.

Similar lines of force exist internal to the frame, where they regulate the play of focus and perspective. It is clear that focal points and perspectival configurations do not occur in infinite space—they would indeed have no meaning there—but rather that they depend on the restrictions operated by the frame in order to function. What occurs with the system of the looks is actually only a graphic representation—one can draw the lines of the characters' gazes—of what exists potentially with respect to any set of elements within the image. A moving picture is precisely that, a constantly shifting visual configuration, whose elements are subject to change in focus and status vis-à-vis one another. This is the case even within the so-called still image, which is a contradiction in terms, for its multiple lines of force always put it into move-

---

[6] This passage is part of the "Postface" to the 1977 French reedition of *Langage et cinéma* (Paris: Editions Albatros), 223.

ment. This collapse of the still/moving distinction removes film from a simple binary, oppositional relation with the other, so-called static visual arts.

It might be argued even that it was a shift in perspective, occurring within "stills," that enabled cinema much more than the invention of the movie camera and projector. For the move from pre-Renaissance to monocular perspective[7] in painting was little more than that, a re-arrangement of elements within the frame that redeployed visual lines of force so as to permit realism, hence the camera, and hence cinema. Thus the photographic still implicitly figures that historical shift and so has the idea of movement within it, before it, in turn, is redeployed within the series of stills that constitute cinema. In "Narrative Space" Stephen Heath argues similarly that narrative contains the movement inherent in the space of the image: "Frame space, in other words, is constructed as narrative space. . . . Narrative contains the mobility that could threaten the clarity of vision in a constant renewal of per-spective; space becomes place—narrative as the taking place of film—in a movement which is no more than the fulfilment of the Renaissance impetus . . ." (*Questions of Cinema*, 36). Barthes, in "The Third Mean-ing," argues for a "theory of the still" that would disabuse us of the notion that the essence of the cinema is the movement of the images. Such a theory would describe "the filmic of the future" in terms of what the image produces as excess, its "obtuse meaning." Obviously referring to Derrida, he asserts that "the still is not a sample (an idea that supposes a sort of homogeneous, statistical nature of the film ele-ments) but a quotation (we know how much importance presently ac-crues to this concept in the theory of the text): at once parodic and disseminatory" (67).

The complications that we have been discussing demonstrate that although the operation of monocular perspective and the disposition created by the vanishing point suggest a very powerful centralization and hierarchization of the elements of the image, as do focus and close-up, such systems of coordination between the frame and its content also inscribe the structures of potential, even inevitable partition.

In the context of relations between technology and cinematic lines of force, we might also mention some recent developments and their consequences for the unity of the image. Thus, for example, the ad-vent of stereo sound, meant presumably to enhance the image's illu-

[7] In traditional art historical terms, pre-Renaissance organization of space is not re-ferred to as perspective, suggesting that the term was invented, or reinvented, with the Renaissance. It is our view rather that there can only ever be changes from one type of perspective to another.

sion of reality, actually serves instead to call attention to its precarious self-(in)sufficiency. Whereas traditional sound has always worked with the image to create an assured self-presence, as we saw in our previous chapter, stereo sound (as, for example, when the hooves of an on-screen horse visually moving from left to right are first heard to the left of the screen and then a second later to the right or when, in the recent *Manon of the Springs* [1987], the speakers in the four corners of the theater cause a reverberation meant to give the spectator the sense of being in a church) actually pulls the spectator out of the fullness of the image on the screen by suddenly constructing alternative loci of representation, and thus other frames.

Another technological development has also troubled the image by transgressing its frame. Here we are referring to "Smellovision," a minor development in the history of cinema—banal enough, certainly, but also in a curious way revealing. Though the historical explanation for its cyclical appearance and disappearance (in different forms, as Aromarama, Odorama, and so on) stresses technical problems (such as the impossibility of completely removing one odor before the next one was required), it is also tempting to see its rejection as a symptom of logocentric anxiety regarding the overturning of the primacy of the visual, a primacy ironically assured by sound. Both sight and sound, but especially sight, Derrida takes to be the quintessential logocentric or "theoretical" senses (cf. "White Mythology") because of their dependence on an "out-thereness" to phenomena, or, more generally, to the reinforcement of the classic subject/object division. The sense of smell, on the other hand, depends specifically upon a "hereness" because it is one of the "chemical senses," that is, a process that occurs inside and that therefore troubles the conventional inside/outside distinction abetted by the dominance of sight. In *Glas* Derrida uses these senses to promote the disseminative power of writing over Hegel's specific exclusion of taste, smell, and touch—because they are not objective enough—from the comprehension of art.[8] Since smell is complexly both real and a representation at the same time, its introduction also troubles realism and the integrity of the film image in a manner similar to stereo sound. It can be an amusing diversion, in other words, but given the close connection between cinematic realism and logocentrism, it is impossible to imagine it ever taking its place in any system of mainstream cinematic representation.

[8] As Derrida eloquently asks, "How could ontology get hold of a fart?" (Quoted in *Applied Grammatology*, 55; an extensive discussion of the "chemical senses" can be found on pages 53–57). For further discussion of Hegel in this regard see Derrida, "Economimesis," in Sylviane Agacinski et al., *Mimesis: Des articulations* (Paris: Aubier-Flammarion, 1975), 55–93.

Finally on our list of divisions of the frame is the Barthesian concept of the photographic *punctum*, as developed in *Camera Lucida: Reflections on Photography*.[9] Here again it can be seen as a type of focal point, but one that does not depend solely, or even principally, on the internal organization of the image. Operating in the profoundest ambiguity both with respect to what Barthes calls the *studium* (a "kind of human interest" found in a photograph that is "of the order of liking, not of loving" [26–27]) and with respect to the viewer, it is also a kind of violence done to the signifying surface of the image, as we shall see.

Barthes introduces the term in this manner:

> The second element will break (or punctuate) the *studium*. This time it is not I who seek it out . . . it is this element which rises from the scene, shoots out of it like an arrow, and pierces me. A Latin word exists to designate this wound, this prick, this mark made by a pointed instrument; the word suits me all the better in that it also refers to the notion of punctuation, and because the photographs I am speaking of are in effect punctuated, sometimes even speckled with these sensitive points . . . for *punctum* is also: sting, speck, cut, little hole. . . . (26–27)

What is of particular interest to our discussion, first of all, is the fact that for Barthes the punctum endows the photograph with the structure of the moving image.[10] In referring to Bazin, for example, Barthes reinforces what we have been saying about the nonintegrality of the image and points to the punctum as an example of the same operation:

> Yet the cinema has a power which at first glance the Photograph does not have: the screen (as Bazin has remarked) is not a frame but a hideout; the man or woman who emerges from it continues living: a "blind field" [*champ aveugle*] constantly doubles our partial vision. Now, confronting millions of photographs . . . I sense no blind field. . . . Yet once there is a *punctum*, a blind field is created (is divined). . . . The *punctum*, then, is a kind of subtle off-screen [*hors-champ*]—as if the image launched desire beyond what it permits us to see. . . . (55–57, 59; translation modified)

The punctum evokes the play of the trace between an absent and a present and signals the dissolution of a clearly demarcated, framed distinction between the outside and the inside. Second, the distinction between studium and punctum is that the former is univocal (41) and

---

[9] Original version *La Chambre claire* (Paris: Cahiers du cinéma/Gallimard/Seuil) published posthumously in 1980.

[10] Elsewhere in *Camera Lucida*, however, the distinction between photography and cinema is clearly drawn (cf. pp. 78, 79, 89–90, and our remarks below).

aligned with the photographer's intentions (27–28), whereas the latter is disseminative and unintentional (47). Third, the punctum can be conceived as perspectival: in the same way that monocular perspective, for instance, evokes the other and now foreign field and system of vision that historically preceded it, so the punctum breaks through the constraints of the assumed direct system of signification that is photography to engage desire and the viewing subject. It punctures what we called the signifying surface and ruptures the space of representation; that is to say it disrupts analogical representation, opening it to its anagrammatical other, in the manner of the hymen.

From another point of view, the punctum functions at the level of the signifying structures of *Camera Lucida* as a whole. As the idea is developed throughout the first section of Barthes's book, it becomes clear to what extent it runs the risk of functioning as a transcendent form of meaning within the image. It is said, for example, that the relation between punctum and studium cannot be regulated other than in terms of a co-presence (42), that the punctum cannot be isolated by analysis (42–43), that it is not coded (51), and finally: "Last thing about the *punctum*: whether or not it is triggered, it is an addition [*supplément*]: it is what I add to the photograph and *what is nonetheless already there*" (55). Now, on Barthes's own admission, the inquiry that leads to the "discovery" of the punctum is informed by a phenomenological bias. Yet this is "a vague, casual, even cynical phenomenology, so readily did it agree to distort or to evade its principles according to the whim of my analysis"; further, "my phenomenology agreed to compromise with a power, *affect*," despite the fact that classical phenomenology never speaks of "desire or of mourning" (20–21). Thus whether it be a transcendent meaning outside of the processes of signification (yet uncannily still within visual materiality) or the supposed prerogative of a preconstituted viewing subject, the punctum seems like a reversion to a precritical idealism.[11]

On the other hand it is from this same ambiguous basis that one can mount a case for the punctum as a form of writing, as the site of a particularly Derridean set of practices. First, its definition contains very explicitly the idea of inscription ("mark made by a pointed instrument . . . it also refers to the notion of punctuation" [26]). But, as we have noted above, the full force of its operation becomes apparent if we look more closely at the structure of the text as a whole. To counter

---

[11] For further discussion of this problem in a number of Barthes's later texts, see Alec McHoul and David Wills, "The Late(r) Barthes: constituting fragmenting subjects," *Boundary 2* 14, nos. 1–2 (Fall 1985–Winter 1986), 261–78.

the sort of hedonistic phenomenological enquiry into the photograph that organizes the first part of the book, Barthes undertakes in the second part what he calls his "palinode" (60), proceeding along contradictory lines and setting up a chiastic structure within the argument. Designed as a type of retraction or recantation, this second part reveals itself as symmetrical to the first. For whereas the first part led to the discovery of the punctum if not the essence (*noeme*) of photography, the second part finds its own punctum, as it were the punctum of the book, and it finds it in an ambiguous play of presence and absence and in the play of death. It is in an unreproduced photograph of his dead mother—one which remains absent and thus only in negative for the reader—that Barthes finds the essence of photography:[12]

> Photography's Referent is not the same as the referent of other systems of representation. I call "photographic referent" not the *optionally* real thing to which an image or a sign refers, but the *necessarily* real thing which has been placed before the lens, without which there would be no photograph. . . . In Photography I can never deny that *the thing has been there.* . . . What I intentionalize in a photograph . . . is neither Art nor Communication, it is Reference, which is the founding order of Photography. The name of Photography's *noeme* will therefore be: "That-has-been," [*Ça a été*], or again: the Intractable. (76–77)

The essence of photography, the structure that allows and explains the functions of the punctum, is seen to reside in the idea of the spectral, as a haunting presence signifying an absence. It is by this means that the punctum comes to trouble the invisible "frontal" frame separating image from viewer and so to rend the signifying surface, by rewriting the relation between the framed rectangle and the viewer by placing him or her within a kind of three-dimensional rectangle or cuboid extending outward from the screen. Even more than that, however, the punctum comes finally to challenge the institutional framework of reference within this system of representation as well.

That, in any case, is how Derrida seems to read the punctum in his obituary article entitled "Les Morts de Roland Barthes" (*Psyché*, 273–304). On an initial level, the punctum and the studium can be seen as instituting a type of opposition that nevertheless disrupts the logic of

---

[12] Barthes had already isolated this denotative sense of photography in his text "Rhetoric of the Image" (in *Image—Music—Text*), which appeared in French some fifteen years earlier. In *Camera Lucida*, of course, the denotative/connotative relation is displaced by the punctum/studium relation, and the argument gains more explicitly Lacanian overtones through reference to the mother's body.

oppositional structures: "Concepts which are in appearance the most frontally opposed, and opposable, he brings into play one *for* the other, in a metonymical composition" (276; our translation).[13] However, this disruption is shown to reach into the conceptual framework itself, where it inscribes an abyssal structure at its center:

> It [the punctum] belongs to it [the studium] without belonging to it, it cannot be situated within it, is never inscribed within the homogeneous objectivity of its framed space but it inhabits it or rather haunts it: "It is a supplement. . . ." We fall prey to the ghost-like power of the supplement. . . . Once it ceases to be in opposition to the *studium* although remaining heterogeneous with respect to it, as soon as one can no more distinguish here between two places, two contents, or two things, the *punctum* cannot be entirely reduced to a concept. . . . This concept of a phantom is as difficult to grasp . . . as the phantom of a concept. (280)

Like writing then, the conceptual problematic that the punctum introduces can be generalized. It not only concerns the specific circumstances of its operation but disrupts the very process of conceptualization itself. For, although the referent can be held in suspense in any system of representation, as Derrida notes (287), the spectral structure of photography means that its referent is always called upon to share its space with a reference to death:

> Now the contemporary possibility of the photograph . . . resides in its conjunction of death and the referent within the same system. Not that this occurs here for the first time, and, on account of its essential relation to reproductive technique, or to technique itself, such a conjunction did not wait for photography. But the immediate demonstration provided by the photographic apparatus or the structure of the *remainder* that it leaves behind it, those are irreducible and undeniably original events. . . . From the moment the *punctum* rends space, reference[14] and death become part

---

[13] Throughout Derrida's article two important "themes" operate: first, references to musical composition, showing respect for the particular style of Barthes's writings and his creative use of rhetoric; and second, plays upon the French word for to return or come back (*revenir*), whose present participle provides a word for ghost (*un revenant*)—both of which relate to the memory of Barthes and to the notions of the spectral being developed in connection with photography. The latter idea is extended through the reading of *Right of Inspection*.

[14] A further precision Derrida introduces is worth repeating here, especially given Barthes's insistence that "Reference . . . is the founding order of photography" (*Camera Lucida*, 77) and its links to our discussion of Mallarmé's mime in the previous chapter: "But should we say 'reference' or 'the referent'? Analytic precision should be up to the

and parcel of photography. . . . This does not occur—not in the same manner in any case, the implication and form of reference taking other turns and detours—in other types of image or discourse, let us say with respect to marks in general. (291–92)

That death is inscribed as structure within the concept of the *technē* is something that Derrida has long insisted upon and something we shall take up again in our final chapter. This is obvious in the "paradigm" case of writing, whose structural possibility (and thus production) is always dependent upon the absence or death of its author. But the "immediacy" of photography means that the structure of death becomes as it were visibly apparent on the representational surface itself. This double and contradictory referent—of presence and death—occurs in the context of a particularly explicit type of reference. Once again, the "concentrated" form of reference that the immediacy of the image is supposed to install, far from making for a privileged form of representation, actually produces an intensification of the crisis of representation. And hence if photography indicates a tendency toward less mediated forms of representation, it is also accompanied by a tendency toward an insoluble tension between the conflicting structures constituting representation.

Now we are not forgetting that Barthes expressly distinguishes cinema from photography in this matter, claiming that "in the cinema, no doubt, there is always a photographic referent, but this referent shifts, it does not make a claim in favor of its reality, it does not protest its former existence; it does not cling to me: it is not a *specter*." For Barthes, the cinema is "protensive, hence in no way melancholic," always oriented toward the future, unlike photography, which is "*without future*" (*Camera Lucida*, 89–90). First of all, for us the structural distinction that Barthes finds, and that tradition maintains, between still and moving image does not hold once the image is analyzed as a dynamic of inside/outside relations. More specifically, we would argue, a dual operation occurs in cinema. On the one hand, given its insistent temporality, it does inevitably move toward the future. On the other hand, this is always a future that is foreseen, that we know will come to an end within the space of a screening; its finality imposes a kind of past upon it. In documentary footage, we know or are told that this or that building no longer exists; in a fiction film, we know that these clothes are out of date, this actress is now dead, that actor is

level of the stakes involved here, and photography puts it to the test: the referent is visibly absent, suspendable, having disappeared into the unique past time of the event, but reference to this referent . . . implies just as irreducibly the having-been of a unique and invariable referent" (*Psyché*, 292).

now old. Within the present space and present time of the film, in other words, one is incessantly reminded of the past, and the past is a specter, the past is death.

A further argument might even be made that the common insistence upon a standard conception of movement as integral to cinema and as a mainstay of the impression of reality works to mask the extent of the image's relation to death. This relation arises from the play of death within desire, a connection explicitly developed by writers from Bataille to Lacan. For movement, or the insistence upon it, can be read as yet another configuration of the subject effect that in Baudry's terms is cinema, that is, the subject figuring his or her own desire: "the key to the impression of reality has been sought in the structuring of the image and movement, in complete ignorance of the fact that the impression of reality is dependent first of all on a subject effect . . ." ("The Apparatus" in *Narrative, Apparatus, Ideology*, 312). In fact, it is discontinuity that, as much as movement, is recognized as constitutive of cinema from the very beginning—in the development of its technology, in the ideas of retinal retention or the phi-effect, and in Eisenstein's theory of montage. In addition, what is recognized as constitutive of the spectator is a certain immobility, or better, sub-mobility. Now both discontinuity and sub-mobility can, rhetorically at least, be related to death. Thus whereas Baudry points to the coincidence between the perceptual and the representational as a type of contrived continuity within the workings of the impression of reality (314–16), we note that movement effects a similar contrivance there. What Baudry analyzes, in his comparison between dream and cinema, as the bringing into play of a libidinal apparatus within which perception and representation need not be differentiated can, like the insistence upon movement, be read as a compensation for the spectator's immobility and as a disavowal of the effect of death within the apparatus of desire. The spectator, in taking pleasure in a privileged form of perception that represses its own discontinuities, compensates for the actual discontinuities between representation and the world, and between the self and the image; and so enacts a form of desire in which death is both represented and disavowed. It is, after all, the very absence or discontinuity implied by representation, as dramatized by the event of the mirror stage—that is, the subject's perception of self operating across or through an absence—it is this very matter that cinema, like dream, might be seen as attempting to circumvent.

To return to the operations of reference and representation enacted by the photograph, it should be made clear that they continue to relate to the problematic of the frame. The matter of reference is itself after all the very frame of representation, that which articulates its inside with its outside. It is important to understand that the process of reference or referral is the institutional support that enables a material signifier such as an image to be related to a referent understood to reside elsewhere. Reference is thus the pivotal armature within the operations of representation. The play of the punctum as described by Barthes, once reactivated as a form of writing, folds reference in upon itself to place reality in a kind of chiastic symmetry with death, presence with absence, confounding inside with outside to the extent that the signifying surface of the representational process is opened to a less strictly institutionalized play of meaning than that prescribed by mimesis. In fact, this disturbance is anticipated by Barthes in his original definition of the punctum, where he supplies a further sense for the Latin word that we have not yet mentioned: "a cast of the dice" (27). The disorientation effected by the punctum within the signifying system of the photograph can thus also be seen as opening its meaning to the play of chance and so to the full force of dissemination.

It is not without contrivance then that we chose to treat of four functions of the frame: the play between analyst and text, the signifier/ signified relations, the work of the second wave of semiological analysis, and the punctum. Indeed the categories overlap and the last brings us back to the first. But the number four is obviously pertinent, four being the number of sides of the frame, the word for which in French (*cadre*) is closely related to that for a square (*carré*) from the Latin *quadrus*. Four is a constant throughout *The Truth in Painting*, shorthand finally for the whole inside/outside problematic.

Thus, though our claim that these matters divide themselves neatly into four is a pure artifice on our part, it is an artifice that serves—as much in its failure as in its success—an important purpose. The precise division of internal coherence operated by the frame is that of quadripartition, its regularity and symmetry allowing not so much for a finite and neatly circumscribed set of functions but conversely laying the groundwork or grid for unlimited subdivision. The four-sided square can also be seen as existing in a relation of excess to other paradigms of geometrico-rhetorical operations: one and the circle with concomitant ideas of centrality, unity, and controlled circulation; the straight line with two ends, origin and telos, dialectics and pivotal equilibrium; and three and the triangle, models of the Oedipal. The square, by contrast, Derrida relates to the domain of writing[15] and most specifically

---

[15] Exercise-book writing paper in France is like our graph paper, *quadrillé* rather than simply lined.

to the rhetorical figure of the chiasmus,[16] from the Greek word *chi*, for the cross or letter "x." It is in his words "the thematic drawing of dissemination" (*The Truth in Painting*, 166), because it erases the center and shoots off in four different directions. The cross or "x," figure of erasure, is formed precisely when the four sides of the square or frame collapse to divide diagonally the internal coherence of whatever resides within that frame, bringing about what is referred to, in Derrida's essay "Living On: Borderlines," as a "crisscross double invagination" (*Deconstruction and Criticism*, 100). Following the model of the Greek "χ," as Derrida notes, this is not an exactly symmetrical subdivision but an erasure that is also a rewriting as *différance*.[17]

The effect of the collapse of the four-squared frame into a cross or an "x," the mark of cancellation, is therefore far-reaching for readings of the image. This would be so for any similarly radical redeployment or rewriting of institutional boundaries. This should not be understood to mean, however, that the image can henceforth be read as an ideal free space immune from relations of power or conflicts of sense. On the contrary, the chiasmatic collapsing of its frame calls for specific textual and reading practices, free yet operating according to a rigid internal "logic" of their own, that continue to work against the dominant institutional structures of the signifying system.

———

Relations between the image and writing have been developed in two important, already often cited contexts outside of what Derrida himself has written. The two principal texts here are Marie-Claire Ropars's *Le Texte divisé* and Gregory Ulmer's *Applied Grammatology*. Whereas our discussion above outlined in broad perspective the sense of the frame for the image, in these texts that perspective becomes the background for a more specific series of reading practices based on the idea of the image as essentially heterogeneous, graphic as well as pictorial, and not subject to a single mode of signification. Those practices can

[16] "Diagonal arrangement, especially of clauses within a sentence. A grammatical figure by which the order of words in one of two parallel clauses is inverted in the other" (*Oxford English Dictionary*). For a full discussion of the chiasmus, its importance for classical thought, and its relation to invagination, see Rodolphe Gasché's introduction to Andrzej Warminski, *Readings in Interpretation: Hölderlin, Hegel, Heidegger* (Minneapolis: University of Minnesota Press, 1987).

[17] "The form of the chiasmus, the χ, interests me greatly, not as a symbol of the unknown but because there is here a sort of fork . . . which is moreover unequal, one of its points extending its scope [*portée*] further than the other" (*The Truth in Painting*, 166).

be summarized as effects of the signature, the rebus, and the hiero-glyph, all means by which writing is read upon, or into, the image. In *Le Texte divisé* the hieroglyph, whose mixture of signifying systems makes it especially appropriate to the study of cinematic signification, is related to Eisensteinian montage in order to describe film as a writing machine. Ropars then goes on to analyze from that point of view Marguerite Duras's film *India Song*. Ulmer, on the other hand, emphasizes Derrida's deconstruction of the borders between speech and writing and between graphic and figurative images, in order to develop what he sees as the more wide-ranging applications of a possible program of grammatology.

Let us first examine the idea of the signature. It is the basis of the strategy by which the reductivist concept of meaning becomes irrevocably problematized. Historical examples, from the deciphering of hieroglyphs and cartouches to Saussure's investigations of Latin poetry bear witness to the importance of the proper name as a form of inscription that, however much it might seek to control and direct hermeneutic interpretations in the form of an authorial intentionality, in fact insures that the singular coherence of meaning within a text will always be undone. As Derrida showed in the early essay "Signature Event Context," a signature (on a check, for example) must always claim to be unique, thus testifying to a present intention, yet must always be repeatable or "citable" as well, since the idea of a single signature is a structural impossibility. Yet this very necessity of iterability insures that the absence of a signifying intention is also an essential part of its structure.

The same thing holds true for a work of art, whose "internal" meaning and coherence are in part guaranteed by the "external" signature appended to it and that as a mark of intentionality acts as its frame. In a painting, this relation is made explicit when the artist's signature is placed near the frame, thus doubling it. The signature or proper name, the very essence of the idea of identity and self-presence, is reciprocally supposed to point directly to a referent, without any remainder that signifies (Austin sees the signature as indexical only).[18] It is thus sup-

[18] An obvious aspect of the signature problematic—one that we do not take up—concerns the relation between an author's life and his or her work, and the meaning of biography and autobiography as effects of the signature. Derrida discusses these questions in the context of an examination of Nietzsche in *The Ear of the Other*. Freud is the other important figure here, for much of his work is heavily autobiographical, providing a possible model for the signatory inscription of the self in theoretical writing (cf. "To Speculate—On 'Freud' " in *The Post Card*). For further discussion of autobiographical

posed, like the frame, to expend itself at its moment of greatest use. But because it too is part of the system of language, it immediately begins to signify beyond the constraints of pure reference.[19] The proper name is also that which remains, accumulating meanings after the author dies. Again, as Culler has pointed out: "In theory signatures lie outside the work, to frame it, present it, authorize it, but it seems that truly to frame, to mark, or to sign a work the signature must lie within, at its very heart" (*On Deconstruction*, 192). Once the proper name is inscribed within the text—as a signature at the bottom of a painting or printed name at the head of a book or a film—there is nothing to prevent its being considered a signifying element in that text. In this way, the proper noun can also be regarded as a common noun that signifies, a situation that occurs frequently in dreams, for example. As Ulmer puts it, "the proper name occupies the masterpiece like a body in a tomb, decomposing" (*Applied Grammatology*, 63).

In his attempt to overturn a logocentric model of meaning, in which all signifying possibilities are guaranteed in advance by the author through the attestation of his or her signature, Derrida instead tries to discover the workings of that signature, now transformed into another textual element, as it disseminates throughout the structure of the text. All writing obviously shows signs or marks of the individual—the idiomatic, in other words—that then become part of the overall working of the text; the disseminative operation of the signature makes it even more intrusive. A number of Derrida's texts have put this into practice, working with such names as Blanchot, Hegel, and Genet.[20] Another well-known example of this operation occurs in *Signsponge*, Derrida's imaginative reading of the name of the French poet Francis Ponge throughout his poems. In that book Derrida specifies three distinct senses of the word "signature": (1) the proper name, articulated and readable in a language; (2) "the set of idiomatic marks that a signer might leave by accident or intention in his product. . . . The style, the inimitable idiom of a writer, sculptor, painter, or orator" (54); (3) the "signature of the signature," a self-reflexive pointing in the text to the act of production—"I refer to myself, this is writing, I am a writing" (54). This last is perhaps most productive, as Derrida relates "Ponge"

---

inscription, see Gregory Ulmer, "Sounding the Unconscious," in John P. Leavey Jr., *Glassary* (Lincoln: University of Nebraska Press, 1986), 65.

[19] As early as *Of Grammatology* it was made clear that a proper name could never signify only a uniqueness since it is (1) part of a classificatory system, and (2) composed of repeatable phonemes (110–11).

[20] For Blanchot, see "Pas" in *Parages* (Paris: Galilée, 1986), 19–116; for Hegel and Genet, of course, see *Glas*.

to *éponge* (sponge), a common noun-object that turns out to have something of the undecidability of writing: it is poised between animal and vegetable, full of air or water, solid and plastic, and so on (*Signsponge*, 70).

If the proper name is indeed the means by which authorial intentionality is disseminated throughout the text, it follows that the signature will be a structuring force within that text. This playing with the author's name is serious, in other words, for the signature can be related to various meaning effects arising from the text, as the proper noun takes its place in other signifying textual chains. Yet Derrida has also asked himself in *Signsponge*: "Will I myself have caught the whole drift of his work from the accident of his name? That would be a bit too simple, and I said at the outset that the question of his name would never be more than a little, insignificant piece of the whole corpus" (116). And again, carefully choosing his words, he states that the signature "doesn't explain anything" (118), because of course it is no longer a matter of explanation. Tracing the signature effect, as well as the "procedure" of anagrammaticality in general, in other words, is a complicated mixture of chance and necessity in every text, an opposition which that tracing always seeks to displace and to rewrite in another register. Intentionality is also rewritten in the process. Thus, answering a question concerning the play of his own signature in *Glas*, in the multiple forms of *derrière le rideau* (behind the curtain), Derrida explains that the question of intentionality is finally an undecidable one:

> Playing with one's own name, putting it in play, is, in effect, what is always going on and what I have tried to do in a somewhat more explicit or systematic manner for some time now and in certain texts. But obviously this is not something one can decide: one doesn't disseminate or play with one's name. The very structure of the proper name sets this process in motion. That's what the proper name is for. At work, naturally, in the desire—the apparent desire—to lose one's name by disarticulating it, disseminating it, is the inverse movement. . . . [The operation is] naturally different and singular every time. . . . (*The Ear of the Other*, 76, 77)

The general strategy (though not the specific results) of Derrida's analysis of the presumably unintentional "+R effect" in Valerio Adami's drawings and paintings, discussed below, differs only slightly from the play of the presumably intentional "+L effect" in *Glas*. The point here is that the question of intentionality is displaced in favor of a general procedure of reading (and hence, writing). It should also be obvious at this point that the signature effect is not to be considered only as a function of marks left by an authorial presence but rather as an invaginated inscription of any autobiographical mark, for instance that of a *reader*. For a reading itself is always a form of writing.

There are a number of points to be made if the signature effect is to be applied to film. On one level, of course, there is a change in medium—writing to image—but this amounts to a difference in the type of inscription that does not negate the structural similarity between the two, given that the film image is also a type of writing. However, it should be noted that the signature of writing is used by Derrida to produce effects of heterogeneity in a seemingly homogeneous medium, whereas film, as we have said, is more explicitly structured by heterogeneous elements. Second, a film does not normally have a single author and so works through a more complicated idea of intentionality. As a general theoretical principle, what must be common to both media is an idea of signature that describes the means by which the cohering structures of a text are challenged by its disseminative functions and the rewriting of authorship within that dynamic. Just as the signature is a function of the competition between intention and dissemination in a written text, similar competing forces, such as the pictorial (itself the site of a complex play of heterogeneity) and the graphic, are at work in the image.

Thus the case can be made for more specific signature effects in film. Arguably the most obvious example is the regular "signature" appearance of Hitchcock in all his films. Generally, of course, the sight of the rotund director is taken as little more than an amusing "in joke" for Hitchcock cognoscenti, but there is nothing that authorizes such an exclusion from the more "serious" meaning effects arising from a Hitchcock film. Like a signature on a painting, the sight of the director assures us, even more directly than his name in the credits, of the authenticity of the product, but since this intervention from the "outside" has necessarily to be written "inside," it becomes the cinematic equivalent of a common noun, with disseminative effects that must be read along with the film's other elements. Even though Hitchcock always disappears from the frame within seconds, textual chains have been put into motion and cannot be unwritten or arbitrarily stopped. For example, Hitchcock's appearance knocking on the bus door in *North by Northwest* (1959) is linked by Raymond Bellour to important thematic structures of castration and sexuality working through the film as a whole.[21] In Bellour's analysis, however, the image of Hitch-

---

[21] "Le Blocage symbolique," *Communications*, no. 23 (1975), 235–350.

cock's appearance is co-opted for its cohering effect, whereas we would stress its disruptive potential.

Hitchcock's appearance is an obvious exemplification of the first type of signature mentioned in *Signsponge*: the director authenticates the fact that it is indeed he who is making the film, claiming it as his own. Much more than this, however, his appearance creates the structure of the third type of signature, the self-reflexive pointing to the fact that "I am writing." For he is unavoidably writing his "proper name" with his body, and writing visually, in the image and in the other signifying loci of the film. He thus becomes a writing, an "excess" in more ways than one, and the simple appearance of his image irreparably disturbs the primacy of the naturalizing, logocentric forces of narrative and consistent characterization.

An interesting case is the way in which Hitchcock writes his image into the film *Lifeboat* (1943) by means of a newspaper advertisement. This indicates that for the purposes of the signature there is no distinction between a profilmic Hitchcock and a once-removed, already represented Hitchcock, for the signature is rendered possible by the very structure of citation, that is, its possibility of being repeated. The newspaper image of Hitchcock does not so much guarantee a product as place his image within an abyssal structure of citation, which ultimately folds the levels of representation in upon themselves.[22]

But it is not only Hitchcock who thus writes his signature on the film; besides the obviously illusion-destroying appearances of Godard in his films, John Huston when he appears briefly in *The Treasure of the Sierra Madre* (1947) and Pier Paolo Pasolini as a Theban in *Edipo Re* (1967) or as a painter in *Canterbury Tales* (1972), to take three examples from many, also overtly put the play of the signature into operation. It seems no accident that with both Huston and Pasolini the appearances are brief but intense, as though the films themselves were foregrounding the violence of the reversal that is accomplished. On the other hand, with a director who is also a principal actor in a film (say, Jean Renoir in *Rules of the Game* and Woody Allen) the effect is at once more consistent and more banal, because less forcefully intrusive. In these films, the fixity of their placement in normalizing structures of narrative and characterization tends to neutralize the disruptive force of the signature. In the Hitchcock films, on the contrary, the very fact that the question "Is he a character in these films?" is unanswerable reveals the undecidability of the inside/outside dynamic of the signature and

[22] Given his alleged proclivities, the sexual dimension implied in Hitch/cock's signature is obvious and could be traced through many of his films.

calls into question the status of character as an integrating structure within narrative.

Given the visuality of film, as well as its usual reliance on narrative and character, it seems particularly appropriate to consider directors who write themselves into their films in the ways suggested above. However, it should also be remembered that a film is written in more traditional ways as well, for example in its script, dialogue, subtitles, and credits—not to mention the "accidental" pieces of written language appearing in many of its images—and in this sense more closely resembles the textual signature effects that Derrida finds in Genet, Ponge, and his own writing. At the risk of appearing less than serious, then, one might also investigate the workings of the director's proper name, as inscribed in the credits, throughout the film. Thus the names of "Ford," "Re-noir," "von Sternberg," "Welles," and so on can be regarded as generative of particular readings of individual film texts or bodies of films, provided that these names are not taken in isolation but inscribed within a carefully developed textual logic. Complicating this particular application of the signature effect is the fact, mentioned earlier, that film's intentionality, because of its collaborative nature, has long been recognized as dispersed and disseminated. In other words, there is no reason for limiting the investigation of the signature effect to the director's name, for in principle all the names in the credits are written on and into the film and thus have the potential of signifying as common nouns.

As we have said, the question of the signature is part of the larger question of what in the image escapes the dominance of the graphic, the visual, or whatever dominant mode of representation is in practice. For Ulmer, the importance of the image resides in its ability to resist the ascendancy of verbal language operating in the Western tradition. When it comes to problematizing the dominance of the phonetic—with its supposedly closed circuit of meaning from mouth to ear—emphasis is placed on the graphic and the pictorial, elements involving the visual rather than the auditory sense. The point, as Ulmer has argued, is not that the phonetic will be replaced by the pictorial or the graphic but that the operations of meaning will be opened up to less limiting possibilities. As we have seen in our brief earlier discussion of such a technological aberration as Smellovision, the visual can even be deconstructed by the olfactory, creating a "picto-ideo-phonographic Writing." As Ulmer puts it:

> Derrida's anti-books, at the same time that they work theoretically and thematically to subvert the final obstacle to grammatol-

ogy—the metaphysics of logocentrism—also demonstrate a certain "graphic rhetoric," the essence of which is a double-valued Writing, ideographic and phonetic at once, which puts speech back in its place in relation to non-phonetic elements. The importance of Derrida's example for an applied grammatology is that it provides a model for articulating in one presentation both verbal and non-verbal materials—the kind of Writing needed for classroom performance and for audio-visual presentation in film and video—in a way, however, that is not dominated by the philosophemes of sight and hearing (theory and voice). (98)

Nevertheless, it is important to understand the subtleties involved in Derrida's enterprise. For the dominance of the phonetic is only one of the possible paradigms for the operations of logocentrism in general, rather than a single practice that can easily be subverted. For instance, in a written text, certainly, but also in an image meaning is still generally assumed to be communicated from a single source that guarantees its arrival in the mind of the reader or viewer, still within a closed circuit. In other words, although phonetic dominance may be displaced by recourse to the audio-visual media, logocentrism will not necessarily be. In discussion of written texts or of images, Derrida has consistently used one to complicate the other, accompanying writing with images like postcards, finding "writing" of one sort or another within and around the image—in its forms, titles, discourses on it, and so on.

Thus, as comprehensive as his understanding of the Derridean enterprise is, Ulmer seems to us overly optimistic when he heralds the arrival of grammatology, the removal of its "final obstacle," and its application through the audio-visual media. This ignores the fact, implied if not made explicit by much contemporary film theory, that the audio-visual media—and in particular film—contain their own very entrenched logocentric assumptions. While it is true that a medium like video might open new possibilities for writing, these possibilities are not clearly developed by Ulmer, and his discussion of cinema (restricted to the example of Eisenstein) does not satisfactorily relate to current audio-visual practices. As a result, the cases treated in the second part of his text—Lacan, Beuys, and Eisenstein—read more as studies in the comparative literature mode than as "applied grammatology . . . already under way" (xiii–xiv).

Having now considered the signature, in the following discussion we approach the question of representational hierarchies by considering the models of the hieroglyph and the rebus. Given its importance

in the functioning of dreams, the rebus seems to relate automatically
to cinema. From a Derridean perspective, as a "written image," it
could be considered as the model for images in general, although the
possibility of its being a kind of puzzle reducible to a meaning that is
graphically representable in its entirety is never allowed. In the comparison between dream and cinema the visual is of course already dominant, and as Derrida points out in "White Mythology," the metaphor
of the truth as light, that is to say a model of the truth based on the
dominance of the visual, is well entrenched within our thinking.
Clearly, then, what also occurs in both dream and cinema is the apparent reduction of speech to a mere support for the visual medium.
However, once the dream is treated as a rebus, as a complex network
of meaning generated by relations between the image, words spoken,
and words "written" within the image, a simple communication of
meaning by means of the visual is no longer possible. Our model in
the following discussion will be the hieroglyph more than the rebus,
but since we are both treating Derrida's work with images and seeking
to extend it to the case of film, we shall take the one to be synonymous
with the other.[23]

In "+R (Into the Bargain)," an essay in *The Truth in Painting* on
Valerio Adami's drawings and paintings, Derrida offers what Ulmer
calls "the best account available . . . of a drawn writing, taking the
letter as a line, divisible . . . letting the semantic or representational
effects fall where they may" (123). Derrida's reading of the pictorial
image is replete with references that cut across any possible reduction
to the purely visual. Conversely, the written discourse that is the medium for his discussion becomes all the more graphic and visual. It is
important to realize that what is at stake here is more than just a discussion of certain drawings by Adami inspired by Derrida's *Glas*.
Rather, the essay represents a systematic intervention across the institutional boundaries separating writing from painting, just as *Glas* operated a similar systematic intervention across the boundaries of philosophy and literature.

Perhaps the most important element of that intervention is the material inscription of rupture within the word. One possible reading of
Glas would investigate the effects of the unpronounceable "gl" left

---

[23] We should note here one other important Derridean use of the visual to create a
complex signifying machine. We are referring to the models discussed by Ulmer (98–
124)—umbrella, matchbox, postcard—which rely to some extent on a visualization of
their functions but which also draw in wordplays across the phonetic/graphic interface,
to act as relays for the dissemination of meaning. They work for Derrida as the rhetorical
equivalent of the dream-rebus.

hanging once the "as" (anagram of the acronym of *le savoir absolu* [Hegel's "absolute knowledge"]) has been amputated from it, that is to say the disseminative effects of a fragmentary signifier extracted from its relation to a transcendental signified, and thus the effects of utterance in general once they are no longer underwritten by the concept of absolute knowledge. In Derrida's essay on Adami the remainder from this rupture engenders "ich," truncated in turn from the Greek word for "fish" (*ichtys*). The pretext for this play is a drawing of Adami's containing a piece of a quotation from *Glas* (in which the fragment "gl" appears) and another quotation in Derrida's own hand, as well as a drawing of a fish half out of water. And it is here, with "gl" and "ich," that the transgression of the phonetic/graphic distinction can be most clearly seen:

> This barely pronounceable writing is not a morpheme, not a word if one restrains oneself (nothing authorizes this) from taking the step [*le pas*] of meaning. *Gl* does not belong to discourse, no more does it belong to space, and nothing certifies the past or future of such a belonging. . . . A rebel . . . to the regulated exchange of the two elements (lexical and pictural), close to piercing a hole in the *arthron* of discursive writing and representational painting, is this not a wild, almost unnarratable event? (*Truth in Painting*, 160)

"Ich" is then transformed anagrammatically into "chi" or "χ" and as we mentioned above, "chi" is shorthand for the chiasmus. This remainder then comes to be related to the title of the essay through the fact of truncation. In turn, " + R," considered in its graphic form as a variant of "tr," relates to the initial letters of the French word for a brushstroke,[24] and finally to a whole list of words and ideas—"*train, trait, trajet, tramé . . . tressé, tracé, trajectoire, traversée, transformation, transcription*" (*La Vérité en peinture*, 195; cf. *The Truth in Painting*, 169–71)—that Derrida regards as directly descriptive of Adami's themes and motifs. The "t" of "tr" is also a cross, then, the cross of the chiasmus and that of intersecting lines, the "tr" the invaginated intersection of drawing and writing, the *definition* of the drawings under scrutiny, an alternative—but equally "valid"—description of Adami's work: "And by drawing the +, you will have quoted along the way all Adami's crosses, especially the itinerary of the red crosses, the badges of

---

[24] Fr. *trait*. See our discussion of genre in chapter 3 for the importance of the *trait* as *retrait*. As we mentioned there, the trait describes a stroke of the brush or pen and is indistinguishably pictorial and scriptural. Besides that, it is a word for a personal characteristic, hence related to the signature, but also a graphic mark or sign of writing that exceeds the pure idiom of that signature in disseminating it.

nurses, of fantastic ambulance men marking simultaneously war and peace, undecidable neutrality in the topography of political Europe" (174). Furthermore, since "ich" is German for the first person subject pronoun, and since a fragment of Derrida's signature appears in the drawing in question along with that of Adami, a further effect of the irruption of signatory writing upon the signifying surface of the image is demonstrated.

We have dwelt on this example, which of course suffers from being summarized, in order to point to the richness of effects that can be generated from a reading of the image that starts out from the principle of its radical heterogeneity, through the play of the pictorial "against" the scriptural and the signature "against" a centralized meaning residing within the work. Let us now turn our attention to a similar type of reading applied to film.

In *Le Texte divisé* and in "The Graphic in Filmic Writing: *A bout de souffle*, or the Erratic Alphabet"[25] Marie-Claire Ropars attempts to trace the materialities of signatory writing within the film image. She thus provides the most reasoned application yet of Derridean theory to the cinematic medium, carrying over into textual analysis the grammatological principles she derives from Eisensteinian montage. We have already made various references to *Le Texte divisé*, where Ropars discusses Benveniste, Derrida, and Freud, outlining their common development of a theory of meaning that undoes the Saussurian theory of the sign. Thus in Freud's *Interpretation of Dreams* dreams are sometimes said to be meaningful according to a more or less fixed system of symbols, a system that models itself on the sign and a *semantic* view of meaning, while elsewhere Freud seems to favor a theory of writing that privileges the particular composition and articulation of each dreamer (in other words, a *syntactic* model of meaning). The former model presupposes the existence of the latent content of the dream, an originary meaning that the dream itself is said to translate, and in translating distort and disfigure. A theory of writing, on the contrary, would hold that an originary latent meaning can only come into existence through the dream's translation by the analyst. (The dream's "cause" paradoxically being caused by its "effect.") Meaning is thus a product of the textual process itself, rather than a process of translation of a previous signified through a collection of individually signifying words or images, and it is here that Ropars finds important connections with Eisenstein's theories of cinematic montage.[26]

---

[25] *Enclitic* 5, no. 2/6, no. 1 (Fall 1981/Spring 1982), 147–61.

[26] Ropars mentions that Derrida, in "Freud et la scène de l'écriture," translates Freud's

For Eisenstein, each shot had figural meaning, of course, but he also insisted that meaning lay in the nature of montage itself, which gives rise to a textual process that undoes the meaning of the individual shots by neutralizing, fragmenting, and making them conflict with one another. "Produced abstractly by the juxtaposition of images, the concept cannot in any case be linked with a particular image. . . . It is the original division of shots—equally removed from representation and signification—that produces a signification not only irreducible to representation but even, at the extreme, independent of it" (*Le Texte divisé*, 39; our translation). It is important to stress that the conflict at work in montage also functions within individual shots—called "internal montage" by Eisenstein—in the arrangement of forms, lines, and volumes.

For Ropars, what links Eisensteinian montage even more closely with Derridean writing is the director's insistence on the role of rupture in the signifying process. Thus, even the so-called invisible editing of classic Hollywood cinema, as Eisenstein pointed out, must both maintain an illusion of continuity and linearity, which implies the effacing of editing, and make each shot *different* enough from the preceding one to justify its inclusion in the construction of its own invisibility. Continuity and rupture, in other words, are simultaneously foregrounded (48–51).

Derrida and Eisenstein are further related in their common interest in the hieroglyph, which is both figural, dependent upon a pictorial code for its meaning, and operational within a conventional system of signs. Derrida has defined the hieroglyph as "the organized cohabitation, within the same graphic code, of figurative, symbolic, abstract, and phonetic elements" (quoted in Ropars, 61), and he argues that Western languages, though basically phonetic, contain elements of opposed systems. For Ropars, the hieroglyph is both figural and conceptual and can be likened, through montage, to what she calls the "scriptural vocation of the cinema" (37, n.29). When the principles of hieroglyphic writing and montage are combined, the image discloses a heterogeneity derived from a tension between "a mimetic current through which figuration would support an adequation between sign and thing, and a process of montage whose only definable motivation remains internal to the play of signifiers" (73). This in turn allows readings of the cinematic image that resist a single definition of cinema

---

Zusammensetzungen as *montages* (*Le Texte divisé*, 33). She notes this as a cinematic reference, and her remarks might be seen as complementing Freudian references to the *camera obscura* that others have discussed (see for example Sarah Kofman, *Camera obscura: De l'idéologie*).

based on its audio-visual specificity (18) and promote instead the sorts of textual analyses Ropars practices on individual texts.[27]

In the second part of *Le Texte divisé* and in the article already referred to, Ropars takes up Duras and Godard. In choosing their films as objects of analysis she benefits, in the case of *India Song*, from an "overflow of agreement with Derrida's conceptualization" (*Le Texte divisé*, 161), but we see no theoretical obstacle to treating any film text on the same basis. In any case, the major point of departure for a comparison between Duras's films (and from a different angle Godard's) and the ideas of Derrida lies with the explicit ruptures within their construction. In Duras, this is most obviously that between image and sound tracks; in Godard, within the sound track, certainly, but also between different genres. Now such ruptures can be read from a Derridean perspective as inscriptions of the signature, a synecdoche of writing. It is first of all the effect of the signature that institutes rupture and prevents unity within the text in the terms already detailed. To repeat, the signature itself cannot be considered written as a unitary sign, however much the institutions of signing, entitling, copyright and acknowledgment might try to give it a monumental aspect; rather it is written to disintegrate within the text as a function of a generalized *writing*.

The scattering of meaning associated with the signature can in fact be set in motion by any proper name in the text. Ropars details this operation through the enunciation of the proper names of *India Song*, which are seen as an inscription of writing that resists, up to a point, the narrative linearity of the film. When Anne-Marie Stretter's name is first uttered it raises the possibility of stabilizing, through the imposition of character and the matching of image with name, the play of voice and image that preceded it, thus allowing for the narrative to take hold. Instead, the name becomes implicated, through the play we referred to in the previous chapter, with the "anti-narrative" of the Beggar, whose incomprehensible words and cries "off-screen" are the most extreme sign of the disruption of the image track by the sound track. Elements of that sound track thus come to represent the structural disunity upon which the text is constituted: "By actualizing a rupture within the proper name, the dissemination of letters strikes a blow at the referential question par excellence, that of identification, which allows the person to be tied to the name, the word to the thing" (159–60). For Ropars, it is of strategic importance to reinforce the Durassian separation of image from sound by further radicalizing its

---

[27] Besides the long analysis of *India Song*, *Le Texte divisé* has shorter pieces on Lang's *M* and Renoir's *The Rules of the Game*.

effects as she does here. She wants to exploit what she calls "privileged fracture zones" ("The Graphic in Filmic Writing," 147) such as that between image and sound, especially in view of the failure on the part of most cinema to recognize this profound structural disunity.

If the analysis of *India Song* is limited to the auditory signifiers of what is easily recognized to be a very poetically resonant sound track, however, Ropars's analysis of *Breathless* (1959) undertakes a more complicated tracing of *writing* with respect to the image. Concentrating this time on the written texts ("written" in the conventional sense) within the cinematic image, she concurrently treats the film as written text. The image is thus read as a hieroglyph "in which the figure's thrust causes signification to shatter into heterogeneous networks" (147).

Those networks include relations between sound and image, between the phonetic and the vocal, between semantic and figurative elements. Ropars's analysis treats each as it mounts incursions over the boundaries of the other, so that what is involved is a radical division of the textual whole and of the unity of individual images. The communication of meaning therefore cannot be restricted to the linear development of the film, and indeed from the very first Ropars declines to establish a standard syntagmatic division of the film into narrative sequences, preferring instead to treat units called "chapters." Since the film deals with a relationship between an American woman and a Frenchman as well as with American film noir in a variety of ways, it might be said that the relations between the film's hieroglyphic elements are those of an unfaithful or incorrect translation, exemplified by slips in Patricia's use of French and her questions about words such as that which closes the film. Translation is after all the means by which language attempts to compensate for its heterogeneity—there being intralinguistic as well as interlinguistic translation—and in the Derridean schema translation uncovers, as much as it conceals, that heterogeneity. Faithful translation, like self-present meaning, is always a structural impossibility.

Although Ropars declines to give her analysis any unitary conclusion, her most important point for us refers more to the principle than to the details of her study:

The hieroglyph hypothesis, which has served as a framework for the analysis, has been reinforced by the film's paragrammatic density, the editing's ability to make the alphabet err into protean anagrams: when scriptural activity gets intense, we have seen the title and meaning come undone, and we have circulated fragments thus taken up from language along multiple channels—iconic or verbal, literal or vocal. ("The Graphic in Filmic Writing," 158)

What began then as an analysis of the effects of written language within a film text—although it was clear from the start that the tactic would irrevocably complicate itself—leads to a form of reading of the image (and of the film as a "whole") based on any available pretext to radicalize its disunity, continually crossing internal and external borders of image, of sound track, and of elements of both, thus deploying a whole range of critical possibilities. Starting from the basis of the image itself, any utterance, whether iconic, graphic, or vocal, is taken to be always internally fragmented.

The implications of Ropars's work on Eisenstein as the basis for her own textual analyses are clearly spelled out in an excellent article by David Rodowick entitled "The Figure and the Text":[28] "A textual system constituted by montage, or what Ropars will later call "hieroglyphic editing," would therefore have an epistemological status different from that of narrative-representational film" (43). We would want to insist once again that *any* film is constituted by montage—and this implication should also be drawn from Ropars's work—whether it has been organized according to Eisensteinian principles or not. For the heterogeneity of the film as signifying system, recognized by semiotic as much as by grammatological theory, demands that its construction never successfully cover its differences, however much classic narrative cinema might try to do that. The ultimate implication of the recognition of film as a form of Derridean writing would therefore be to disqualify the privileged epistemological status of narrative-representational film, to disqualify it as a coherent and intact cinematic category. To demonstrate this it would be necessary to apply a reading such as that Ropars undertakes on *India Song* or *Breathless* to films whose "fracture zones" are not so explicit.

It is important to recognize, however, that Ropars's treatment of *Breathless* does not after all suggest that that text is without structures of relegation or control over the dissemination of meaning that she has tried to outline. On the contrary, the heterogeneity of elements implies a very complex system of competing forces, of plays of power, and she finds, as Rodowick notes, that the "radical potentiality" of the registers of cited texts and image/sound relations, is "superintended" by rela-

---

[28] *Diacritics* 15, no. 1 (Spring 1985), 34–50. For further discussion of Ropars's work, see Laura Oswald, "Semiotics and/or deconstruction: In quest of cinema"; and Dana Polan, " 'Desire shifts the Differance': Figural Poetics and Figural Politics in the Film Theory of Marie-Claire Ropars," *Camera Obscura*, no. 12 (Summer 1984), 67–89.

tions of sexual difference that control "the dissemination of letters in the film" (46). In other words, it is not an ideal space of textual free play that is opened up by the hieroglyphic image but an institutional struggle, and the more powerful the institutions of meaning are, the less likely they are to permit a reading to pry open their fracture zones.

According to Rodowick, Ropars's reliance on a paradigm of sexual difference, as well as the privilege that he finds that she gives to the modernist *poetic* text, means that "the epistemological standard of logocentrism . . . has not been 'deconstructed' " ("The Figure and the Text," 48). His principal objection is that the Derridean definition of writing upon which Ropars bases her analysis is undercut by her recourse to "models of literary speech and communication" (49). Indeed Ropars does concentrate her reading on the play of literary allusion and the figure of Patricia as woman, but she maintains that the disturbing forces of femininity and of the poetic are both inscribed and deleted within the text, as signs of writing: "The written, in the strict sense of the term, is refused, even deleted, without ever being definitely abolished. Warded off, the graphic sign still returns, both desirable and prohibited" ("The Graphic in Filmic Writing," 154). And if she finds that the repression of woman brings about a regression of writing from its Derridean to its conventional literary sense, her argument is similar to that advanced in her analysis of *India Song*, where the eventual dominance of the narrative involved the closure of a certain play of writing. Given the complex network of writing effects that Ropars examines in *Breathless*, we find Rodowick's objection to represent more of a reduction of the force of her analysis than a discovery of its blind spot.[29] He is finally led to conclude that "for Ropars, the textual system is *intrinsic*: neither historical nor materialist, this conception designates the text as an empirical object whose form would preordain certain types of reading" (49), whereas for us the importance of her reading is its very resistance to structures of textual closure.

The first part of Rodowick's essay deals with the work of Thierry Kuntzel[30] as offering another recasting of "textual analysis as a problem of filmic 'writing' " (36), and in this case he concludes: "Kuntzel's theory on the other hand is *extrinsic*. It presupposes the fluidity of the semiotic process, and rather than predetermining the system of the text, it opens the text onto a discursive field where its potential mean-

[29] We agree more with Rodowick when he questions whether Ropars's recourse to Benveniste is compatible with the development of a Derridean notion of writing (cf. "The Figure and the Text," 48).

[30] The essays Rodowick examines are "The Film-Work," *Enclitic* 2, no. 1 (Spring 1976), 38–61; and "The Film-Work, 2," *Camera Obscura*, no. 5 (Spring 1980), 6–69.

ings and subjective relations are capable of critical transformations as well as stabilization" (49). Indeed Kuntzel's relation of textual signification to that of dream raises the possibility we referred to earlier of the image's being treated as a rebus, and the first essay treated by Rodowick (on *M*) explicitly refers to a Derridean model of reading ("The Film-Work," 38). In the long essay on *The Most Dangerous Game* in *Camera Obscura* the question of reading is discussed at length. A tension arises in the essay between a proleptic analysis of the first images into which "almost the entire film can be condensed" ("The Film-Work, 2," 24) and a "perturbing, perverting, mixing . . . a way of writing which is sufficiently labile to render the fluidity of film, its movement, its mixedness, and the specificity of its signifying process" (56). A tension therefore between a "static" application of Freud and a more dynamic one through which Freud's attention to wordplay and the *Nachträglichkeit* can be read as functions of writing in the Derridean sense. It seems to us that this tension is structurally very similar to that which Rodowick criticizes in Ropars, between writing and the literary. Given this, Kuntzel's reading is as susceptible as Ropars's to being reduced to an essentializing gesture that sees in the image a stabilization rather than a dissemination of its meaning effects. It is true that to the extent that Kuntzel allows his analysis to become the site of an interrogation of reading itself, he is more Derridean than is Ropars. On the other hand, and to return to the emphasis we have been developing in this chapter, Ropars insists that the immediacy imposed by the image as iconic entity is contradicted by its inscription within the montage chain, that is to say that the frame that encloses and defines it also cuts it off from any originary coherence: "The shot can be considered as a unit of writing, to the extent that it challenges any claim made by sense to constitute units. Homogeneous in terms of its substance, and closed upon itself, heterogeneous in terms of meaning, and open to multiple hieroglyphic tracings, it imprints upon the film the contrariety of rupture and of the network—which constitute the trace" (*Le Texte divisé*, 116).

In conclusion, it may be useful to examine a recent text of Derrida's in which he comes closest to writing "about" the cinema. In this text Derrida provides a reading (which is the term used on the title page) of a series of photographs called *Right of Inspection*.[31] First, reading here

[31] The French title (*Droit de regards*) can translate as both "the right to look" and "the law(s) of looking (of the looks)," but the expression *avoir droit de regard sur* means "to

is, as always, concerned with institutional boundaries and is therefore a juridical matter. As the title indicates, and as film theory has been long aware, the image is still in the business of positioning its reader, still exercising power over the right to look: "A text of images gives you, along with its 'characters,' a right to look, the simple right to look or to appropriate with the gaze, but it denies you that right at the same time: by means of its very apparatus it keeps for itself the authority, the right of inspection . . ." (24). Derrida's text accompanying the photographs thus sets out to avoid the inevitable positioning operated by the images. He refuses first of all to subscribe to the protocols of narrative and instead writes a sort of polylogue with himself (or selves), with the photographer, or with someone else.[32] Taking as a pretext the appearance of a checkerboard in one series of images, he inscribes the figure of the diagonal across the carefully posed and framed images. At the same time of course, the checkerboard with its even and institutionalized distribution of black and white, its negative and positive—the background against which the game of checkers or of ladies (Fr. *une partie de dames*), and hence the narrative, takes place—comes to represent the images. The checkerboard is itself simultaneously being subdivided and transformed into the site of a game whose dominant rule is not straightforward but diagonal.

It seems to us that any attempt to extend Derrida's ideas concerning the image to the domain of the cinema will come back to the matter of how strategies for reading film might challenge, more radically than semiotics did or does, the institutions that determine and restrict such reading(s). It will not be by simple fiat that the ideological and historical framework of photography or cinema will collapse to allow for the rewriting of textual and institutional relations that we envisage here. A minute and systematic critique of history and theory has been necessary for the problematic of writing to assume the configuration

oversee." A recurring wordplay in Derrida's text is on the word *demeure*, from the verb meaning "to stay" or "to rest." It is also a noun meaning "a large house"—the setting of many of the photographs—and occurs in the legal term for "serving notice." Marie-Françoise Plissart's images deal with a series of sexual encounters, mostly between women, one of whom is a photographer and whose photographs (some *en abyme*) play an important part within the narrative. For further discussion of Derrida's text, see David Wills, "Deposition: Introduction to *Right of Inspection* [*Droit de regards*]," *Art & Text*, no. 32 (1989), 10–18; and idem, "Supreme Court," *Diacritics* 18, no. 3 (1988), 20–31.

[32] This device is used in the essay on Van Gogh's shoes in *The Truth in Painting* ("Restitutions," 255–382), described as "a polylogue of n + 1 voices, which happens to be that of a woman" (10), as well as in other texts such as "Pas" and *Feu la cendre/Ciò che resta del fuoco* (Florence: Sansoni, 1984). The latter has been republished by Des Femmes and is also available on cassette read by Derrida and actress Carole Bouquet.

we recognize since Derrida. And above all, that critique has deployed
a variety of reading practices that challenge the imposition of institutional forms. *Right of Inspection* thus implicitly outlines the task ahead
of a deconstruction of film:

> —If I understand correctly, one has to bring enormous atten-
> tion to bear on each detail, enlarge it out of all proportion, slowly
> penetrate the abyss of these metonymies—and yet manage to skim
> through diagonally [*en diagonale*]. To accelerate, speed up the
> tempo, as if there were no time.
> —That's right, it's the law of draughts [checkers] and of pho-
> tography. (68)

and suggests the difference that is to be gained by a theoretical rein-
vestment:

> Here everything demanding *inversion*, that of the sexes,[33] that of
> the order of the series or temporalities, calls for a certain reversi-
> bility, the time to leaf back through, to move the sequences about
> like *dames*, to calculate other possible trajectories within the space
> of the labyrinth and the simultaneity of the board, to traverse or
> cross through the narrative sequences in several directions, always
> according to the rules . . . obliquely. (41–42)

The sense of what that reversibility might entail in the case of film is
something we have tried to sketch out in this and the preceding chapter.

As Derrida develops them, the terms "inversion" and "reversibility"
mean something other than a simple idea of opposition, referring instead to a more complex deployment of resistances to the institutional
constraints in force. These ideas relate more to the diagonality of the
checkers move, both obeying the rules of the game and exploiting
them to make abrupt and oblique interventions such as seem to exceed
those rules. This is especially relevant to the question of speed as it
relates to photography and cinema. The precise technology of the
camera—perhaps the very definition of technology as we understand
it—resides in its speed; the speed of the shutter, the reproduction process, and so on. Yet the ideology of technological advance has reduced
speed to notions of linear ordering that privilege directness, notions
from which any idea of obliqueness is excluded. Taking the lead from
Derrida's writing on photography, however, we might begin to imag-

---

[33] *Un inverti* is a homosexual, thus this is a reference to the content of the photographs
as well as to the questions of difference and *différance* that Derrida raises.

ine a type of writing on film whose rhetoric borrows something from the technology of the medium; a rhetoric of cinema (perhaps later of the video clip) informed by angle shots, double takes, shifts of focus, and close-ups:

> Breaking down [*Faire pièce*], that is what is happening here. No single panorama, but simply parts of bodies, torn-up or framed pieces, abyssal synecdoches, floating microscopic details, X-rays sometimes focused, sometimes out of focus, hence blurred. The zooms, the dolly shots . . . never deliver the whole, it is never before her eyes in its entirety. The whole retreats, and in its retreat only leaves traces in the forms of fragments. (74)

As always such a strategy cannot be a simple or unitary one—the idea of speed, of course, should not be adopted too quickly as an excuse for lack of attention.

In *Right of Inspection* Derrida manages to force open the image in spite of the laws it imposes. Visual language, no matter what privileges it might claim, is undercut by its verbal other when the *photogrammes* composing the text are shown to set up a *photogrammaire* that lets one syntactical configuration through its net. For a photograph, as studies of point-of-view and eyeline-match shots have discovered, cannot *show* two people looking at each other, at least not right into each other's eyes. Thus the senses of *elles se regardent* ("they are looking at each other") that verbal language allows cannot all be rendered by individual visual utterances. That single *aporia* is all that is required for the introduction into the circuit of the photograph's meaning of elements over which its institutional restraints have no control. It is the sufficent difference that allows Derrida to divide the image *en abyme* or chiastically like the squares of the checkerboard represented within it; to play on its blacks and whites diagonally or obliquely and beyond the reach of the simple physics of vision; to introduce the spectral (34) and the violent through the same game of checkers pieces that oppose and devour each other;[34] and to digress to Poe's *Murders in the Rue Morgue* (43–53) and so to the whole frame of the literary. By reaffirming what we call the image's fundamental incoherence, that structured by its (non-)originary divisibility, Derrida's reading of the image becomes in more ways than one inseparable from writing upon the image and opens the way for a whole new body of writing upon film.

---

[34] In French, one uses the word *manger* (to eat) to mean "to take" (another piece in checkers).

CHAPTER FIVE

BLACK AND BLUE

In the preceding chapters and in the chapter to follow we have tried, as academic protocol dictates for a collaborative effort, to disguise our individual voices, to offer the illusion of a single, seamless flow of thought that has arisen naturally from our work together and even, perhaps, without great effort. Needless to say, whatever smoothness and seamlessness this book may demonstrate is the product of a great deal of discussion, debate, compromise, revision of each other's revisions, and so on. In this chapter, in which we attempt to read (on facing pages) François Truffaut's The Bride Wore Black *(1967) and David Lynch's* Blue Velvet *(1986), we want rather to unmask this fiction of a unity in favor of the duality it is (or rather, multiplicity, for, like everyone else, both of us are ourselves traversed by multiple voices) by foregrounding the heterogeneity of our thinking, our personalities, and our texts.*

The two films we have chosen are hardly canonical texts in the history of film studies, and that is one of the reasons for their selection. We felt that offering a reading of a classic film like Welles's Citizen Kane, *for example, would inevitably be taken as an explicit model of how deconstructive analysis was to be "done," in other words, as an example of a deconstructive methodology.*

Our purpose is quite different. For one thing, the very nature of deconstructive thought (assuming, momentarily, that such a self-present entity exists) insures that no "proper" or "correct" methodology—complete and procedurally explicit—can ever be formulated. Thus, for example, we take the title of Christopher Norris's introductory book Deconstruction: Theory and Practice *to be profoundly misleading even though, in a logocentric world, perhaps inevitable. Rather, we offer what follows as strategic events, readings that are explorations of certain problems seeming to arise in the texts—two idiosyncratic styles of approaching a text, two signatures. Finally, we should point out that though our names do not appear over our individual texts, these texts are of course "signed" throughout.*

François Truffaut's *The Bride Wore Black* announces its binary, structuralist project in its title. Most immediately, of course, a certain duality is manifested structurally and even materially in that title's position vis-à-vis the film it is said to represent. Since it is always known first, the title in a sense can be said to precede the film; it is that part of the film that is "most" outside it, if such things can be quantified. It exists independently, beyond the film's frame, and is similar in this regard to certain film clips, previews, and so on, which themselves are never really part of the film "proper," nor ever the property of the film. Rather they are *exergues* or prefaces, both part of the film and not part of it, which stand in a complicated synecdochic fashion in relation to the film. The title will be cited in newspapers, magazines, film histories, and analyses like this one. As such, it repeats the parergonal relation that exists between such texts and the film. A piece of writing graphic, phonetic, and pictorial all at once—and thus a kind of hieroglyph—the title exists inside the film, that is, inside the credits. (But are the credits themselves inside or outside the film proper?) Outside the film, the title is a piece of writing that will enjoy a life of its own, becoming grafted upon and into other texts, producing additional meaning effects that can never be completely controlled or even catalogued.

A title in some sense also exercises control over what it is meant to represent, a certain delimiting or shaping of expectation obviously, but also a restraint of a potentially rampant textuality. Thus the binary logic of the title of *The Bride Wore Black* functions most powerfully in its generation of an inexhaustible set of oppositions that attempt to master the text's nonbinary heterogeneity. (The title can also of course be seen as the *end point* of this textual operation.) These oppositions are, in conventional terms, formal as well as thematic and include, in different registers, white and black, character and plot, love and death, chastity and sexuality, and genre and anti-genre. Just as the parergonal logic of the title puts it inside and outside at once, however, the film's oppositions themselves are, as we shall see, always undone through their own continual process of internal division. In fact, the sheer number of oppositions produced by the film becomes inexhaustible—for example, open form/closed form, sound track/image, realistic treatment/formula treatment, and so on—and thus paradoxically reflects the generative power and ultimately heterogeneous force of the text at the same time that an attempt is being made to harness this force through a binary logic.

Black and/or blue, the visual signifier always has its moments of un-decidability though rarely does theoretical reflection make them its fo-cus. A female voice asks out of a dark black to blue background whether he is the one who found the ear. One has no need to stop the film, thus incurring the reproach that this analysis is going to reduce cinema to a series of stills, in response to which in any case I might try here to counter with a kind of moving analysis; one has no need to stop the film, for the black and/or blue background is suspended there for a few seconds. I say 'blue' because the faint weeping willow branches are strongly reminiscent of the warp and weave of the blue velvet curtain of the credits (which does indeed fade to the brilliant blue of the Lumberton summer sky); then there is the television, the curtain in Dorothy's apartment, not to mention the dressing gown and of course the film's title, of which more to follow. I could say 'black' since the signified, at least one necessary signified, is darkness. Unless black be the signified of the signifier 'darkness', for do we really know which way it goes, which comes first, in a case of analogical significa-tion? Where is the referent? That night – lost to all except a handful of artists and technicians (lost no doubt to them also) – of the precise date when the scene was shot? Is that night the referent for the spectator? Or, as a more sophisticated theoretical approach has taught us, is it rather one night in Lumberton, USA, a fiction the film invents? Would that be its denotative sense, clearly distinguishable from some conno-tative darkness? But did we ever even agree that it was night and not darkness denoted by those few seconds during which we wait for Sandy Williams to appear? Did we agree that it was black rather than blue? I was saying 'black' in the light of other images or scenes, the interior of the ear, and later the 'Now it's dark' of Frank's manic scenes and Dorothy's own sadomasochistic vortex.

So, early in the film, she, blonde Sandy Williams is undecidable black and blue in the shadows of the trees on her father's front lawn. And then near its climax, she, bruised and naked Dorothy Vallens, black and blue scarecrow, a flailing apparition from Lincoln, stum-bling delirious down the path out of the night of those same small-town streets. As if, between the two, the undecidability of signification in visual terms that occurs in the first were to have found an echo in an idiom brought from outside of the film to describe Dorothy's battered body in the second. But what does it mean to say that the idiom 'black and blue' is brought from the outside when both black and blue are

On one level, these oppositions are set in motion by the director's stated intentions, for Truffaut clearly means for there to be a binary structure embodied in the film. His many interviews concerning the film thus become further attempts to control the textual diaspora. Truffaut signs and resigns the film through these interviews and tries to take responsibility for its proper signifying. Yet the effects of this application of intentionality cannot be sustained for it can never authorize a meta-level standing outside the text and adjudicating between warring elements inside. Rather, the director's remarks become transformed into signatory textual interventions that are inevitably written upon and grafted onto the film text and that themselves must be brought to bear upon any construction of the film's meanings. They become more textual "material" circulating within the general economy of sense and sense making, within a certain field of reading and writing. This operation is exemplified most strikingly perhaps in the manner in which the director's signature, "Truffaut," itself becomes an effect dispersed throughout the text, inevitably becoming rewritten "True/faux," following the film's (and his) insistent attempt at a binary (and inevitably hierarchical) structure.

A principal opposition posed in this film concerns the genre or genres in which it can be said to participate.[1] By overtly trying to make a film that is both thriller and love story at once, Truffaut troubles the usual generic tyranny, and when the film first appeared in this country in 1968, critics seemed at a loss about how to classify it. Some called it a thriller, others called it a love story, but all insisted on placing it *somewhere*. What is interesting in all this is the obvious discomfort critics feel when faced with texts that foreground a certain duality or undecidability and that refuse to submit to an easy either/or placement. A kind of will to categorization reigns here, for to establish genres is always to essentialize, to repress signifiers that do not fit, in order to "understand" and thus master the text. However, because *The Bride* offers two essences, two centers, the process of genre assignment is derailed, and the critic's repressive force is laid bare. This attempt at

---

[1] The film's plot is unusually straightforward. Jeanne Moreau plays a young woman named Julie Kohler who is bent on avenging the wantonly careless slaying, on the steps of the church, of her husband of five minutes. Obsessed by the loss of the only love of her life, she relentlessly tracks down each of the five men present at the drunken stag party that occasioned the accidental shooting. She plays to the amorous fantasies of her victims by disguising herself as each one's image of the "ideal woman." Thus the film's general narrative and its mini-narratives are constructed and motivated by phallic desire and its representations. Made vulnerable by this desire, her would-be lovers are dispatched one by one by means of elaborate, individually designed murder plots.

highlighted in the film and even, I am suggesting, appear in undecidable simultaneity like bruises on the body? What does it mean when image and referent are articulated as tightly as we are told that they are in film – does that not threaten to disturb irrevocably relations between inside and out? Since we view the film as if it were all there, within the frame – Lumberton, the black and/or blue night, Jeffrey Beaumont and Sandy Williams – how far out would we have to reach to find a colloquial expression for a victim of violence? As long as we are using words to describe what occurs within the frame, would we be going any further out than the words 'Lumberton', 'night', 'Jeffrey', and 'Sandy' to produce the words 'black' and 'blue'? Since we know anyway, in spite of appearances, to what extent a film depends on suturing with its outside. Is this our presumption: the importation of a single common conjunction 'and', thus imposing a syntax whereas the image speaks only in concrete terms? Of course not, it is also a long time since we agreed that there is no future in expecting an image, or part of an image, to correspond to a word; that any image, any part thereof, like this black and/or blue, can speak volumes. But would we, for all that, have closed discussion on relations between image and word, once we went looking for the structure of the film in terms of a narratology rather than a linguistics of the sentence? By doing so, we may have sidestepped a problem of immense proportions: because we use words or writing to talk about images (and about words and writing also – that should have had us wary from the start), unlike literary criticism, which uses writing to talk about writing, has that enabled us to rigorously dissociate one from the other? Given that our institutional situation requires us to write about film, not to mention our desire to write, which may or may not reduce to a politico-institutional form. Even assuming the image is 'there' before this discourse comes to write about it – not a self-evident assumption in spite of the fact that we may be able to lay our hands on certain lengths of celluloid – is there any sense in which it is here before us now, without my writing on it? For if I were to stop writing now or had never even begun, but had instead shown the film *Blue Velvet* or a still from one of its early sequences, would that have precluded the discussion? I can imagine the reply that of course not, and that that only serves to demonstrate that what you write comes from outside the image. But on the other hand, now that it is uttered, now that the question of black and blue is raised, can the image resolutely close itself off from that question and resort to being unequivocally image? Unequivocally black or blue? Blue black, I seem to remember, was the name for a colour of ink, thus its undecidability here a sign for writing.

the repression of difference,[2] even if necessary to achieve "understanding," is also necessarily an act of violence, an act that produces its own black and blue marks in the text. These hermeneutical marks are repeated in those inflicted as part of the ongoing psychosexual violence against *The Bride* as woman who is constantly humiliated in Truffaut's film.

But while Truffaut wants to trouble genre classifications through his binary structure, the end result is nevertheless the maintenance of the individual terms of the opposition as undivided and whole. It is a duality that is always two unities. As we have seen, in Derrida's formulation even the notion of "mixing" genres in effect confirms "the essential purity of their identity" ("The Law of Genre," 24). Truffaut's strategy of division, in other words, has as its covert project the maintenance, finally, of the serene unity of each of the divided parts of the binary opposition, just as the train tracks that appear early in the film announce their relentless duality and alterity (and that of the film) yet go to exactly the same place.

Perhaps we could say instead that, rather than manifesting two genres, *The Bride* inhabits the border between them. But can anyone or anything ever inhabit a border? Where would such a border and such an inhabitant *be*? Where would this border *take (its) place*? Perhaps, then, *The Bride*, both as film and as character, is the hymen, Mallarmé's *entre/antre*, his between and his cave. Perhaps it is she/it who distinguishes genres or in whom genres can be distinguished, yet who collapses such distinctions, leaving them no place. The representative of marriage and divorce simultaneously, she/it is perhaps the confounder of love and death, the true and the faux (merging the two languages of the subtitled text) and, indeed, of all oppositions, in a single gesture that has a contradictory double effect.

Now it is of course possible to take Truffaut's opposition between love and death as being between a conventional genre, the thriller, with its set of presumably clear-cut (though in practice, impossible to specify) expectations, and a non-genre, or even anti-genre subject, the love story. Fully in complicity with this distinction, Truffaut himself provided an example of it when he told an interviewer from *Le Monde*, in the course of discussing *The Bride Wore Black*, that "if two different directors made *The Bridge on the River Kwai*, they would make the *same* film, whereas if they both made *Brief Encounter*, they would make *dif-*

---

[2] Defending his love for Julie at one point, the painter Fergus, one of her victims, insists that *"elle est différente."* Corey, the cynical ladykiller, replies *"Je n'aime pas ce mot-là."*

Would it be reaching too far out altogether to introduce a further complication that I could not promise to resolutely separate from this discussion? If I were to keep silent about it, would I for all that have prevented its organising or disorganising the analysis? Or by including it here do I manage any more to control its effects throughout this reading? How to resolutely separate a filmic image, already subject to the 'inscriptions' of the verbal coming from the sound track, from the play of the verbal in general? How to resolutely separate this analysis, and hence the film, from the text of the subject performing it – the subject(s) producing it and the subject(s) reading it? My further complication is this: for as long as I can remember the word 'velvet' evoked, for me, both a texture and a colour, presumably by catachrestic confusion with 'violet'. Thus one ear of mine is determined to hear the title *Blue Velvet* as a contradiction in terms, one colour corrected by another rather than a colour qualifying a fabric; 'blue velvet', as that ear hears it, homologous to 'blue black', inevitably running, like one colour into another, into a reading of the film;[1] inevitably running into the idiom 'black and blue', wherein the question of colour may be seen to either preserve its undecidability or resolutely separate its terms through recourse to violence.

Considered again, my idiosyncratic reading of the title falls within the structure of a title, always an opening towards a supposed outside and posing the question of belonging, a sort of converse signature. But especially so this one. Should we read in it the title of a film, of a song, a quotation from a song, the name of a curtain or dressing gown? For according to how we choose, the words may either lose themselves in the textual network of the film or rebound into the unbounded context of the lines of force that traverse it. Unsettled with respect to its origin, the title will always bear quotation marks, not just the ones that my reading gives it but those that signal a graft and inscribe the possibility of repeated recontextualisation.

Hence the question raised by the black and blue read every which way in this film is a question posed on the limits of reading. The question is what it means to interpret a part or whole of a film as a rebus, to read a fact of the diegesis as a type of wordplay encouraged by cer-

---

[1] It does not concern me to answer the question of colour in what might be called empirical terms. If the black or blue of the darkness serves to signify night, it refers only to a play of presence and absence of light that allows for a whole range of colour modulations. The undecidability on which I am concentrating is not one which might derive from the lighting used for shooting the sequence, from the chemistry of film stock and developing processes, or from the viewing apparatus (cinema or television screen) but from a disturbance in the play of signification.

ferent films."[3] In the context of the Romantic aesthetic fully indulged by the *nouvelle vague*, an aesthetic valuing originality and personal expression above all else, the director's sentiments are clearly with the love story. Thus despite his desire to evoke both halves of the opposition and hold them in tension, the love story has already become the favored term in the oppositional hierarchy.[4]

But how is it ever possible for two different directors to make the "same" film? Same in what way? Such a notion of sameness can only become operative by positing an unchanging essence that can never, by definition, actually be manifested in the specific, material signifiers of the text. Even harder to understand is how two directors could make the "same" film in different ways. Furthermore, if it is possible to label a given film as a "love story," is this not itself already a genre distinction? It might be argued that there is no set formula for a love story and hence that it cannot be considered a genre. So many different situations and outcomes are possible, and since the settings, characters, plot and iconography are unpredictable as well, the love story may be thought of as a good example of what many critics have called "open" form (which brings forward another set of oppositions). But what is the formula or the genre trait for the thriller, other than that the film must be thrilling? (And one can easily imagine a thriller that is not thrilling.) Can anything more specific than that be properly individuated as a mark of that genre? Someone is usually chased, yes, but in a love story someone is always in love.

The director made it clear in the *Le Monde* interview that he very consciously set out to tell two different stories in *The Bride Wore Black*, to construct "two parallel films which move forward simultaneously." Again, this fascination with duality, this immense binary energy. "Two parallel films": a bizarre formulation and strange economy when we remember that they must always be enacted within the physical (and narrative) actuality of a single film. The idea is difficult to decipher even on a loose, figurative level. The effect of claiming to have intentionally bifurcated the original unity of the film is, of course, to construct analeptically such an original unity. What we have now, in effect, is *two* original unities, for very firm borders are also in the process simultaneously established between these two stories, and it

[3] *Le Monde*, 18 April 1968. (All translations, except where an English source is given, are mine).

[4] This hierarchy also appears in *Mississippi Mermaid*, a film he made two years later with Jean-Paul Belmondo and Catherine Deneuve. After seeing Nicholas Ray's *Johnny Guitar* (1954), one of them says, "You're right, it wasn't just another Western." The other replies, "No, it was a love story, with lots of feeling in it."

tain explicit or implicit thematic elements. By what right and according to what parameters can one impose upon an image or a film an
organising, or disorganising, device derived from verbal language or
from the text of the reader; and what difference finally would such a
chance and peripheral observation – the fact that Dorothy's body,
white within the visual medium, is black and blue in linguistic terms,[2]
or the fact of an idiosyncratic catachresis – make for a reading of *Blue
Velvet*?

My premiss is that the undecidability of black and blue leads, if not
to an outside within the image, to an abyss at its centre, like that of the
ear serving as entry to the perverse, violent, yet invisible other of
sleepy Lumberton.[3] Once that abyss is uncovered – and I could therefore have come here through the earlier image where the camera enters
the ear, or no doubt through any number of other images – once the
image divides itself, how does one successfully negotiate between its
inside and outside? What else might one expect to emerge from the
black and/or blue darkness?

A reading of *Blue Velvet* that would concentrate on textual fissures
in order to problematise the self-constitution of the text's meaning,
and more directly the self-constitution of textual borders, raises the
question of the negotiation of difference on which that reading depends and whether it is complicit with the resolution of difference by
violence that dominates the film. That is to say, does my problematisa-
tion of textual borders amount to a reduction of their difference, analogous then to the violence perpetrated against the female as difference
in the film?[4] Is it possible, or desirable, to conceive of a practice of

[2] It might be argued that it is not until she appears in a medium shot that she can be
described as black and blue and that then she appears so 'visually' as well as 'linguistically'; in other words that we can describe her only when we see her bruises. But it must
be remembered that I am not proposing an analysis of an intact still image; I do not
privilege this moment as some integral equivocality whose reading can be performed
out of the context of the rest of the film. It is Dorothy's stance that, as much as anything,
marks her as injured when she first appears out of the darkness, but in any case she has
been the victim of violence from early on in the film, thus what this scene portrays is
the starkness or the naked revelation of what has until now been a secret shared only by
those within her circle of violence; it is the coming-into-the-light of her always-already-
black-and-blueness.

[3] It could be said that the black screen, which usually serves as a form of punctuation
between sequences, has come to operate as a division internal to the sequence; but more
than that, the punctuation here takes on semantic instead of syntactic significance, such
that a division of the same is also a division of the other.

[4] Though there may be discussion as to whether the violence perpetrated against Dorothy Vallens in the film is necessarily a violence perpetrated against woman as representing difference, any analysis of that question would have to turn on the matter of her

becomes important to insist upon their total separation so as to keep
them uncontaminated by one another and thus intact within themselves. The strategy is clear: two unities are constituted within one, but
each remains self-present and complete.

But what were the conscious reasons behind Truffaut's careful elaboration of this tension between opposites? Were they important
enough to run the apparent risk of a bifurcation that refuses to resolve
itself and become one, the traditional goal of an organicist asthetics?
For the director, the playing of genre against anti-genre seems itself, in
fact, to have been part of a dialectic of personal expression and self-
concealment: "In *Baisers volés* [*Stolen Kisses*] . . . I had constantly to
cover my tracks, camouflage myself, and transpose so that I wouldn't
be too recognizable. In short, I wore a mask. In *La Mariée* [*The Bride*]
or *La Sirène* [*Mississippi Mermaid*], on the contrary, the mask existed a
priori, and behind borrowed characters I felt freer to express my own
personality."[5]

The implication is that a mask can be a screen—neutralizing, insubstantial, at least compared to the fullness it ostensibly cloaks, something both there and not there—which shields both author and viewer
from the powerful yet potentially embarrassing spectacle of the true
self in operation. In this sense, then, Truffaut consciously inscribes his
own personality into the dialectic of meaning in the work: it comes
out, again, as True/faux, a dynamic between what is seen as genuine
and what is seen as artificial. He clearly privileges the personalized,
"true-to-life," art-film themes associated with character and its unpredictable, multiple permutations. What becomes less important for
Truffaut is the satisfaction of viewer expectations through the traditional generic mode of variations upon a theme, which presumably
does not involve the artist's most personal concerns. Ever the romantic, he proudly admitted in the *Le Monde* interview that "to speak of
love demands a greater gift of self and forces you to go beyond the
framework of a told story." Thus, the True-/ self is that which
breaches or transcends the /-faux frame of a story. Like Kant's inessential parergon, the genre story seems there to provide some sort of neg-
ligible material base, a necessary evil perhaps, for the real story that
must be both hidden and visible. But where can this speaking of love
ever *take place* except within the frame of the story, i.e., within its particulars?

Of course we cannot take Truffaut at his word when he dismisses

[5] Quoted in James Monaco, *The New Wave: Truffaut, Godard, Chabrol, Rohmer, Rivette*
(New York: Oxford University Press, 1976), 70.

différance as erasure that is not underwritten by the violence of correction, the repression of difference? If that violence is everywhere in the film, why obscure it by referring to some undecidable black and blue?

'Don't you fuckin' look at me!' screams Frank as his arm cuts a diagonal across the screen to strike Dorothy's face; 'Heineken? Fuck that shit! Pabst Blue Ribbon!' he shouts at Jeffrey, after asking what sort of beer he likes. His is a form of correction designed to resolve not only externalised oppositions. He will have himself called 'Daddy' so that he can call himself 'Baby' shortly after; or he will tell Jeffrey 'You're just like me' before pommelling him senseless. Difference is asserted and violently repressed, created in order to be violently repressed, and denied but nevertheless repressed, which serves to assert it, and so begin again the circle of violence. Given that, what would be the investment in seeking out an 'erasure' that was a rewriting putatively different from the violence of correction? How could it be anything but complicit with such an endemic violence that seems to preempt every possible position for the production of difference?

The position of this reading is that there exists another deployment of the repressive control of difference within the textual system, also analogous to the violence of a text such as *Blue Velvet*, namely that which calls for a singular sense, for the inevitability of a certain reading. To counteract that the aim here is to investigate other possible means of multiplying textual effects in the hope of producing an excess that even the most refined and multifarious power machine will not always contain.[5]

Let us not forget. The film has its answer to the violence exercised by Frank Booth, it represents an official form of resistance, and it is simply more of the same violence. Even the most traditional form of criticism can recognise that.[6] But given that the text is composed of

---

rape, on the matter of sexual violence. That in turn would seem to depend on a notion of domination, a form of repression of difference.

[5] There are no doubt grounds for arguing that if *Blue Velvet* so foregrounds violence perpetrated against (a) woman that she is not permitted any form of resistance, to the point where she is herself condemned to sadomasochistic responses – or alternatively, that the film vindicates the sadism of the male by suggesting that the female derives a masochistic pleasure from it – grounds for arguing that if such is the case, then a critical response that does not foreground the enormity of such a violation of (a) woman is showing itself to be complicitous with that violation. Without denying that, however, it also needs to be argued that the film as text similarly seeks to dominate the readings it generates and that the call for a singular reading is not so much a form of oppositional resistance as an abdication of strategical possibilities, at worst a form of critical masochism.

[6] The film also performs its own simple division of the world between bourgeois

the genre element of the film as merely a "mask" behind whose "borrowed characters I felt freer to express my own personality." For while this mask is innocently meant to conceal in a neutral, unproblematic way the more "important" themes that must remain obscured because they are too autobiographically revealing, it, like all mediations, in fact forms the spectacle itself and cannot be so easily discounted. As Jean-Louis Baudry has pointed out in "Writing, Fiction, Ideology," the mask "is a surface which conceals nothing but itself, and yet which, insofar as it suggests that there is something behind it, prevents us from considering it as a surface. The mask implies a depth, but what it masks is itself: it simulates dissimulation in order to dissimulate the fact that simulation is all there is."[6]

Truffaut's is yet another example of the logic of the supplement, a "logic" in which a full signified is constituted by distinguishing it from a signifier or "outward" manifestation that is itself always incomplete, discontinuous, false—like a mask covering a presence that is somehow beyond direct representation and that can only manifest itself through its own absence, through what it is not, through that which has been written off as unworthy and superficial. At any rate, in this film the mask is irrevocably in place and is, after all, what the viewer sees. It is the locus of all the signifiers, and meaning must finally manifest itself here, if anywhere, by way of the mask's particulars.

This mask also bears a striking resemblance to Truffaut's mentor in genre, Alfred Hitchcock. For one of his "two films," Truffaut chose a cheap thriller written by William Irish (Cornell Woolrich), the same writer whose novel Hitchcock had adapted for *Rear Window*. This, along with the presence of Bernard Herrmann's score, is what writes Hitchcock's signature into the film as much as any supposed self-conscious emulation of or *hommage* to the master that many critics have mentioned.[7] Mere citations, it might be said, overt signs and signals of a certain indebtedness—but these are citations with effects as well. They come with invisible quotation marks around them and sit uneasily within and without the text.[8] Thus *The Bride* is constantly assailed

---

[6] Jean-Louis Baudry, "Writing, Fiction, Ideology," *Afterimage* (London), no. 5 (Spring 1974), 27.

[7] Also, by pointing to Hitchcock, Truffaut is pointing to himself, structurally, as "author-in-the-text." He thus signals the constructed quality of the text through his own signature in it—Hitchcock is countersigning for him, as it were—a textual presence that says, "Look, I am writing here."

[8] In fact, this same process can be seen in the way in which quotations are incorporated into a written text. For example, British style and American style punctuation differ on whether to put the quotation's own punctuation marks within or without the incorporating text's marks that signal a quotation, and thus act as a kind of frame. This is not a

layers, discontinuities, self-reflections, given that it harbours at its centre a confusion of primary colours and the abyss of the inner ear,[7] gate-
way to memories far more numerous and complex than any already
referred to here, given all that and more, a traditional reading might
be difficult, if not impossible, to locate.

On the other hand, where would one locate the edges of a reading
that took account of references to sexuality and voyeurism, among
others, and related them to concerns of contemporary film theory, a
reading inspired by psychoanalysis? Firstly, would that be an application of a body of knowledge from 'outside' the film and thus any
more relevant than an analysis that played with the words of the title
or with a memory playing through this reader's ear? That is, after all,
the question that haunts any reading that answers to an idea of relevance underscored by an always assumed and possible reduction to a

---

small-town ordinariness and the perversion and criminality inhabited by Frank and Dorothy. Though within the narrative framework of the film the latter underworld seems
to threaten Jeffrey's existence to the extent that he, like Inspector Williams, can only
answer its violence with more of the same, the viewer is reminded that it is only detec-
tives and perverts who seek out the difference that the calm surface of the normalised
world serves to conceal. There is a strange duplicity here. Since difference is distinguished in Manichean terms, concealed and confined to the absolute evil perpetrated by
the likes of Frank, those who, like Dorothy, Jeffrey, and Inspector Williams, are forced
or desire to confront it cannot but become a part of it. All that is standard for the thriller
genre, and to the extent that *Blue Velvet* is a standard thriller, it follows the formula.

On the other hand, the film multiplies the ironies and self-parodies from the first
images – the too brilliant flowers against a too white picket fence, the parading fire en-
gine, the television images, Lumberton radio – and to the one-dimensional character of
Inspector Williams, the trite comments of the adolescent protagonists, not to mention
Sandy's dream. On another level one finds the zany touches such as the dog yelping at
the upturned hose when Mr. Beaumont has his stroke (or whatever it is), Ben's performance, Frank's disappearance from the frame just before they leave Ben's, the dead but
erect Gordon, and so on. All that is sufficient to take the film out of the confines of its
genre and open it to a variety of self-reflexive readings, somewhat in the style of *Diva*,
to name but one example of a category that is perhaps becoming a genre in itself. From
that point of view, a 'first' reading of such a film might not be at the level of the 'surface'
narrative but rather in terms of a thematic development – sound, for instance, in the
case of *Diva*, perhaps sexual initiation in the case of *Blue Velvet*.

[7] The ear, which will impose itself as important to any reading of the film, including
this one, is already problematic on the level of the narrative, since the question of how
it came to be lying in the grass implies a whole set of possible scenarios that the film
does not care to follow through. Other narrative 'lapses' include Jeffrey's recounting of
how he, presumably, followed Frank and the well-dressed man to another part of town
where they climbed a fire escape and looked off into the distance, whereupon he describes what they saw in the distance although it was physically impossible for him to
be sharing their perspective; and the uncertainty concerning the circumstances under
which Gordon meets his death.

by the same aggressive male gaze that spies through the *Rear Window* (the camera and the script are obsessed with women's legs in Truffaut's film) and can be regarded and understood in the context of that other text's problematizing of vision and voyeurism and violence against women. This other text is a place where wives are seen as those who nag, where Miss Lonelyhearts is deluded and brutalized by men, and where Jimmy Stewart, forever ogling Miss Torso (as *The Bride* is forever ogled) is threatened with castration by his butch nurse when she tells him that Peeping Toms used to have their eyes put out. Herself having been positioned and fixed by the telescopic rifle lens of her husband's killers, *The Bride* will in effect carry out these castrations on her five victims, thus revenging the women seen through the *Rear Window*.

Bernard Herrmann's score for *The Bride* also strongly resembles many of those he wrote for Hitchcock, especially *Marnie* (both seem to have been taken from Puccini's *Gianni Schicchi*), and thus that other bride is written on and into Truffaut's film as well. Actually, it is clear that *Marnie* is continually being quoted in this film, consciously[9]—especially in the bright red that often appears, a reference to the color associated with Marnie's trauma—but what is equally clear is that Truffaut means these quotations to signal little more than a desire to honor Hitchcock. Once in the text, however, these citations have their own effects and the virulent anti-male sentiment and consequent female revenge of both films can be read together as mutually reinforcing and complicating. Truffaut's murdering, castrating *Bride* thus acts out the anti-male violence that Marnie sublimates by stealing from them, castrating them by taking their money. Furthermore, these citations from Hitchcock's films have the effect of destablizing *them* as well; anagrams that simultaneously recall one context and introduce another when seen again in the context of Hitchcock's films, these citations that "began" in these earlier films will always inevitably cite the Truffaut film as well, producing another *mise en abyme*. Their working, forward or backward, cannot be restrained by some (external)

---

sign of yet another quaint difference between the two cultures but an indication of the undecidability of the citation's status within the citing text.

⁹ Early scenes in both films show a woman packing or unpacking a suitcase, stuffing or unstuffing it with money, and walking on a train platform (interestingly, the order of the scenes is reversed in the two films); a little girl plays near Julie's front door, and several little girls play near Marnie's front door; both pull their skirts down under the pressure of the male gaze (one of her victims says of Marnie that she was "always pulling her skirt down over her knees, as though they were a national treasure").

central truth. Yet although the elements that invite a psychoanalytic reading have never been more explicit,[8] it is doubtful that a rigorous and comprehensive reading along those lines could be performed. There seems to be too much concentrated within the closet scene, too much ambivalence in the role played by Dorothy, especially when one doubles psychoanalysis with a feminist critique of spectatorship as one must inevitably do in the context of contemporary film studies. What I mean here goes further than it appears (hear that statement as if echoed against a mirror). It is not just that an informed film analyst cannot fail to raise questions relating to feminism about a film such as *Blue Velvet*, given the sexual violence perpetrated against women. Nor is it just that the informed film psychoanalyst cannot fail to raise questions concerning the feminist critique of spectator positions, given the fact of Jeffrey's voyeurism, questions that are reinforced by the scenes of violence against women within the scene of voyeurism. The structure of object relations obtaining in voyeurism is, after all, the necessary structure for the perpetrating of violence against woman as object.[9] In

[8] Dismemberment, falling trees, scissors, knives, a man playing with a snake, the absent, emasculated father, the detective surrogate – the sorts of combinations that have given rise to close critical attention to the films of Hitchcock in recent years are all here. Central to such a reading would be the episode of voyeurism as Jeffrey watches Dorothy from behind the closet door, is discovered, and then witnesses her rape by Frank. Remember that he is drawn into this by the discovery of the severed ear; he determines to find out for himself the truth about such a castration – 'I'm seeing something that was always hidden,' he will later tell Sandy, 'I'm in the middle of a mystery and it's all secret.' After witnessing the semi-nakedness of woman, the suggestion if not the fact of her castration, his attention is drawn to the frame Dorothy pulls out from under the couch. Later revealed as that of little Donny, it means that mother and son, although within different representations, were together on the plane of visibility exposed to Jeffrey, as if in the mirror. The scene is interrupted by Dorothy wielding a knife. 'What is your name?' she asks. 'Jeffrey,' he replies. 'Jeffrey who?' 'Jeffrey nothing,' comes the answer as he declines to assume the name of the father. Then, encouraged by a nick across the face from her knife, he fills in the gap. It is his turn to stand naked in front of the mirror – 'Get undressed Jeffrey Beaumont! I want to see you' – and her hands, mouth, and the knife come more dangerously close to the genitals. She invites him to consummate the incest wish, but he becomes instead the spectator of a primal scene more perverse than that of the Wolfman, and so on and so forth. Later, of course, there will be a song about the Sandman, who threatens in Hoffmann's tale to rip out children's eyes, which Freud reads as a fear of castration in *The Uncanny*.

[9] The matter of Dorothy's violence against Jeffrey and treatment of him as object may or may not irredeemably complicate matters for such a reading. On the one hand, there is simply a reversal of sex roles so that the woman becomes perpetrator of violence, but there is no change in the subject/object relations. The subject in the relation looks at, controls, and takes pleasure from the other as object. In fact, the reversal of sex roles is offset by the preservation of an adult/child power relation, in terms of which there is not even a change of role. On the other hand the reversal of sex roles is not sustained: Jeffrey

principle of propriety, and after *The Bride*, *Marnie* can never be the same. No original here, either.

It is important to understand, however, that these Hitchcock films are not written into the Truffaut film *in toto*, nor as self-contained wholes that can continue to keep their own borders and internal divisions intact. Rather, fragmentary citations of one film inside another have the effect of recalling bits and pieces of themes, forms, characters, and various other textual fragments that necessarily become unmoored from the narrative structure and other formal divisions anchoring them in the "original" text. They have dispersed effects in the new text in a variety of ways that cannot be predetermined. The task of an intertextual reading, then, would be to resew these fragments into new patterns with their own logic beyond the specific internal logic, guaranteed and policed by the many institutional supports we have already discussed, of the films from which they are said to originate.

Let us now return to Truffaut's structural oppositions and the ways in which they dissolve themselves. The director was especially attracted to the Woolrich novel, he claimed, because the plot was so very clear and simple that the murderous genre story could be told through the visuals alone. This left the dialogue and the other components of the sound track "completely independent" to tell another tale, one with different, presumably more personal meanings that transcend the bounds of the thriller. Truffaut's remark points to a split that in fact is always there, for the relation between the sound and the image is already a grafting of disparate entities. In the context of mainstream cinema, however, such a clear-cut division is as impossible as any other in this film; Truffaut is obviously overstating the independence of the sound track from the visuals, and his boast that "if the soundtrack were played over the radio, people would be totally at a loss. They would have no reason for ever imagining that murders were taking place"[10] is simply untenable in the face of the film's particulars.

In any case, the neat division between love story and thriller is already undermined from within. The love story, for example, is itself bifurcated into opposing elements that conflict. Elements of the thriller, elements of genre, in other words, are already within the love story, thus destroying its integrity and unity. On the one hand, the love story concerns the love between Julie Kohler and her dead husband, which actually only exists in the past as preserved in flashback through Julie's mind (and which is the only way it is made present to the audience). The film's barely articulated past—which itself can only

---

[10] Quoted in C. G. Crisp, *François Truffaut* (London: November Books, 1972), 98.

stating that psychoanalysis must inevitably be doubled with feminism in a reading, I mean that the context of one has been radically altered by the context of the other, their outside borders irreparably breached, those of Freud first by those of Lacan, then those of Lacan by those of Mulvey – although I am reductively circumscribing things by means of such a lineage – and so on. We are back to our original problem such as exists in any discourse upon a text, namely that it cannot be a matter of bringing one coherent and integral body of knowledge to bear upon another coherent and integral body of text, but if not, then how is one to regulate or negotiate relations between the bodies involved?

Perhaps most obviously, a psychoanalytic reading of *Blue Velvet* is disturbed by the bugs. I could say disturbed by the excess represented by the bugs, but it is doubtful that representation as we know it is what is in play henceforth; it is doubtful that it is in play once it is a matter of excess, since a representation cannot by definition represent that which exceeds without calling into question the limits of representability. The bugs are an excess in terms of the diegetic structure of the film from the time the camera seeks them out in the grass immediately after the collapse of Jeffrey's father.[10] But to say that the bugs are excessive with respect to the narrative, to suggest that they signify a

---

is not raped by Dorothy in the same sense in which Dorothy soon is by Frank. Yet a feminist definition of rape would presumably want to include the circumstances under which Dorothy constrains Jeffrey to indulge in sexual activity under threat of violence, irrespective of his avowal of pleasure. 'Do you like that?' is a common question uttered by rapists anyway. To some extent rape of a male by a female must remain inconceivable, in the sense of being unable to be fully theorized, within the current sway of sexual politics; but that is the same as saying that it is that which, as the outside of a feminist reading of sexual relations based on a certain empiricism of male domination, threatens to irredeemably problematise such a theoretical position.

[10] It is the sort of digression that is repeated when the camera enters the ear. They set up a counter structure to the narrative, in terms of which the supine and unconscious father is echoed by Jeffrey sleeping or daydreaming on the garden chair at the end of the film; in terms of which the major part of the film could be held to be within parentheses, those of a dream or fantasy. There are discrepancies with such a reading, namely the appearance of the father in hospital within the parenthesis and of Dorothy and Donny outside of it in the closing shot. Besides, the shot of the bugs in the grass precedes Jeffrey's first appearance; the ear is entered later, as an autonomous shot once the narrative is under way. Imagined bugs play an important part in the narrative when Jeffrey sprays Dorothy's apartment and participate in a different system of reference when one is seen in the mouth of a robin at the end. All of which to say that the bugs may set up a structure counter to the narrative on the same plane but that they are also indicative of another signifying order, call it symbolism, metaphor, or whatever; and that finally they disturb the separation between such planes. Of course, within dream or fantasy the separation of such levels of signification cannot be preserved either.

be manifested through its always impossible present, moving toward its future—is thus the locus of what might be called the pure form of the love story, but, as the past, it is also inextricably linked with its supposed opposite in the binary scheme, death. This love can only remain pure because it has been stopped (or started) by death. We also realize in retrospect that Julie's great love is precisely what, denatured and warped by obsession, has turned her into a ruthless killer. The priest in the confessional asks the appropriate question: "How can you get to love through hate and murder?"

But love also exists in what the film offers as its present tense of genre and death as well, even if all that we see of love are the more or less miserable approaches that the five marked men, each in his special fashion, make toward Julie as she lures them to their deaths. The earlier love, perfect because not of this world, serves as contrast to the decidedly imperfect, but real, amorous possibilities now being offered her, and both can be seen as part of the love story. This is especially true in the case of Fergus, the woman-obsessed painter, who becomes true love's last representative near the end of the film. Since he seems genuinely to pursue Julie because he has fallen in love with her, unlike her other victims, he becomes a kind of combination of his lust-minded friends and her husband, calling the distinction between them into question. Thus even what Truffaut wants to see as the anti-generic part of the film, the love story, is itself split from within by a structural opposition genre/anti-genre represented as casual sex/pure love. In the textual entity "Fergus," the term "casual sex" is itself further split into casual sex/pure love. For which can he be said to stand? The *mise en abyme* is clearly not far away.[11]

In any case, little of this "love material," of either sort, was part of the original novel; virtually all of it was added by Truffaut, and, within the binary terms that we have been using and that the film demands,

---

[11] The textual confusion created by the continual self-division of the love story elements is reflected in Truffaut's own ambivalent, divided comments on the love theme in the film. For example, he told a German interviewer that it was not really a film about love, because the love had taken place before the story began (Hanns Fischer et al., *François Truffaut* [Munich: Carl Hanser Verlag, 1974], 63). When asked by the interviewer from *Le Monde*, however, if it was another film about love, he replied, "Yes, I don't think there's a better subject. . . . *The Bride* is indeed a film about love, but a love of pure feeling since for Julie, it's a love in the past." But in his interview with Charles Thomas Samuels, Truffaut makes it clear that he means the term in its widest, and perhaps least appealing, sense. Samuels asks the director if he is right in thinking *The Bride* is "about the meaning of love." Truffaut, responding affirmatively, says, "It is a film which illustrates five different ways of comporting oneself with a woman" (*Encountering Directors* [New York: G. P. Putnam's Sons, 1972], 40).

realm of desire lying beneath the surface of things, a realm that is also that of violence and perversion, is not yet to establish that they are excessive with respect to a psychoanalytic reading of that narrative, inasmuch as psychoanalysis is able to account for desire and perversion. On the other hand, if it were to be maintained that what the bugs signify is a domain, or rather a means, of signification reducible neither to narrative sense nor to processes of figuration – at least not as traditionally conceived – but is rather a function of what have been called elsewhere operations of writing, then the point will have been made. For the psychoanalytic gesture remains a hermeneutic one, in spite of its attention to figuration.

The question that I am posing here is whether there could be a reading that is not grounded in narrative sense nor processes of figuration, and if so, what such a reading might look or sound like. Since it will inevitably continue to refer to textual material and rely on a certain organisation of that material, what is there to save it from surrendering to the hermeneutic impulse, to save it from reducing to a further, more arcane elucidation of an always present coherence? That question is raised in Barbara Johnson's 'The Frame of Reference' (*The Critical Difference*) and remains no doubt the question haunting any deconstructive reading practice. Still, a reading practice is just that, a set of strategies devised for a particular text. Perhaps starting from what are normally considered peripheral textual elements, a deconstructive reading may or may not repeat some of the findings of a reading starting from a supposed centre. But its devices are designed so that they cannot of themselves establish a new centre, more likely revealing themselves as expendable, as having no more nor less validity than another set of strategies. Furthermore, if a reading practice starts out from the *question* of its cohering impulse, then the latter cannot be conceived of as its outside threat but should be understood rather as an example of its motive force.

If the bugs escape the spaces of narrative, of thematics, and of readings like psychoanalysis that rely on such structured spaces, it is perhaps because they inhabit the space of the ear, the severed ear lying open-ended in the grass posing a logistics problem for hordes of ants, like a threshold granting access to the world that crawls to be entered by the camera two sequences later. One could say more accurately, then, that the bugs play on the surface of the tympan,[11] perhaps even

---

[11] Cf. 'Tympan', in *Margins*. See also our discussion of the hymen in chapter 3. I do not wish to overstate the obvious return to the hymen as undecidability that underscores this analysis; its negotiation of difference and violence, its play with the will to resolution and positionings in general, and so on. Nor do I probably need to remind the reader of

the effect, not surprisingly, is to strengthen character. In an ordinary genre film, of course, especially a thriller, the plot is usually thought to outweigh the attention paid to character, but here they enjoy a more equal status, forming yet another unstable set of structural oppositions. In the novel, for example, Julie's victims are only sketchily portrayed and seem largely to exist to become empty, anonymous targets of her vengeance. In the film, considerable care is taken to create individualized portraits of the men on her list. Truffaut self-consciously sees this as a strategy, an effort to mitigate the genre elements by making the film more "realistic," thus introducing yet one more set of oppositions: "I began with the assumption that the structure was so strong that there's no danger of weakening it, that on the contrary it's better to introduce a touch of reality. I tried to make the characters live, and I think it works from Michel Bouquet [Julie's second victim] on."[12]

Similarly, Truffaut has further accentuated the nuances of character in the film by subtly and ironically de-dramatizing many of its emotional encounters, ostensibly in the interests of greater realism. As he admitted in the Le Monde interview, he deliberately avoided concentrating on the "big moments" (which, though he does not say it, usually serve to emphasize predictable, situational emotion for its own sake rather than the idiosyncratic complexities of specific characters, thus becoming, by implication, less "realistic") or on leading the audience gradually up to great explosions and discoveries in the plot line. To further this anti-generic emphasis on "realistic" character portrayal, he also filmed the bulk of each episode in the realist manner of long takes and medium shots. The editing, likewise, as the realist aesthetic demands, is often strictly functional. By C.G. Crisp's account, The Bride has only some 400 cuts, compared to the 800 of La Peau douce (1965). Again stressing his concern for what he sees as realism in this film, Truffaut repeats Bazinian dogma that "a character can exist much more realistically as part of a long-take sequence, including some calculated dead-spots, than as part of a fragmented montage."[13] Since realism is itself a style that can be shown to be only tangentially and in heavily conventionalized ways related to reality, doubt must be cast

---

[12] Quoted in Crisp, *François Truffaut*, 98. Paradoxically, however, it seems to be precisely through the intense individualizing of each figure that he becomes free to emerge as a specific type.

[13] Quoted in Jean Collet, *Le Cinéma de François Truffaut* (Paris: Pierre Lherminier Editeur, 1977), 126. In C.G. Crisp's version of the quotation (which he translates rather ambiguously) Truffaut continues his remarks by confessing that "This procedure is rather unnatural to me, but I like forcing myself to do things I'm not used to" (97).

that the whole film plays on such a surface, which is the surface precisely of the rebus whereupon this whole discussion began. I speak not of the particular rebus of black and blue but of the idea of a differential articulation between the inside and outside of the image and between the composite discontinuities that comprise it. If there is a thematics to which such ideas relate, it is that of the severed ear as a breach within the circuit of language, as that which, by virtue of being removed from its original site as receiver of the spoken word, opens up the space of non(-linear)-sense, of perversion (of sense), and of criminality (infractions against the law and name of the father). The space, in short, of writing, of a conception of language that is without origin, whose differential surface is exposed in all its vulnerability and potential for resonance.

Here then there would be a correspondence between bugs in ears and mouths stuffed with blue velvet. In each case there arises a problem of the articulation of speech. When 'Baby [Frank] wants blue velvet' he wants obviously to return to the imaginary of an umbilical plenitude that binds him to Dorothy, and in doing so he also acts out the violent reduction of language to the logocentrism of bodily communication, the violence of undifferentiation and nonmediation. But by the same

---

the whole sexual mythology of the ear as female organ compared with the nose as male organ (cf. *The Life and Opinions of Tristram Shandy*), which relates the tympan to the hymen apart from the simple physiological comparison between two diaphragmatic membranes. It would seem to be an obvious reference in *Blue Velvet*, Don's torn and decaying ear echoing Dorothy's abused sexual parts and Dorothy's 'He put his disease in me' concerning Jeffrey apposed to 'They have hurt his head' concerning her husband, of which more below. In terms of bugs, the ear has its own privileged one, namely the earwig, which burrows into fruit, presumably leaving worms and rot at the core, but which is also supposed sometimes to burrow into the ear. In French the earwig is called *un perce-oreille*, and the word is an explicit pun in *Persephone*, the text by Leiris constituting the right hand column of Derrida's 'Tympan'. Persephone, daughter of Demeter, was abducted by her uncle Hades, and having taken a bite from a pomegranate while in the underworld is required to return there for a period of time each year during which the earth endures the barrenness caused by Demeter's wrath – and during which, no doubt, there are no robins. All that I shall let resonate through the connections between the tympan, the hymen, and the film *Blue Velvet*. Furthermore, the French word for 'to burst', used in terms of eardrums, eyes being put out, breaking hearts, and so on, is *crever*, which is also a word for dying ('To pierce the hymen or to pierce one's eyelid [which in some birds is called a hymen], to lose one's sight or one's life...' *Dissemination*, 214). In the climax to the film the sexual abuse of Dorothy, generalised to render her whole body black and blue, corresponds again to the violence against Don's head – 'They have hurt his head,' she whispers, delirious, her statement a metonymic confusion between his missing ear and the bullet through his brain, itself synecdoche for a bursting of the eardrum. Note also how much Jeffrey's bruised head has the make-up of the severed ear after he is beaten by Frank.

upon such schematic formulations concerning what is more realistic. In fact, it could easily be argued that since the long take is highly abnormal (in relation to most conventional films, which contain a great deal of cuts), it is more often perceived as unrealistic because it calls attention to itself in a Brechtian manner, thus disturbing the illusion upon which all realism depends. For his binary purposes, however, Truffaut needs to see the putative realism of these techniques as essentially opposed, and utterly different from, the putative artificiality of genre.

In a further attempt to soften other generic aspects of Woolrich's novel and thus simultaneously sharpen and equalize the genre/anti-genre contrast, Truffaut greatly minimized its important police procedural element: the emphasis is resolutely centered on Julie rather than the police, as she moves through a streamlined series of events. In the novel, what occasional importance Julie does have over the police is clearly focused on the more or less uncomplicated factual *why* behind her metamorphosis into killing machine; Truffaut, on the other hand, reveals her secret motivation after she murders her second victim and in so doing forces us to attend to her as a person, a constituted self, rather than as an empty locus and instigator of activity or a shallow riddle to be solved with a single sentence.

This last change was clearly meant to enhance the anti-generic, character-oriented aspect of the film, and it does; paradoxically, however, Truffaut's early revelation of Julie's secret also heightens *plot*—and thus genre—by laying it bare, revealing its goal, and making it march, machine-like, even more inexorably to its only possible conclusion. Truffaut's decision to emphasize the separateness of each episode of this already skeletal plot, perhaps in order to foreground, for the purposes of realism, the uniqueness of each character's personality, has the contrary effect of slowing the plot down—making it somehow more rather than less relentless—and thus reducing it to its starkest essentials, further foregrounding it. The primary, if unintentional, effect of these manipulations is to counter the emphasis on character and thus to heighten the contrast between character and plot by enhancing the stylized, "fairy-tale" aspect of the generic side of the film. Thus introducing yet one more set of binary oppositions, the director has said that "there are two sorts of film: films of situation and films of character. It struck me that it should be possible to mix the two, so I tried to make this rather extravagant story realistic. It's sort of Walt Disney for grown-ups. I like making films that resemble fairy-tales."[14]

---

[14] Quoted in Crisp, *François Truffaut*, 94. Another aspect of the film's heightened styl-

token the cord of blue velvet inserts itself as material spacing (*espace-ment*) such that it becomes a party to the operations of textual play that I am calling writing, not the least of which being the title of the film, the song (of which more shortly), and the rebus and signature effects with which we began. And of course bugs, when they are not in the ear, are listening devices that function as extensions of the ear, but the space that they open up within the circuit of communication is again that of writing. Bugs involve misunderstanding and interruption of communication, they are a form of deceit (an 'aural' voyeurism) or criminality. Once discovered, they provide for more complicated forms of deceit and misinformation and ultimately risk destruction. The correspondence between bugs and ears and blue velvet and mouths providing the context of writing has its culmination in the climax to the film and in the image of Dorothy's mutilated husband bound and gagged and sitting dead in their apartment. Not because writing needs to violently destroy speech in order to come into being – although writing seems born into violence, that of its repression – but rather because Don is the link to writing throughout the film, as I shall shortly argue in detail. His violent death here also reads as the death, or a death, of writing, as much as the death of speech.[12]

But it is not only the blue velvet that is the fabric of Dorothy's dressing gown and Frank's fetish object that circulates between mouth and ear to open the space of writing. There is in addition the 'Blue Velvet' of the title song, and also involved, by extension, are the film's songs in general. The play between extra- and intra-diegetic music is one of the most important factors acting counter to any rigorous homogeneity among the elements of the film – divided, let us remember, between image and sound and then, within the sound track, dialogue, ambient noise, and music. But we should probably maintain a further distinction, since it is in play here, between 'theme' music and songs.

---

[12] I don't wish to pursue too literal a reading of this sequence, nor indeed of the mouth-ear connection as representing speech. One could say that the blue velvet stuffed in Don's mouth here acts as a form of closure that does not permit an opening of the communicative process to dissemination but is merely the imposition of an unmediated prelinguistic imaginary such as Frank has always sought through violence (cf. my comments above concerning the repression of difference). But the risk of such literality is that it reverts to a simplistic conception of writing as opposite to and competing with speech, as being involved in the violence of correction that is such a dominant structure in the film. Writing must be understood as being always already a function of speech, not its exterior other, hence my previous references to bugs in the ear and velvet in the mouth, to the externalised inner ear of the severed organ as space of writing, and the velvet as spacing of speech as it 'falls' into the operations of writing as much inside as outside of itself.

Throughout, then, Truffaut wants to posit a tension between the stylized and "realistic," a conflict that thus enacts the same structure of
opposition as that operating between plot and character, genre and
anti-genre.

But just as the love story side of the film, as we saw earlier, is itself
internally divided between casual sex and pure love, genre and anti-
genre, death and love, so too the portrayal of character, presumably
associated, in the terms I have been tracing, with the anti-generic, is
itself further divided into the stylized (and thus generic) and the "realistic." For while Julie's five victims have been fleshed out "realistically"
into something at least resembling human beings, Julie herself, even
though her individuality is insisted upon, is more a deliberately
flaunted product of the imagination than a real person. Her suicide
attempt near the beginning of the film, for example, is so highly stylized that it seems an arbitrary bit of narrative shorthand not meant to
be believable at all. Nor do we ever see her go to bed, eat, drink, or
perform any of the other mundane chores of everyday life; she seems
rather to inhabit a fantasy world removed from these petty concerns.
This distinction is maintained in camera movement and editing as well;
for while Truffaut went to great pains to increase the Bazinian mise
en scène of long takes and sparse cutting for the five men, Julie most
often appears magically before us—fully created yet other-worldly—
through some disturbing and decidedly anti-Bazinian trick of panning,
jump cut or subjective camera. She seems also to know in advance,
without having had the slightest contact with them, exactly who the
guilty parties are, where they live, and what their weaknesses are in
respect to women.

It is possible, in other words, to divide the film's heightened sense
of characterization—supposedly a sign of increased realism—between
the stylized Julie and the more realistically portrayed men. The portrayal of the men, however, is also internally divided. If they are in
some ways made more realistic, the director's use of the principle of
enumeration that, according to Truffaut, is what makes fairy tales so
fascinating, makes them simultaneously more stylized. Thus Julie
meets five different men in a row, just as Goldilocks encounters three
bears and the wolf, three little pigs. Truffaut has said that he deliberately tried to heighten the fairy-tale atmosphere through a constant
effort of simplification and visual stylization: "For example, at the end

---

ization is the fact that the setting is deliberately left vague in order to increase what
Truffaut calls the film's "dreamlike quality," a quality "reinforced by the musical score
of Bernard Herrmann . . . which pulls the film toward opera" (*Le Monde* interview).

Although using popular music in this way has become a rather common practice in recent American cinema, *Blue Velvet*, as I read it, takes the practice much further, setting up structures of rupture on the surface of the text that help to authorise the sorts of shifts the present analysis is exploiting.

What if it were to be suggested that the whole film were derived from its title song?[13] Not that everything would relate back to an exegetical reading of the song's lyrics, banal as might be expected for the genre, but that the film could be conceived of as a reading of the song no more nor less inadmissible than the present reading of the film. The song itself opens up a network of signification within which the signifier 'blue velvet' shifts back and forth, although not in simple binary alternation, between person and decor ('She wore blue velvet...bluer than velvet was the night...bluer than velvet were her eyes...gone was the glow of blue velvet...I still can see blue velvet through my tears'), functioning more like the generalised fetish Frank exploits it as than the simple adjectival phrase it starts out being. But that doubling or troubling of signifying functions is compounded by the performances of the song, the extradiegetical snippets of the original recording, and Dorothy Vallens' renditions, all of which remain fragmented. Then of course there is the complex use that Frank makes of blue velvet in his rape scenario and his keeping of a fragment of the dressing gown. But one does not have to depend on a theory of fetishism to understand blue velvet, especially the song 'Blue Velvet', as introducing a problem of signification that is more specifically a problem of naming. And while that idea might lead us back again to psychoanalysis and to the question of Jeffrey's assumption of the name of the father, it is my intention once again to follow a different tack.

For 'Blue Velvet' is not the only song performed in the film, nor the only song that raises the problem of naming. 'The Candy Colored Clown They Call the Sandman' poses the problem with its title; firstly because the title Frank gives it in quoting its first line is not the title Roy Orbison gave when he named it 'In Dreams'; and secondly because that false title is explicitly about a problem of naming. It too has its idiosyncratic performances, first the lip-synch mouthing Ben puts on for Frank, then the ad lib Frank himself performs in Jeffrey's face. In that same scene Frank tells Jeffrey he will send him 'a love letter straight from my heart, fucker. Do you know what a love letter is? It's a bullet from a fucking gun, fucker,' renaming thus the subject of a song that will be played in extradiegetic performance over shots of the

---

[13] I thank Roberta Belulovich for making this suggestion.

of the only scene in which the five men are together, the text says: 'They decide to separate and to never try to see each other again.' And the image shows, in spite of a total lack of verisimilitude, the five friends who rush down the iron stairs and who, once they're at the bottom, take off in all directions" (quoted in Crisp, 94). In other words, they literally (and humorously) take off in five completely different directions, instantly losing their painstakingly sketched individuality to become mere pawns of the film's stylized design. Their dramatic particularity is called into question but not destroyed by their ongoing symbolic function as types. They are realistic and stylized at the same time and cast serious doubt on the integrity and thus viability of these terms.

This unstable differential structure that seems to organize and disorganize the film at its broadest levels can also be found reduplicated in many of its smaller formal details. A closer look at some elements of the very beginning of the film will suffice to make the point, for the polarities are stated and yet implicated within one another from the opening credit sequence. The title itself suggests that most basic duality of all, white vs. black, that reoccurs throughout the film. In the simple declarative "The Bride Wore Black" (or "La Mariée était en noir") the two terms seem to glare at one another from opposite ends of a line. The bride of course stands for the anti-generic love story. This half of the equation comes also to represent an open form resisting closure, a place of possibility and hope that has implications for the artist and aesthetic practice as well. The bride is the very embodiment of love and traditionally suggests the promise of the new life that will come from her body. Continuously threatening this promise of life and eternal possibility is the blackness of the title's final word. Its connection with death and limitation is inevitable, of course, but here these terms become associated with genre *per se*, and not only because the film is a thriller with plenty of dead bodies. Rather, the very notion of genre suggests the limited possibility of closed form, impermeable in its dark, obsessively repetitive vision, never open to influence by the quick and the fresh. Here the artist works from an already written script that, no matter how different its surface manifestations might appear, is always the same underneath. Nothing new is possible, says genre; the same grim fate awaits all beginnings. Love too will have its day and be lost.

But if the two terms of the equation stand opposed, they also reinforce and even create one another—just as black and white in any context always depend upon each other for existence—both frozen in the unresolved dialectic of the title. Syntagmatically, the second term seems poised to annihilate the first: blackness, absence, and death overshoot-out at the end of the film – 'Love letters straight from your heart, Keep us so near while apart, I'm not alone in the night, When I can have all the love you write...' Hence love letters, sandman, and blue velvet, shifting signifiers of absent signifieds, circulating in the space opened by language in its performative function, help to establish a generalised context of unstable sense identifiable even in the most basic of linguistic operations that is naming.

When it comes to the characters themselves this effect is more generalised still. Irreducible to the purely supplementary function of the nickname, unless the supplement be understood in its sense of standing in for and replacing an always already lacking originary name – a failure of the law of the father in establishing a single, undivided signature – the multiplication of names foregrounds again the activity of violence as correction while raising the possibility of a form of erasure we can call *différance*. As long as this naming is a function of Frank's power, it represents a form of violence. One of his gang claps his hand in Jeffrey's ear and repeats 'I'm Paul,' as if such a declaration could only be made by opposition to, and denial of, the other. Frank himself is variously 'Sir', 'Daddy', and 'Baby', all turns of the Oedipal screw; Jeffrey is 'neighbour', 'fucker', and 'fuck'; Dorothy is 'tits', Don is 'Van Gogh'; a single Ed is 'Ed' unless he is half of 'Double Ed'. There is a name without a face, uttered within snatches of conversation when Dorothy is on the telephone talking to a combination of Don, little Donny, and Frank. 'You mean Madeleine?' she asks, and the name remains suspended there for the duration of the film.

It is the name of Don, Dorothy's husband, that is 'performed' as writing, like the signifier 'blue velvet', at different times during the film. First that name is repeated in that of Little Donny – yet another Oedipal scene – with the paradox that the diminutive Donny inevitably requires an amputation to form Don. But for my purposes what is amputated is the binary choice of the n(o) and the y(es), so between Don and Donny there is evoked more violent correction. The context for this is given by what the spectator knows of their being held hostage and subject to Frank's sadism and reinforced by the confused anxiety of Dorothy's phone call during the mirror/closet scene. As the most innocent victim of that violence, Donny has it imposed upon him, he is named in order to bear its effects. On the other hand, Donny, always Little Donny, is doubly diminutive and in the second epithet the stricture of 'ny' may be said to be erased (as it is doubled) by another *différance*.

In another doubling the name of Don, and with it the violence of the binary, is disseminated throughout the syntax of the film's dialogue. It raises the possibility of undoing, by means of a rewriting, the

whelming whiteness, presence, and life. The insistent temporality of the medium adds to this impression, with its constant rush toward the future (both in the film in general and in the title's syntagm), toward the opposite term of the equation. Yet it never happens, and the past tense verb that occupies the center of the sentence and acts as the proposition's third term—Kant's bridge of analogy over the gap between two apparent heterogeneities—is a sign of this non-event, this Keatsian immobility, this refusal of the future. The film's title both moves forward and stays absolutely still. Its second term has always already been there as well, and the future turns out to be the past, death.

Beyond the title, the textuality of the film continues to dismantle its proffered binary structure by showing that the opposed terms are riddled with the presence of each other. During the opening credits, for example, we see what appears to be a police or newspaper printer turning out hundreds of photographs of Julie's nude painting as she had been fantasized by the painter Fergus, while on the sound track an organ loudly proclaims Mendelsohn's "Wedding March." The visual image—Julie naked—reveals the pristine bride as a fully mature sexual being, initiated into sin and death, a natural denizen of the closed-form generic world of corruption against which she is meant to stand. The "Wedding March" theme itself will continue to be heard throughout the film in flashback as the aural accompaniment to the irresponsible rifle shot that kills her husband on the steps of the church. Played bombastically and used as a kind of violent punctuation at key moments, it thus becomes a dual signifier—representing both halves of the equation, the love story and the thriller, at the same time—and thus further entangles its presumably opposed signifieds.

Similarly, the film may offer the bride as the eternal possibility of love, but Jeanne Moreau's puffy face and obvious heaviness[15] (she was nearly forty when the film was made)—signifiers constantly before us—work simultaneously in the opposite direction, never allowing us to take this idea of "new life" very seriously. In fact they signify death, especially considered in relation to the text of Truffaut's earlier film *Jules and Jim*, which contains a Moreau of five years before—whose character in this earlier film thus also becomes invaginated into the later film—and the years have not been kind.[16] As we saw earlier, the referent of all photography is called upon to share its space with death,

[15] Who knows the biographical reasons? Would such reasons also affect the reading of the text? Would they be "relevant?"

[16] The earlier text is explicitly invaginated into the later one also because "Julie" is a feminized version of "Jules" and her last name is clearly a German one, Kohler, which marks its difference in this French film. This differential relation is of course an important topos in *Jules and Jim*.

structure of correction that otherwise dominates and serves as a contrast to Dorothy's assumption of violence as masochism. Her sexual relations with Jeffrey reduce ultimately to alternations between 'hold me', 'hit me', 'hurt me', and 'help me', so that even if her mouth as sexual object is privileged by the camera in these scenes, which produces an eroticisation of the body through the voice that is almost absent in mainstream cinema ('Do you like the way I feel? Feel my nipple, it's getting hard, feel me'),[14] the close-up on her mouth serves also, perhaps only, to accentuate the effect once the lips that speak their desire also utter the phrase 'Hit me'. In a simple chain of consecution the words 'hold' and 'feel' come to be corrected by their violent others 'hit' and 'hurt'.

But such is not the case after the first attempt at sexual relations between Jeffrey and Dorothy, which is also his first encounter with 'her' violence, that which Frank inflicts upon her and that which she wishes to inflict, indirectly, upon herself. 'Don't!' she calls out as Jeffrey starts to leave, and Isabella Rossellini's accent coupled with the emotion in her voice cuts the final consonant and lengthens the vowel to put in her mouth, equally possibly, the name of Don. It is a moment of chance, a slim, feeble, perhaps obscenely frivolous counter effect to the overwhelming violence of the scene. It might be said to trivialise the victimisation that a responsible reading cannot avoid, to divert attention from the facts of sexual violence against women, which, I have already suggested, may need to be spoken above all else here.[15] But as the chance that the text gives to escape that circuit of violence and the strictures of its structures of correction, which go all the way to the insistence upon a correct reading acting as a kind of deafness to the differential details within the text, it asks, however obliquely or negatively, for attention. One might argue that it would be a case of turning a bad ear to Dorothy's plight and that of her husband not to hear her calling the name 'Don' within the entreaty 'Don't'. In any case what the reader encounters is an undecidability on the sound track similar

---

[14] I am obviously excepting the porno from the category of mainstream cinema, for that is perhaps the only genre in which 'desire' is commonly spoken within the sexual act.

[15] It might also be objected that there is no undecidability that recourse to a script cannot resolve and that, as I have just observed, does not derive from the vicissitudes of the casting process. But that would be to revert to the same sort of diachronic empiricism I rejected earlier, in the case of the blue-black night. It is once again a reading effect that I am following here, and there is a series of other such effects – naming, the shots of Dorothy's mouth – to bring this one into focus, as the preceding discussion serves to argue. But finally, the extent to which 'Don't' is heard as 'Don' is regulated by the matter of hearing that has been a problematic for me throughout this analysis – a matter then, of bugs in the ear.

and a differential temporal relation between photographic texts can make the effect all the more immediate, though it does not alter the reference itself. Everything else in the film, especially the insistent narrative, tries to subordinate, insists on subordinating these visual facts concerning Moreau's body to an organic reading. One might try to explain them away, in practical terms, as a matter of casting, box-office economics, and so on, but in fact Moreau's face, no matter how we might marshall arguments based on intentionality to dismiss its importance, is itself always a textual element whose meaning is as legitimate as any other even if not homogenizable to a totalized reading. And the meaning to which it leads is a conflation of love and death.

Other structural contrasts meant to support the basic binary structure include the fact that in a color film Julie wears only dresses that are either completely white or black or various expressionistic combinations of the two. At times she wears a pair of striped pajamas resembling a prison outfit or a striped apron, clothes that blatantly work against the film's realism. (Thus, color vs. black and white becomes another opposition generated within the film, but again, one in which the oppositional terms can never be kept separate). Such unsubtle choices underline the stylized fairy tale always at work, which never ceases to threaten the open-form film of character. But can the stylized and the realistic ever really properly be demarcated from one another? The stylized element itself, in other words, expresses the host of opposites that congregate around white and black, including presumably the conflict between stylization and realism.

Color itself functions as a kind of third term that suggests the possible reconciliation of opposites. An exceptionally bright red—the homage to *Marnie* mentioned earlier—blatantly reappears throughout the film (walls, kitchen bricks, a cleaning rag, a tablecloth, a car, a rug, a bathrobe, a towel, a sweater, a fire extinguisher, etc.), clearly foreshadowing violence and death each time. Yet this textual detail quoted from Hitchcock also throws off the binary scheme, for red can of course equally stand for love and passion, the other pole of the antinomy, and sometimes seems to work this way in the film. (For example, the sympathetic little boy "Cookie" and Fergus both wear bright red sweaters.) Truffaut's use of red cannot be any more stabilized than any other entity in the film and demonstrates that the color could be just as easily aligned along one axis as the other, according to the logical demands of the critical reading set into motion.

In the film's last scene, which is claustrophobically closed and utterly death centered, it seems that genre will triumph despite the demands of the hierarchical opposition. Apparently, we have come to the end of the title's sentence. The visuals show the interior of a prison and

to the blue-black night of the visuals that began this discussion. And just as there the darkness opened up an abyss at the centre of the visual track that fractured its relations with itself and with its supports to allow a reading of the image as rebus, so here the unity and coherence of the proper name is fractured first into the competition of forces that operate throughout the film, the violence of its dos and don'ts; but then it introduces excesses that escape the constraints which that violence would seek to impose. For the proper name is now given the structure of any utterance and disseminated through the textual fabric; and conversely the singularity of the imperative is countersigned by the name that I hold to be the name of writing; a name divided as it is uttered since it is misaddressed as long as she speaks to Jeffrey, as long as she addresses the always absent Don.

The name of Don as it is written here within the utterance 'Don't' functions thus as a signature for the film, not so much the mark of an author as a cryptic rendering of its scriptural effects. But as some uncanny chance (whose?) would have it, this 'writing' of the name in the undecidability of Isabella Rossellini's accent has had a much more explicit manifestation in the film. The scissors that cut the yellow 'Police Line – Do Not Cross' tape in the first shot of the short sequence showing the police combing the area where Jeffrey found the ear slice exactly through the 'o' of 'Not,' in place of an apostrophe, to have the name of Don violently produced in graphic explicitness. And as the camera moves to reveal more writing, it pauses on the suspended 't' and the following word 'Cross', giving repetitions with a difference of the chiastic effect that divides the pictorial with the graphic.

Thus the name Don functions as signature effect for the film first because it is produced in self-division, as we have just seen, but more explicitly because of its material differences. If between 'Don' and 'Donny' there is the alternation of binary opposites, between 'Don' and 'Don't' there is instead the apposition of speech and writing: the speech of apostrophe, of direct address to a fully present addressee; and the sign of writing as chiasmus, quadripartition of the coherence that speech assumes. Or again, there is a double writing: the apostrophe as sign of an elision, as the mark of absence written on the supposed fully present surface of speech (divided yet again in this case since what is elided is 'o') and the 't' as erasure that does not so much correct as produce more writing. Thus 'Don' might be read as the undecidability that divides the binary alternative of do/don't, and 'Don't' heard as 'Don' as a mitigation of the will to violently impose truth as correction. Or, to return to the earlier image, Don and a double cross, the written remainders after the decisive cutting of the scissors through the word, echo of the diagonal sweep of Frank's arm across Dorothe slot of the sound track, formerly the site of the love story, according to Truffaut's schema, is now almost totally empty, having been drained so that it may be refilled with death. We discover, solely through the visuals, that the shady Delvaux, Julie's final victim, whom she had earlier just barely missed when he was taken off by the police for another crime, is an inmate. Suddenly we realize why she has been so seemingly careless as to leave intact Fergus's incriminating wall portrait of her; the temporary enigma that the police (and the audience) have pondered in the previous scene is now solved. When we see Julie hide the kitchen knife as she is about to begin her rounds doling out the prisoners' dinner, we understand what is about to happen. By mixing male and female prisoners in the same cell block, Truffaut seems at this point completely to turn his back on realism, toward the stylization of genre. The director plants the camera at the end of the hall as we watch with tense fascination the ritual sameness of distributing the food at each cell, an act that recapitulates the mechanical series of murders and the obsessive fairy-tale mood and mode of so much that has gone before. Julie turns the corner with her cart, out of our field of view, yet the camera remains rigidly still.

The visual field, while completely taken over by the empty prison hall, has thus become as curiously empty as the sound track. It is "filled" of course, as all images must always be, but there is nothing to see; a lone guard enhances rather than diminishes its emptiness. The sound field continues to be devoid of dialogue and is occupied with the meaningless, dully repetitive sounds of cartwheels and clanging soup pots. It is as though the film, exhausted by the demands of its binary project, now hesitated before the ultimate choice it must make between love and death, genre and anti-genre. And then—Delvaux's blood-curdling scream. The anguished cry fills the sound track to bursting, but the visual remains unchanged, filled with everything and nothing. After Delvaux's cry the sound track, momentarily filled, quickly empties. Then, a second later, the camera still rigid, a bitterly triumphant blast of the organ playing the "Wedding March," the signifier of the love story, perhaps, but a signifier also deeply complicitous with death. What triumphs? Thematically, is it love or death? Modally, is it genre or anti-genre? This is where the film ends, poised between all of its oppositions, within and without them as well.

thy's mouth. But there is more to the comparison of this utterance
with that play of visual undecidability. The two senses of apostrophe
may be read in the absence of the image of Sandy, voice out of the
darkness before she is blonde in a pink dress on the one hand, and the
direct plea for attention that is Dorothy naked in the garden on the
other; and again, the abyss Sandy's emergence has identified in the centre of the screen counterpoint to the scarecrow Dorothy as human chiasmus coming from the side to inhabit that centre as sign of originary
incoherence. For with this 't' the image invades the space of the verbal – counterpoint to the writing within the pictorial just mentioned –
and there is a picture within the word responding to the verbal idiom
previously seen or imagined within the undecidable darkness.

As it is spoken, the final 't' of the word is not heard. It comes from
outside, from the outside edge of the sound track where it may or may
not exist as a trace; it comes from the outside of the image track to
divide internally the coherence of the images, the consistency of their
imposition of violence. The limits of the image fall chiastically in
upon themselves to rearrange it as writing. It is true that it remains a
feeble chance against the force of violence and that the way the lines
are drawn may be all there is to separate erasure from correction, to
prevent erasure from being a correction of correction, for it to be instead a rewriting. But it (read it as 'I"t"' or 'I/t') is also the chance that
reads *Blue Velvet* as text, that reads it as texture, that allows a piece of
its rent fabric to colour the night where all this began, in a title, in a
song, in a word. It goes like this: there may be a name – or just the
chance and gamble of a name – for that undecidability of colour, and
it might point to a certain unrepresentability on the filmic surface, that
of texture as a mode of writing not reducible to either the imagism of
the visual track or the verbalism of the sound track, such that it is velvet we are seeing in the blue-black night, except that simply seeing is
no longer what is involved here, we need to listen also, listen where
we are used to seeing and look where we are used to listening, I hesitate
to say we need to feel, in view of all that word has been put to, and in
any case it is not just that either, this will not resolve in the feel of
velvet, it is whatever is required to read a night bluer than velvet like
the song says, reading the borders where colour is called by the name
of texture, calls the name of texture, 'bluer than velvet was the night'
goes the song, apostrophising a reader whose catachrestic memory
confuses velvet and violet anyway, reading those doublings and trans-
versals as the rewriting that remotivates the play of difference that a
corrective violence would seek to foreclose, reading black in blue and
blue in black, violet in velvet and velvet *in violet*, and so on.

CHAPTER SIX

CINEMA AND THE POSTAL

It might seem surprising that the book in which Derrida makes the most explicit comments about relations between technology and the media, namely *The Post Card*, is also his book on psychoanalysis. An interesting parallel thus exists between the emphasis of current film theory and the ideas developed by Derrida. However, the perspective from which Derrida approaches the domains of psychoanalysis and the media is quite different from that adopted so far by film theorists. Rather than developing a metapsychology that links psychoanalytic functions with those of spectating, or analyzing diegetic relations according to a Lacanian model, Derrida investigates the conceptual underpinnings common to the two domains. Thus his work again opens up new ground for film theory, some aspects of which we shall develop in the following discussion.

For Derrida what connects psychoanalysis and the technological media is a most basic philosophical "concept" called the "postal." Since much of what follows involves an attempt to develop the idea of the postal in at least some of its complexity, we would resist giving a ready definition of it at this early stage. Suffice it to say that the domains of its address include conceptualization itself, the operations of technology in general and of the relaying of communications in particular, and forms of textual analysis. The model for the operations of the postal is the form of writing textualized by the postcard. Obviously, the technology of communications is common to the postal and to cinema, and the postcard, as a discontinuous combination of written word and visual image, is analogous to film in ways that remain to be developed.

There is a characteristically logocentric opposition governing all operations of technology, of the machine, and of mediation in general, and that is the opposition between *physis* and *technē*, between nature and art—the former being considered prior to the latter, the latter seen as a fall away from, or an unsatisfactory substitute for, the former.[1]

---

[1] Heidegger was the first to consider the particular constellation of terms that Derrida develops in *The Post Card*—the technological, the technē, destin(at)ing, and *Ge-stell* (usually translated as "en-framing," its roots are in *stellen*, "to put" or "to place," an

This opposition comes into play most obviously in an extreme case such as cybernetics, where something inanimate like a robot is perceived as a threat to the human or where we are told that computers can do anything that we tell them to but that they cannot think on their own, cannot "create." In fact, however much Derrida's work has brought to our attention the logocentric assumptions at work in the treatment of speech versus writing, the physis/technē opposition is perhaps a far more obvious case of the same assumptions, one more deeply ingrained in our thinking and thus more difficult to unseat. There would seem not to be a more certain opposition than that between the natural and the artificial, between animate and inanimate.

Now Derrida's analyses have clearly demonstrated that the machine and the unnatural have always shared a common structure with the written and received similar treatment. As Derrida explains in "Plato's Pharmacy," writing was indirectly criticized by Plato for being an artificial memory aid, a sort of prosthesis to the mind that would breed bad "live" memories. With Freud's mystic writing pad, analyzed in "Freud and the Scene of Writing," the shared structure between writing and a mechanical apparatus is even more obvious. As one of Derrida's translators, Alan Bass, writes:

> It was this series of questions [in "Freud and the Scene of Writing"] that helped me to understand the importance of the *machine* for Derrida. Writing is always treated by philosophy as a *technique*, as part of the technology of communication, which always means the communication of truth and meaning. According to the traditional view, technology has no life of its own, and is to be kept below and apart from the living truth. Like writing. It is no accident, then, that the machine—the dead mechanism which endlessly produces the same thing—should be as unthinkable for philosophy as writing. ("The Double Game," in *Taking Chances*, 77)

Derrida's work also makes clear that the domain of the technical or technological is also that of art in general, the Greek word technē being the word for "art" among other things, so that once again the distinctions are not to be drawn between the "natural" arts on the one hand— poetry (writing), drama, dance, and so on (those which supposedly only require a voice and a body)—and the "media arts" (those depending on technology) on the other. Rather, differences are to be found

---

important nexus for Derrida here)—but always, of course, in the context of the Question of Being. See Martin Heidegger, *The Question Concerning Technology and Other Essays*, trans. William Lovitt (New York: Harper and Row, 1977).

among these various art forms, all of which are mediated and whose model in Derrida's terms remains writing. After all, poetry was already seen by Plato as enough of a misapplication of thought to be banned from the City. The threat that underlies the logocentric attitude toward technology is extreme, for not only does the lifelessness of technology foreshadow death but, as we saw in an earlier discussion, its very structure represents an articulation of death. For Derrida the effect can be generalized. To repeat what we quoted earlier: "Now the contemporary possibility of the photograph resides in its conjugation of death and the referent within the same system. Not that this occurs here for the first time, *and given its essential relation to reproductive technique, or to technique itself,* such a conjugation did not need to wait for photography" (*Psyché*, 291; our translation, our emphasis). We can note then that it is the principle of reproducibility that defines technology and points toward death and that this possibility resides even in a form such as writing.

Derrida's reference here, repeated in other instances,[2] is to Walter Benjamin, especially to his essay "The Work of Art in the Age of Mechanical Reproduction." Benjamin there discusses how photography has brought about a fundamental change in the relationship between original and copy, eliminating from the work of art what he calls its "aura" or its ritual element and introducing instead the political. Expressed another way, the cult value of the work has been superseded by its exhibition value. This in itself has important political implications for Benjamin, who finds the vocation of cinema in "the promotion of a revolutionary criticism of traditional concepts of art."[3] Derrida would disagree with Benjamin where he treats as a historical innovation what for Derrida is a structural fact of any work of art, namely its detachability from any original context, its essential iterability. It is suggested in "Les Morts de Roland Barthes" that reproductive technique is not, as Benjamin implies, structurally different from technique, the technological, or the technē in general. The very "event" of the technē, its introduction of supplementary or prosthetic relations, of modification and detachment, and of altering of contexts represents the same structural possibility as repetition.

However, he would be more likely to agree with Benjamin on two other important matters. First, Benjamin interestingly points to a similarity of structure between film and psychoanalysis, comparing the

---

[2] See " + R (Into the Bargain)," in *The Truth in Painting* (175–81); and *Right of Inspection* (73).

[3] "The Work of Art in the Age of Mechanical Reproduction," in *Illuminations*, ed. Hannah Arendt (New York: Schocken Books, 1969), 231.

revelation of details in the close-up with the symptoms of the unconscious: "The film has enriched our field of perception with methods
which can be illustrated by those of Freudian theory. Fifty years ago, a
slip of the tongue passed more or less unnoticed. . . . By close-ups of
the things around us . . . the film . . . extends our comprehension of
the necessities which rule our lives. . . . The camera introduces us to
unconscious optics as does psychoanalysis to unconscious impulses"
(235, 236, 237). Thus we have further reinforcement, although from a
different perspective, of what might at first have seemed to be an un-
usual combination of subject matter in *The Post Card*, that of media
technology and psychoanalysis.

Second, Derrida would agree with Benjamin concerning the political force of what photography represents, structurally or historically,
that is: the absolute political importance of the technological or more
generally of what we are developing here as the postal. This is made
most explicit in a later reference to Benjamin: "*If* Ps.[Psychoanalysis]
and Ph.[Photography] form a single event by belonging to the same
historical field, to the same epoch . . . then in fact [they] pose and
repose, independently and in unison, the same question, that of the
right of inspection. They displace the foundations of an established
jurisdiction, they call for another . . . (*Right of Inspection*, 74). However
one looks at it, the postal, the political, photography, and psychoanalysis form a complicated nexus that intersects more generally with the
whole question of the technological media. We shall develop these
matters in a more detailed discussion of *The Post Card* below.

Whether or not one is able to situate a qualitative change in the notion of the work of art with the advent of the mechanical reproduction
represented by photography, as Benjamin does, and whether it is useful or not to refer to that change as a loss of artistic "aura," the technological media certainly accentuate the idea of a work's detachability
from its supposed original context. For Derrida again, the artistic
event, which he calls writing, cannot be defined as such without that
idea. Writing, destined or designed to function in the absence of its
originator, already displays the sort of "exhibitionism" that Benjamin
attributes more particularly to photography. It may be worthwhile to
say, then, that photography represents a case of the writing principle
that can be situated historically—and we have argued at length for the
same to be said of film—but it is doubtful whether the structural distinction Benjamin draws between a cave painting and a photograph,
between art as cult and art as exhibition, can still be maintained. As we
have said, for Benjamin "Artistic production begins with ceremonial
objects designed to serve in a cult. One may assume that what mat-

tered was their existence, not their being on view. The elk portrayed by the man of the Stone Age on the walls of his cave was an instrument of magic. He did expose it to his fellow men, but in the main it was meant for the spirits" (224–25).

There are obvious inconsistencies in this view when considered from a Derridean perspective. The existence of the work of art, here distinguished from its being on view, could as well be said to be constituted by its being on view. If a work was meant for the spirits, it would presumably not need to be communicated in materiality. In fact Benjamin's last sentence in the quotation above sums up the paradox of art as writing and also represents the familiar logocentric occlusion of that paradox. For once the work has sufficient materiality to be seen by the caveman's fellow men, once it exists as remainder, its meaning and the circulation of its sense can no longer be controlled by any original intention the caveman artist might have had. To say that "in the main" it was meant for the spirits, in no way prevents it from being viewed by others and thus becoming "exhibitionist." It makes obvious sense to say that the cave drawing was "meant for the spirits," and it makes obvious sense to say that intentionality or destination is a function of a work of art, as indeed of any utterance. However, as long as the work is "exposed to his fellow men," that must also be an intention of sorts, or rather a constitutive gesture. It is not consistent to maintain that a specific intention is the overriding consideration in determining the effects of a work of art; it can never be established as *the* prior or governing function. One could just as easily say in the case given by Benjamin that the man of the Stone Age did mean the work of art for the spirits but that in the main he exposed it to his fellow men. Neither event can be established as the originating act or intention relegating the rest.

The question of reproduction as it concerns mimesis and the relationship between reality and photographic image have been the subjects of an extensive earlier discussion. Benjamin's comments are directed rather at the idea of proliferation that is the mark of media technology. But for Derrida the difference between reality and image would have the same structure as the difference between one reproduction of an image and another reproduction of the same image, for where there is no origin there is always already difference, and repetition implies that difference. Two of the "same" photographic images are as different from one photographic image as one photographic image is from its referent.

Reproduction as proliferation is a central topic of discussion in Derrida's essay on Titus-Carmel's *The Pocket Size Tlingit Coffin* entitled

"Cartouches,"[4] in *The Truth in Painting*. The work in question consists of a matchbox-sized model and 127 drawings of it. The model is a box containing a mirror and a pliable wooden oval, partly covered in fur, that is attached to the box with laces. The box is closed with a plexiglass lid. Although no reference is made to Benjamin in Derrida's essay, the model of the Tlingit Coffin could be interpreted as having mystical or religious significance, like pretechnological art, whereas the drawings of that model raise the question of mechanical reproduction in and of art, even if they do not rely on the same process. It should also be pointed out that these are not 127 identical drawings but a series including pencil sketches, watercolors, and engravings, from various angles and perspectives, executed and dated over a period of slightly more than a year.[5] A system of original model and derivative series is thus very much in play, and in Derrida's discussion the priority of the one term over the other comes under scrutiny.

Derrida chooses to call the coffin itself a "paradigm" rather than a model. This term is interesting considering its use in semiotics, where the paradigmatic—as the set of all possible choices—can be seen as a non-originary series, unlike the syntagmatic, whose ordering requires a beginning and an end and whose beginning determines that ordering and that end. Derrida exploits the ambiguity of its Greek root, which refers to "the sort of artificial model which already proceeds from a *technē*" (*The Truth in Painting*, 195). But the Greek word also gives verbal forms meaning "to propose as a model or give as an example" as well as "to make an example of, to condemn, to blame, to cover with infamy" (196). Derrida thus implicitly takes the approbation usually reserved for the copy and applies it to the model. For he shows how the model/copy series is set up and at the same time deconstructed by *The Pocket Size Tlingit Coffin*. Or, if one prefers, Derrida deconstructs the paradigm set up by Titus-Carmel's work. This can be seen from a number of different perspectives.

First, the model or paradigm is not itself a natural object but an artifact: "The paradigm was not at the origin, it is itself neither producer

---

[4] The word "cartouche," literally "cartridge," refers also to a system of decoration in heraldry and to a means by which the names of royalty are emblazoned in hieroglyphics. For Derrida it becomes another function of the parergonal or the signature effect. The explanatory text that Titus-Carmel attaches to his series raises again the question of the frame—does it belong or not?—and illustrates the incursion of the graphic upon the pictorial (205).

[5] Derrida's essay is in the form of a series of diary entries executed over a six-week period, thus mimicking to some extent Titus-Carmel's series of repetitions. The period in question (30 November 1977–11 January 1978) takes place within the time frame of the letters constituting "Envois" in *The Post Card* (134).

nor generator. It is a *fac-simile* of a model, will first have been *produced* . . ." (194). Much of Derrida's discussion, however oblique, becomes a matter of maintaining that one might just as well ascribe the origin of the series to Titus-Carmel. Such an approach, however, far from assuring a self-present and intact origin, introduces irremediable effects of heterogeneity into the series through the functions of the signature effect. Titus-Carmel signs the *Tlingit Coffin*, and in setting about creating the series (*s'y mettre*) he is putting himself in the coffin (*s'y mettre*), inscribing his paternity, committing parricide, and so on.

Second, it is actually only an effect of writing or of the signature, namely Titus-Carmel's title for the work, which suggests that the coffin was in any sense prior to the drawings. In fact, that title also includes the drawings, thus erasing the distinction: "Now this declaration which *puts order* into the series, this narrative which seals an irreversibility, belongs to the cartouche. This is a cartouche: it puts to work and forms part of the work by inscribing (itself) there (as) the title, the signature and the autobiographical performative of the signatory . . ." (219). However, as Derrida insists, there is nothing to prevent a viewer from considering the coffin to be a reproduction like all the rest or a wooden model built according to the design of one of the drawings, with its own place in the series, perhaps coming in the middle to provide perspective on either side of it or even at the end as a sort of monumental finish.

The possibility of its being displaced along the series leads Derrida to compare the paradigmatic coffin with a cursor—which in the age of word processing has particularly technological connotations—and so suggests also that from a certain perspective it is radically heterogeneous to the series it supposedly engenders. This and our previous point are made clearer when the coffin series is compared with another of Titus-Carmel's works, *The Great Cultural Banana Plantation*. There fifty-nine plastic bananas form a series with a real one that decomposes and so marks its difference for the duration of the exhibition. In this case the real banana has a greater claim to being the originator of the series, since its naturalness seems to endow it with a priority that the coffin does not have. But the more the banana distinguishes itself and its priority, and the more it tends to decomposition, the less it is able to function, the less it is able to be privileged over its synthetic relatives. In other words, the more the banana distinguishes itself, the more it becomes different (from itself), thus losing its identity. The coffin, produced rather than natural, has more staying power; but paradoxically, it cannot distinguish itself as effectively as the banana, it remains qualitatively one synthetic product among 127 others and cannot of itself be assured of the primary place in that series. As it decomposes, the banana can no longer be considered the model within the terms of the series; rather it requires us to go outside the present time frame of the work to be regarded as such. Thus, like photography, the model banana evokes the play of time and death. In fact, it inscribes those structures within the work even more explicitly than photography is able to do.

The banana and the coffin refer to the paradoxical effects of the parergon, the *cartouche*, the frame, and the signature. If such functions are outside that which they supposedly govern, as meta-operational truths, they cannot in fact be said to control the order of the series, the order of any set of effects ascribed to them. If on the other hand they belong within the series, they lose that overriding control, becoming but "piece[s] of the general performance" (220). The model/copy paradigm does not in fact describe a filiation or a descendance along family lines as philosophers ever since Plato have maintained. Rather whatever occurs within materiality (and that term would no doubt require redefinition) comes to be considered as an always already synthetic product of some sort. There can be no pure natural any more than there can be pure speech, for the natural contains within it functions of the synthetic—as potential, as conditions of possibility, as operations that also effect the synthetic. Nor can the natural close itself off from the synthetic, clearly delineating its own borders.

Thus Derrida uses the word "paradigm" and its synonym "paragon" (model, but also an old word for characters in printing) to connect with parergon, pharmakon, and parricide, hence with many of his other texts and as a form of lexical shorthand for the deconstruction of the original/copy opposition. And the technē, supposedly derived from and secondary to the physis, art opposed to nature, can be seen to either coconstitute, exclude, or render irrelevant that which is said to bring it into effect.

———————

Let us now look more closely at the wider range of what is implied by the technē as Derrida elaborates it in *The Post Card*. First, it is worth noting the structure of the book. It consists of four parts: "Envois," "To Speculate—on 'Freud,' " "Le Facteur de la vérité," and "Du tout." The first part, from which most of our discussion will be drawn, is a series of love letters written over a two-year period, centered loosely around a discussion of a postcard the narrator finds when visiting Cambridge, which seems to depict Socrates writing under Plato's dictation, a reversal of what we take to be historical fact. But "Envois" was also intended as the preface to "To Speculate," an analysis of Freud's *Beyond the Pleasure Principle*, and hence is also an oblique discussion of psychoanalysis. The third essay is the well-known reply to Lacan's seminar on Poe's "The Purloined Letter" and is followed by "Du tout," an interview with a group of French psychoanalysts.

A further note is necessary with regard to "Envois." They are written as love letters and function along a whole series of paradoxes that both construct and deconstruct the postal as a concept. Neither the sender nor the addressee remain singular identities. In the case of the sender there are frequent allusions to this effect, to the possibility for instance that the postcards are addressed by their author to him- or herself as addressee. Assuming that there is a separate addressee, a more obvious structural paradox occurs. The love letters are said to be addressed to the object of the writer's love and so contain any number of personal notes and references, but they are by definition open letters, thus also addressed to any reader. They are written in the event of the separation of the "two" correspondents from each other (only one writes however) and written *against* the event of their coming together, for such an event would negate the sense of the postcards. Yet they act as a set of promises, entreaties, and arrangements concerning the togetherness that they also ward off. These mechanisms become extremely convoluted and need to be studied in detail,[6] but the purpose of our raising them is to suggest that even more than other texts of Derrida, "Envois" cannot be easily reduced to a set of concepts or to the elaboration of a theory or thesis. The *thetic* (from the Greek for "to place," which is *ponere/positum* in Latin), representing a pose or a position, is a function of the postal that "Envois" deconstructs. For the placing of posts, the possible and necessary marking of points or positions in a system of relay, is the condition of possibility of the postal, of any system of addressing and sending. By the same token, however, since the post marks a halt that is also a destination, it is undermined by the structural necessity of non-arrival or *a*destination. As will be seen below, Derrida goes so far as to maintain that in fact a message always also arrives elsewhere than at its supposed single address.

Most obviously, the postal refers to systems of communication and more particularly to those systems relying upon the transfer or transport of a material message—a note, a letter, and so on. Different then, at first glance, from oral communication on the one hand and satellite

[6] For further discussion see David Wills, "Post/Card/Match/Book/*Envois*/Derrida," *SubStance*, no. 43 (1984), 19–38.

message transfer on the other. But on closer analysis all of these systems depend upon a notion of destination, a teleological concept of sending; they assume there to be a closed circuit between sender and addressee. Thus, though there are important and obvious material differences between systems of communication such as the voice, the letter, and the electronic transfer, those differences cannot be read as oppositional given their common reliance on the idea of destination. And although we seem to be at a point in history where the materiality of message transfer is about to be superseded—and Derrida quotes at length from observations and prophecies made in this regard by the French postmaster general (105–7)—we also seem determined permanently to repress or overlook the paradox in the idea of communication that the letter or postcard represents. The idea of communicating computers, far from being a radical shift into the technology of the machine and the denial of the human element in communication, in fact reproduces the same model instituted by oral address and allows for a tightening of the circuit of message transfer.

The paradox that the letter represents and that technology, however much it may overlook it, in fact depends upon, is the simple fact that a letter cannot arrive. Not just the possibility that it may not arrive, that it may be diverted, delayed, or irrevocably lost—which would suggest that those occurrences were accidents that befell the operation or threatened it from the outside—but the structural necessity of non-arrival built into the system of address. What is insisted upon here is that the event of addressing and sending can *in no way* guarantee arrival, only arrival can do that. The event of sending is permanently divided, in its constitution, by its other event, that of non-arrival. All this was elaborated in detail by Derrida in his debate with Lacan, who, in analyzing "The Purloined Letter," concluded that a letter always arrives at its destination. But in *The Post Card* it becomes clear that the idea of spacing that Derrida thus introduces into the system of communication is all that is required to institute the possibility or rather the necessity of delay, and hence the postal. With spacing comes the structural necessity of delay—spacing means something other than immediacy—and delay means some sort of adestination, hence the postal principle. A type of *différance* thus comes into effect within every conceivable event: "To post means to send by 'counting' with a halt, a relay or a delay involving suspense, the place of a mailman [/factor—*facteur*], the possibility of going astray or being forgotten" (*The Post Card*, 65; translation modified). Whereas on the one hand the postal, implying the materiality (and the divisibility) of the letter, exists as perhaps the most simple and obvious case of mediation as technē, at

least within systems of communication that are the models for conceptual thinking, on the other hand it shows how the technē in fact inhabits the most fundamental ideas of positioning such as identity, difference, and so on. For if the postal as event, and as event of the technē,
is always divided by the event of non-arrival, then concepts such as
identity and difference that depend on it are similarly divided. If the
addressee cannot be established in its singular identity, neither can it be
distinguished in pure difference from a putative non-addressee. The
postcards, addressed to a lover but that the reader overhears or over-
reads, continually demonstrate that. In this context the technē comes
to be the mark of impurity (the artifice in nature) inscribed as condition
of possibility in any event conceived of as natural or automatic.

   In view of the interconnections between it, the event, and the
technē, the postal, more than other examples from Derrida's glossary,
seems to approach a universal concept, connecting with the most
wide-ranging conceptual networks. To counteract this he adopts the
same strategies used in connection with other "concepts." He posits
for the postal a structural definition that, by virtue of its paradox, cannot operate on the basis of an originating structure; and he immediately inscribes the term within a chain including other terms such as
the position or the event. The quasi-universal status of the postal becomes clear in "Envois" once the letter writer decides to publish the
letters after first deleting from them whatever is "personal" in the correspondence, whatever does not relate to the theoretical concerns of
the postal:

   What is there, rigorously, in our letters that does not derive from
   the *fort:da*, the vocabulary of going-coming, of the step, of the
   way or the away, of the near and the far, of all the frameworks in
   tele-, of the adestination, of the address and the maladdress, of
   everything that is passed and comes to pass between Freud and
   Heidegger, of the "truth," of the *facteur*, "*du tout*," of the transference, of the inheritance and the genealogy, of the paradoxes of
   nomination, of the king, of the queen and of their ministers, of
   the magister and of the ministries, of the private or public detec-
   tives? (222)

Given this tendency to proliferation, Derrida is at pains both to histor-
icize and to deconstruct the postal to prevent it from becoming a master concept:

   this history of the posts . . . cannot be a history of the posts: primarily because it concerns the very possibility of history, of all the

concepts, too, of history, of tradition, of the transmission or interruptions, goings astray, etc. And then because such a "history of the posts" would be but a miniscule *envoi* in the network that it allegedly would analyze (there is no metapostal), only a card lost in a bag, that a strike, or even a sorting accident, can always delay indefinitely, lose without return. (67)

Indeed, the very concept underwriting the possibility of history, the *epochē* (Gk. "pause," "fixed point"), is a particularly "postal" concept: "Now there are also differences, there is only that, in postal *différance*. . . . In the great epoch (whose technology is marked by paper, pen, the envelope, the individual subject addressee, etc.) and which goes shall we say from Socrates to Freud and Heidegger, there are sub-epochs, for example the process of state monopolization, and then within this the invention of the postage stamp and the Berne Convention, to use only such insufficient indices" (191). No master concept then, but an indefinite series of differences that still remain to be analyzed, however interminable that operation might be. Such a rewriting of those differences would no doubt imply a rewriting of the whole of our conceptual system. And however important technological differences might be within that system—and there is no reason why what we understand as technology should not still form the basis of a system of differentiation—it will be found that technology does not "arrive" or occur with the invention of the pen and paper, photographic reproduction, or even "faxing." It is simply a condition of possibility of the postal, which is a condition of possibility of the event, which is a condition of possibility of the technological, and so on, where none of those terms can ascribe to themselves absolute priority:

> The entire history of postal *technē* tends to rivet the destination to identity. To arrive, to happen would be to a subject, to happen to "me." Now a mark, whatever it may be, is coded in order to make an imprint, even if it is a perfume. Henceforth it divides itself, *it is valid several times in one time*: no more unique addressee. This is why, by virtue of this divisibility (the origin of reason, the mad origin of reason and of the principle of identity), *technē* does not happen. . . . (192)

However obliquely, Derrida's critique especially addresses that naive opposition between communication and the modern era of *telecommunications*, for all communication contains within it the notion of the telos, of distance and spacing on the one hand and destination on the other. There is no unmediated communication (and ironically it is

telecommunications with its heightened sense of distance and concom-
itantly of speed that claims to be more and more "direct" these days),
none without an epochal, postal, or technological spacing.

Now what is important in this for a discussion of cinema is the situation of that medium within the "history" of the postal. In "Envois"
the model for the era linking Socrates to Heidegger, as has been stated,
is the postcard. It is also the model for literature both as we know it
and as Derrida would have us understand it. It is material and trans-
portable, precise in form, reproducible, consumable, and it contains
messages with varying degrees of explicitness or implicitness. Yet for
Derrida it is also open and thus an invitation to theft, diversion, and
the like; flimsy yet formally divided (picture, copyright, message, signature, address, stamp, and postmark) and hence problematic in its
relations; verbal and nonverbal, cryptic, and prominently signed but
liable to arrive after the sender has returned home. Thus not only does
the postcard represent the whole of our literary epoch, it also represents the limit of that epoch. For telecommunications dispenses with
the particular materiality of the document upon which literature, and
its attendant industry, depend: "An entire epoch of so-called literature,
if not all of it, cannot survive a certain technological regime of telecommunications. . . . Neither can philosophy, or psychoanalysis. Or
love letters" (197).

How then does cinema fit into this scenario? Following Derrida, we
might say that it falls within the same structural categories of literature
or philosophy, despite the fact that it is less than a hundred years old.
And as Benjamin has pointed out, it is in the same historical and technological category as psychoanalysis. The close-up is a case in point
here, as we saw earlier. From one perspective Benjamin's link between
the close-up and psychoanalysis might lead to some sort of fetishiza-
tion of the message as materiality. The close-up would thus define the
image as a monumental form of representation, larger than life, transmitting details overlooked in reality. But this leads very quickly to a
reinforcement of the familiar logocentrism of the realist position.
From the point of view of a theoretician of the close-up like Balàzs or
a practitioner like Dreyer, such an image elides its effect of distance in
the manner of a telecommunicative apparatus. For them, film com-
municates its essence to the viewer all the more powerfully by bearing
in on the details of an image or visage, revealing a hidden reality and
directly communicating it to the viewer. Now most modern spectators
no longer so enthralled by the magic of cinematic technology would
accept, as *Blow-up* (1967) or any number of suspense films remind us,
that the revelation provided by a close-up is also in an important sense

a distortion. Thus if the power of the close-up as revelation derives from its communicative force, that is, the possibility of its involving the spectator more "directly" in a given experience, then it also points to the role of adestination within the process of communication. A close-up becomes a rhetorical figure like an apostrophe, and cinematic technique in general becomes a matter of emphasis given to particular forms of address.

In this sense cinema is clearly inscribed within the postal epoch of the postcard, of literature. It has claimed since its inception to be an art form with a cultural status similar to that of literature, and its advantages have traditionally been described in terms of its communicative superiority—more direct, more visual, more accessible, more democratic, and so on. Hence if we follow what Derrida says about literature, cinema is just as unlikely to survive in its present form. Here of course technological advance seems already to be proving the prophecy true; first threatened by television, cinema now fears the advances of video. But that is only a surface effect, and the question of cinema's place within the postal epoch does not reduce to its competition with video, even if we could definitively establish that there were a sufficient structural distinction to be made here between a film on the big screen and a film on the small screen.

More pertinent points can be made. First, to the extent that cinema falls, like literature, within the postal epoch, meaning that it provides a support for a material message—words and images—to be transmitted to an audience, film is as susceptible as literature to being deconstructed and rewritten as postcard. Our earlier discussion underlining the strategic advantages of considering film as writing was intended within that perspective, and we shall have more to say in that regard shortly. Second, as we also suggested earlier, other ways of analyzing film might emerge if cinema were to be compared not only with other art forms or other media but also with the operations of the information sciences and telecommunications in general. Yet a problem remains: practically all of film criticism and theory, from auteurism through textual analysis to spectator studies, like the information sciences and telecommunications, repeats even as it analyzes it a model of communication that assumes systems of address based on identity. Auteurism relies on authorial intention and control to ensure arrival of the sense of a film corpus; textual analyses tend to assume a structured core of sense restored to some intact form in order to be transmitted; and spectator studies, however informed by the psychoanalytic conception of a divided subject sutured into the film text, still describe that subject very much in terms of a positionality, failing to deconstruct that term with a notion of the postal or of adestination. We also realize, however, that at a certain point one cannot do otherwise than rely on notions that remain problematic, and Derrida's critical practice, after all, does not claim simply to step outside of a logocentric model even if it undertakes a most radical questioning of it.

Thus cinema's status as a postal event resides not so much in its technological pedigree as in its participation within a whole network of conceptualization that technology continues to render problematic as it naively reinforces it. Such a network sustains the teleology of narrative as much as the linearity of conventional reading practices; it positions the sound track with respect to the image track as much as it situates the viewer; it formalizes textual boundaries so that analysis tends always to a type of stasis.

What cinema or criticism would be without those sorts of bases seems from here inconceivable, and indeed they would simply not be, for the postal is a condition of their existence. However, such speculation might serve to displace the question from that which asks what cinema will become, how it will exist after video or in another sub-epoch, for such thinking remains entirely within the same framework. Even the post-postal would, paradoxically, still be postal, its conception dependent upon the idea of a determinable limit or identity called "the future of cinema." The new question would involve, rather, asking whether (or how, since it is a given) the present or future parameters of cinema compare with the technological or postal apparatuses that have defined them up to this point; whether or how the medium will continue to be constituted by forms of address. In other words, one might well argue that not simply is there no cinema in the future but that there is no future after cinema, no possible conception of it that does not fall within the same technological limits that define it now.

This is the sort of analysis Derrida points to regarding the everyday sense of the postal, after discussing the future technological innovations vaunted by the French postal bureaucracy. New methods of transmission of information are supposed to permit mail messages to be sent from one's personal computer terminal to the post office nearest the residence of the addressee, which would then distribute the same, several within the same envelope. The postmaster general does not say why the message could not be transmitted directly to another computer terminal, nor why and for how long he envisages that the practice will be restricted to business mail only. In any case the formal support of mail as we know it, with individualized envelopes stamped, weighed, and so on will have been superseded. Furthermore, asks the same official, why not consider having the post office, well placed on account of its "omnipresence," deal with any kind of transaction between the population and the administration? As Derrida says: "I can't decide what is most striking here: the monstrosity of this future that the Postmaster General envisages, with a beatific and quite forward-looking *insouciance* (while he calmly converses with us about the worst of State and trans-State police . . .) or on the contrary its ancestral antiquity, the very normality of the thing. In its essence, of course, in its *eidos* it is more than twenty-five centuries old" (106–7; translation modified). For the postmaster proposes no structural modification of the postal system, from sender through centralized network to addressee, but simply a tightening of the operation. And we should not be surprised by the systems of control and censorship he proposes, since such systems have never been any more foreign to the postal than the possibilities of theft and loss. Thus the epochal or technological change that would bring about the disappearance of the letter in its presently constituted material form would not for all that represent a structural change in the technē or postal concept upon which the system relies. The postmaster's blind spots are those of Socrates and Plato, those that will perpetuate the postal beyond its twenty-fifth century in spite of technological innovation: assumptions about the singular identity, the presence to themselves of senders and addressees, and the indivisible nature of messages sent between such private individuals.

In the case of cinema one might envisage an analogous and supposedly radical change from the image as imprint upon light-sensitive celluloid to the image as computerized abstraction not reliant upon any object in the world "having been there" in the Barthesian sense. However, as long as objects as entities continue to be the referents of even computerized images and attendant concepts of spatialization continue to be the frames of reference for the sorts of hi-tech special effects increasingly seen in titles, trailers, advertising, and so on, the parameters defining cinema will not have escaped the perspective of the technological and of the postal. As with special effects in general, it will remain a matter of bringing even "unreal" or imagined worlds within the sphere of the spectator's perception, not of changing those modes of perception. Film here, like any visual medium, seems constrained by the importance given to the visual senses in the operations of conceptualization in general. As Gregory Ulmer has pointed out, referring to Walter Ong, the word "idea" comes from the same root as Latin *video* ("I see") and the idea was considered from the beginning to be a picture in the mind (*Applied Grammatology*, 36). The limits but also the chal-

lenge of a reading of film or cinema that attempts to change conceptualization as much as perception are found in a critique of the articulations of the various support systems for perception, representation,
signification, identification, figuration, interpretation, and so on, as
we know them now. Those conceptual supports for cinema are also its
"posts," and to the extent that deconstruction might replace semiology's analysis of the signifier with an analysis of what we could call
postal effects, it still remains for film theory to address itself to the
pieces of that conceptual framework without or against the bias of the
logocentric assumptions upholding the edifice. At a certain point or
from a certain point of view not only does perception "not exist," as
Derrida posited as early as *Speech and Phenomena*,[7] but there is no identity or figure or concept, and so on. That is to say that they remain to
be redefined against the institutional limits constituting them in their
logocentric bias.

The degree of institutionalization and the extent of systems of control to preserve those institutions are the hallmarks of the political significance of the postal. Derrida is insistent about that, and it is in this
context that psychoanalysis returns as a central topic in "Envois" and
indeed in *The Post Card* in general. In fact there are several categories
of profession (considered as forms of political activity) that fall within
the same rubric, that of "guardians of the letter": "By their very function, those who deny it [the fact of adestination] most energetically are
the people charged with the carrying of the mail, the guardians of the
letter, the archivists, the professors as well as the journalists, today the
psychoanalysts. The philosophers, of course, who are all of that at
once, and the literature people" (51). But it is psychoanalysis that,
apart from philosophy, is singled out as the institution that, though
situated at a turn in the postal era, too readily reinforces its restrictive
power and that, having uncovered the unconscious and the work of
censorship in human psychic activity, itself acts as a policing agency
over this activity. This of course is quite contrary to the avowed aim of
psychoanalysis since Freud, and Derrida is not saying that this is something into which psychoanalysis has degenerated but rather that, acting within the postal conceptual regime, it cannot but reinforce the
laws of that regime.

In general we might say that the *post*al necessarily involves *sta*king
out claims and an obsession with *post*erity, but the political scene of the
postcard more particularly is the relationship between Socrates and

[7] *Speech and Phenomena*, trans. David Allison (Evanston: Northwestern University
Press, 1973), 45.

Plato, their signing of a pact and forming of a private company with a monopoly over Western thinking, to which we are required to pay our dues for activities as diverse as when we make "war or love, speculate on the energy crisis, construct socialism, write novels, open concentration camps for poets or homosexuals, buy bread or hijack a plane . . . teach, or piss against a tree" (100). The whole philosophical institution is constructed by them and is perhaps based on a gigantic hoax, since we only have Plato's word for what Socrates said. In any case it functions through systems of privilege and secrecy assuring the controlled circulation of ideas. The political side of things comes into focus even more clearly when we consider the postal as mail system. There immediately arise the questions of state monopoly (before Louis XI introduced this in France the University of Paris was given the privilege); of censorship and policing (postcards were used in the Franco-Prussian War to facilitate military censorship); of international capital (the prime mover for postal reform in England was a tax reformer and that movement brought about the international convention of Berne now under the aegis of the United Nations).

Derrida's objection to psychoanalysis, then, from the point of view of the postal, is that it seemed particularly well poised to challenge the conceptual framework it inherited. Furthermore, as Derrida reminds us, "there would be neither postal relay nor analytic movement if the place of the letter were not divisible and if a letter always arrived at its destination" (*The Post Card*, 324)—that is, if there were no delay or relay in the circulation of a message say, between unconscious and conscious, latent and manifest, there would be no room for psychoanalysis. It is precisely in its exploitation of notions of delay (*Nachträglichkeit*) and relay (primary and secondary processes, conscious/unconscious, etc.), of readdress (lapsus) and interception (the complex and contradictory workings of the Pleasure Principle), that psychoanalysis fulfills its most radical potential. Yet in failing to sufficiently theorize and develop those ideas against its conceptual limits, psychoanalysis risks becoming another form of policing activity within the logocentric apparatus:

> The past and the present of the said institution are unthinkable outside a certain postal technology, as are the public or private, that is secret, correspondences which have marked its stages and crises, supposing a very determined type of postal rationality, of relations between the State monopoly and the secret of private messages, as of their unconscious effects. That the part of "private" mail tends toward zero [cf. the postmaster general's com-

ments above], does not only diminish the chances of the great cor-
respondences (the last ones, those of Freud, of Kafka), it also
transforms the entire field of analytic exertion. . . . (*The Post
Card*, 104)

As an attempt, however ironic, to redress (readdress?) that situation,
Derrida studies in some detail in "To Speculate—on 'Freud' " the role
played by Freud's correspondence in assuring proper management of
his heritage or that of psychoanalysis. He plays thus between the postal
principle in what might be called its literal sense, concerning letters
and correspondence, and its wider sense, concerning the transmission
or communication of truth, attempts by the father of psychoanalysis
to close or limit the effect of the openings his theories had created
within our conceptual apparatus. By the same token and with similar
irony Derrida develops psychoanalytic concepts where the institution
has fallen short, expanding its scene of writing to include signature
effects at its very basis, holding it to be constituted by an "autobio-
graphic" or "testamentary" writing, especially at its outer limit defined
by *Beyond the Pleasure Principle*. Finally, if one takes "Envois" to be the
preface to "To Speculate," one can see how Freud's rewriting of or
calling into question of the *Pleasure* Principle (or the *primary processes*) by means of the death instinct—described in *Beyond the Pleasure
Principle*—all that is deconstructed or re-marked by Derrida's *Postal
Principle* as elaborated in "Envois."

Remembering again how film and psychoanalysis are historically
contemporaneous and how both develop the possibility of revealing
aspects of the unseen, could cinema not be similarly accused of failing
to live up to its promise? Discussion since the earliest days of cinema—
and we could cite the Surrealists or the 1920s avant-garde in general—
has raised this question, arguing that since film could so effectively
unlock worlds of fantasy, there was no need for it to restrict itself to a
depiction of reality within which any concessions to fantasy were just
that, always seen against the ground of reality. As we suggested above,
given that it could provide new perceptions, one can bemoan the fact
that film is content to reinforce the position of the powerful yet passive
viewer installed since the Renaissance. Film has certainly proved to be
a very faithful and potent force in the relating or relaying of reality to
truth. Though it seems to owe nothing to "autobiographical" writing
or to the rigidity of a network of correspondence assuring heirs and
disciples the way psychoanalysis does in Derrida's critique, not being
a system of knowledge in the same sense, there remains nevertheless
much to be said concerning the ways that it has occluded new possible

relations between art and science, presented as innocent and neutral the ideological bases of technological innovation, and circumscribed its own scene of writing by reducing its literary frame to that of narrative. Clearly, the level of economic and political involvement of cinema, in the strict sense, is superior to that of psychoanalysis, and those concerns need to be more explicitly addressed. Yet the structures operating are the same in both domains, though they operate at different levels and in differing degrees. Like psychoanalysis, cinema can be remarked, if not redeemed, by attention to its institutional articulations, particularly those under strain at present: its address to a supposedly indivisible mass audience; the conflict between a big vision and a shrinking screen; its loss of a ready and sure formula for quick return of capital; the inroads made by high technology image production or effects such as colorization; the problems of archiving and preservation in general.

The answers to these questions may well need to be redefined along less conservative lines than those given by the keepers of the archives. Not that we should not be vigilant to the changes wrought by economics or technology, which will often amount to a further reinforcement of the established institutional forms. However, neither can we resort to arguments based on moral right or truth, the sanctity of the original, the prerogative of authorial intention, and the assumed definition of what we call cinema.

Colorization is a case in point. The Society for Cinema Studies is right to point out, as it did in a recent statement,[8] that this technique is but one of a whole range of modifications, often hidden, that films made for theatrical release undergo before being shown on television—at worst amounting to a complete reediting process—and that the preservation of archives, like the amassing of any information, is important from a number of historical and theoretico-critical perspectives. But hand in hand with "artistic integrity" and the preservation of archives goes a categorization process involving hierarchical relegation, choice and discard, and so on. These are not accidents external to the process, and thus there is always already deformation or modification of documents, even in terms of the frameworks into which they are received. A less theorized reaction to the issue of colorization underlines this point. Writing on the op-ed page of the *New York Times*, Woody Allen says: "What's at stake is a moral issue and how our culture chooses to define itself. *No one should be able to alter an artist's work in any way whatsoever, for any reason, without the artist's consent.*

---

[8] "SCS Statement on Creative Rights," *Cinema Journal* 27, no. 2 (Winter 1988), 5–7.

It's really as simple as that" (June 28, 1987; our emphasis). One could ask Allen any number of questions, such as: If the artist is not alive to give his consent, does that belong to his heirs, as some laws decree? More importantly, what does it mean to alter a work, and do the conditions of reception have anything to do with that? Does spectating not perform an alteration? What about the simple effect of the lamp and mechanism on celluloid that means a film changes—with rips, scratches and so on—every time it is seen? As Paolo Cherchi Usai has pointed out, for each screening of a film "its aesthetic changes, since each copy ends up possessing an identity of its own, distinct from all the others."[9] Does this mean for Allen that a film should only ever be seen once, never distributed in different copies? How can the artist foresee all the possible cases where his consent would be required? For us, a work of art is constituted by an authorial abrogation, and since it exists nowhere in an originary form, it is always already altered.[10]

Cinema as a form of the technē has never existed in a natural form, has never attained a form that could be called natural. It has any number of distinct historical definitions, involving any number of distinct practices. Those distinctions cannot be established once and for all time; they are open to redefinition on the basis of whatever conceptual format is used to constitute them. The postal is one such conceptual format, defining itself in opposition to the historicist, the semiological, the psychoanalytic, and so on. In a more important sense, however, the postal, by deferring its own definition through a series of other terms like the technē, deconstructs its own conceptual support, seeks to be the basis for a history of and a mark of the end of a certain epoch of conceptual thinking. Thus cinema, analyzed as technological halt or

---

[9] "The Unfortunate Spectator," *Sight and Sound* (Summer 1987), 173.

[10] As an interesting counterpoint we read John Updike in the same issue of the *New York Times*, writing on film adaptations of literary works (would this be an "alteration" in Allen's terms, and if so, where and how would consent begin and end? Would it be in simple legal terms by the signing of a contract?). For Updike, "Movie makers, like creative spirits everywhere, must be free; they owe nothing to the authors of books they adapt except the money they have agreed to pay them." Updike encourages alteration as normal, but in the same breath his notion of a "free creative spirit" reinforces the assumptions that allow for Allen's conservative approach. Indeed, a little further along in the same article he refers to "the inner coherence works of art should have, the ultimate simplicity of one voice speaking," and it becomes clear that he tends to share with Allen a most logocentric notion of artistic creation, in spite of the nuance that gave rise to an opposite point of view in one case (although we do not in fact have his views on colorization, they could well coincide with Allen's). More strident views in favor of this "battle to preserve our humanity" are represented by George Lucas and Steven Spielberg in *The Washington Post*, 28 February 1988.

staging post within the postal, promises not to be the same cinema we see today.

If cinema in general can be seen as relating to the postcard in terms of its technology, what of film texts in particular? How might they be re-marked as postcards? We noted in passing at the beginning of this discussion that the postcard shared with cinema a certain heterogeneity of the iconic and linguistic. To evoke again Barthes's categories elaborated in "Rhetoric of the Image," it can be added that the functions of the linguistic or written message on a postcard well exceed what he calls "anchorage" and "relay" (cf. *Image—Music—Text*, 38–41). The two sides of the card function in opposition more than in concert, though that opposition is not simply dialectic, and apart from a caption or legend the written message need not refer to the image. (It is worth noting in this regard that during the early history of postcards, messages were only allowed on the picture side so as not to interfere with the address.[11]) Thus there is a radical discontinuity not only between the two sides of the card, similar to that between image and sound tracks in cinema, but also between various elements within the written message—caption, address, greeting, and signature—suggesting that a similar heterogeneity might remain to be exploited among elements of the visual side, which the logocentrism of monocular perspective and the effects of narrative centering have served to occlude. The written side of a postcard effects a grammatization of the image in the Derridean sense, as discussed in the previous chapter; the image is "written upon," has writing "written into" it, by virtue of the heterogeneity inscribed upon it. If by no other means than an effect of metonymic contamination—the divisions of the written side reflecting upon the visual side—the image is forced to reveal its own implicit structures of heterogeneity explicit in the writing. (Conversely, is not the final destiny of the writing on the postcard to be turned to the wall?)

Thus the relation between image (track) and linguistic (track) in the postcard, which we are putting forward as a model for cinema, is akin to the *double bande* (double band/tape/track, double bind, double erection) that Derrida develops in *Glas*. There the Hegel track, more reasoned, more discursive, more masculine perhaps, lies opposite, or apposite to, the Genet track, more irreverent, more delirious, more feminine perhaps, except that those distinctions do not hold but

[11] See Frank Staff, *The Picture Postcard and Its Origins* (London: Lutterworth Press, 1979), 48–49, 61–62.

change from one track to the other, and the coherence of each is, as a result, internally divided:

> They [the columns] are not opposite, they are, however, hetero-geneous . . . one column does not speak the language of the other, nor does it obey the same rhythm nor the same law . . . however they communicate with each other: because these columns are not intact, because they are double, oblique, because there are peep-holes,[12] shades, a series of exchanges is established between them.
> (Kofman, *Lectures de Derrida*, 148–49; our translation)

In actual fact, in the case of the postcard that is the pretext for Derrida's text, that showing Plato and Socrates,[13] writing comes to invade the image most explicitly, for it is Matthew Paris's labeling upon the im-age itself of the figures represented (perhaps his mislabeling) that has Plato dictating to Socrates and thus gives rise to much of Derrida's discussion and especially the notion of radical reversibility.

Only a gesture of *Aufhebung*, a logocentric onto-theology, would discover a fundamental disunity simply in order to mend it, with the idea that the end of all things is the intact state in which they presum-ably began. Derrida's approach differs from the start, for he finds no originary unity but rather a series of always already fractured effects. In the postcard-cinema disunity is explicit, and it is only that logocen-tric gesture that would seek to deny it, whether in the film production tying dialogue to image in the overwhelming majority of films or in the critical operation reading sense as fundamentally coherent and re-coverable. Derrida takes the disunity of the postcard as a basic struc-ture that proliferates throughout the text, so the heterogeneity of the written message, starting with the fundamental division of the address by the event of non-arrival, repeats itself on both sides of the card. For the card's image is itself divided over and over by Derrida's play on Paris's squares and lines and is cut up to produce new versions, paro-dies, inversions, profanities, and so on, all of those possibilities being inscribed from the beginning. Disunity also enters as a structure fun-damental to both postcard and film as a result of repetition. Like Der-rida's series of postcards, all the same one, all sent to the same ad-dressee, each with a different message, the frames of a film operate a kind of difference as deferral while the sound track inscribes a linearity

---

[12] In French *des judas*, a word that Derrida develops in the text as a shorthand for his signature (JD).

[13] The postcard in question comes from a thirteenth-century fortune-telling book by Matthew Paris, now in the Bodleian Library, Oxford.

over what might well be a static shot, the difference being occluded by a presumed but in fact mythical continuity.

That "Envois" acts as a film is explicitly suggested on a number of occasions, precisely because of its being constituted as a series of images with sound/written track. It is cinematic also because of the farcical or burlesque quality of the relation between Plato and Socrates, like characters from a Marx brothers film, and Derrida's manipulation of that relation that gives it the effect of motion: "Put a filter over *Socrates*, multiply the filters, mobilize them, spread them out in every direction, isolate the parts of each personage, and screen the film . . ." (17; translation modified). Although for the most part cinema is evoked in terms of its fragmentary nature, as though this were an old film we were watching, before the standardization of 24 fps, it also exists as part of a totalizing dream or desire that the narrator recognizes as being as much the outer limit of writing as anything else, "the old impossible dream of exhaustive and instantaneous registration, don't on any account lose a word—for I hold to words above all, words whose rarefaction is unbearable for me in writing—the old dream of the complete electro-cardio-encephalo-LOGO-icono-cinemato-biogram" (68; translation modified). However, we do not wish to develop here a thematics of the cinema in "Envois," nor does explicit mention of film serve, except as an aside, to establish the structural relations between it and the postcard.

Another point of comparison between the postcard and the cinematic text is an effect that, for want of a better term, we could call iconoclastic. Situated as it is on the margins of painting (or the visual arts), and literature (or writing in general), the postcard seeks to deconstruct the monumental pretensions of the artistic genre it represents, as well as those of philosophy for which, in the discussions comprising "Envois," it becomes to a great extent the medium. It is content, like the disputed letters of Plato, to be relegated to the domain of the apocryphal, the minor, and the vulgar. Film, on the contrary, though it has for the greater part of its history actively combatted a similar relegation, now seems poised, with the advent of mass media on a grand scale, either to continue that combat and so inevitably consign itself to history along with literature and philosophy (which does not mean disappearing) or rather to participate in a redefinition of the notion of art, especially in its relations to technology and the sciences.[14] The argument is not finally what constitutes high art or low

---

[14] For Ulmer, film and video are more important from a Derridean perspective in terms of their pedagogical potential. Following what Derrida says in *Etats généraux de la*

art, or the role, however important, economics plays within this medium or that, for economics and politics of one sort or another were
never absent from literature and philosophy, as Derrida has amply
demonstrated. It is rather that, after the postcard, or given the postal,
art, which has always been an effect of the technē, becomes a question
of ends: ends in the sense of positions and order, and ends in the sense
of address and destination. Within the realm of art or culture, cinema's
position or order (and thus that of film as document), is not a given,
nor even something that it will merit or achieve by virtue of its possessing a certain set of attributes. It is instead a position that derives
from a political configuration, a result of the shifting relations it has
with its outside—not just other forms or genres, other media, whatever we have come to call the extracinematic—but a veritable postal
network. Furthermore, film's end in the sense of destination opens the
whole question of critical and theoretical approaches, and it has been
our aim throughout this discussion to encourage what we take to be
the most radical and most productive of those, call it deconstruction.
A certain body of criticism risks consigning film, or restricting it, to
an automated logocentrism that presumes to have known film's address before it was even sent. Even, and perhaps especially, those critical approaches inspired by psychoanalysis still depend upon an idea of
spectator positioning that seems to assume arrival, a configuration or
network of looks that directs sense, in spite of its detours, to a singular
destination. The sorts of readings we are promoting here, seek, on the
other hand, to send film's messages further along the path to dissemination.

In "Envois" the most far-reaching potential of the postcard lies in its
reversibility: "My postcard naively overturns everything. In any event,
it allegorizes the catastrophically unknown of the order. Finally one
begins no longer to understand what to come [*venir*], to come before,
to come after, to foresee [*prévenir*], to come back [*revenir*] all mean—
along with the difference of the generations, and then to inherit, to

---

philosophie concerning the need for philosophy to concern itself with the media instead
of viewing them as the threat of contamination, Ulmer rightly compares such an attitude of condescension toward television to Plato's deprecation of writing as bastardiza-
tion (*Applied Grammatology*, 69). For him, following Derrida again in his deconstruction
of conceptual thinking based on the "philosophemes of sight and hearing (theory and
voice)," the audio-visual media offer the possibility of teaching "within the enframing
of a sensorium reorganized to reflect the contact qualities of the chemical senses" (98).
What is not really clear in Ulmer's discussion is why those media should be any more
useful from a pedagogical perspective than others, apart from their mere novelty. We
would argue that the visual media need to undergo a more thorough deconstruction
before they can be assured of any particularly revolutionary pedagogical potential.

write one's will, to dictate, to speak, to take a dictation, etc." (21). And that arises not because Matthew Paris may have made a mistake and assigned Socrates' name to Plato and vice versa but because the message is always already divided in its address by the event of misaddress, non-arrival, or adestination. It is the notion of order underwriting that of the end (or vice versa) that is called into question by the postcard, for if the end does not "arrive," does not sit well, does not provide the assurance that metaphysics has always sought in it, putting the seal on its coherence and keeping it intact; if that does not occur, then everything that came before and whose order presupposed that end is undone.

Film as postcard, must, in the final analysis, be read as an adestined text, despite its provenance in certain shifting political and economic configurations. The context in which film—film in general and any given film—is viewed, read, consumed, analyzed, and so on need not be that which film itself determines, for in the end film cannot so determine its own destination. What we have been proposing throughout this discussion as a possible new destination for film—though by no means a settled one, not a destination in fact—namely the context of the writings of Derrida, might seem to some to be a manipulation, a forcing of film and cinema into a direction that is not normally, or not naturally, theirs. It would be our contention, however, that it is only by starting from that context, that of a radical conception of context, of detachability or reversibility, that film and cinema can continue to be important in a shifting field of visual media and media in general. For film never was simply visual, nor the visual ever simply that.

Derrida refers to the notion of reversibility as "catastrophic" (*The Post Card*, 22), with all the apocalyptic overtones that that word conveys. But he also mentions the rhetorical sense of the word, that of the "fall" at the end of a line of poetry—*cata/strophe*. And here it is related to the "apostrophe"—a form of personal address within the context of a discourse to a wider public—that sets up the basic divided structure of "Envois" with its public and private addressees. Catastrophe, then, suggests a sort of inevitability that does not come to language from the outside but that is envisaged from its beginning, in its beginning. It is within that perspective that we envisage radical changes in the concept of cinema and the critical discourses that take it for their object—neither as an accident nor a harm that we would wish upon the medium; rather, as both an event within a wider context and an apostrophe (an interpellation or provocation even) that seeks to have cinema respond from an unexpected position, thus bringing about change in the conceptual framework enclosing it.

What Derrida's postal principle insists upon is that even the visual as idea, as mental representation, depends on and participates in the technē; that there never was anything that was not already mediated, not already in the same structural space as writing, film, and media; and that there never was truth without its postmen or factors to expedite it, assure its delivery, and in the same movement open the possibility, the structural necessity of its diversion: "There would only be '*facteurs*,' and therefore no vérité [sic]. Only 'media,' take this into account in every war against the media. One can never substitute the immediate for the media(ted) but only other apparatuses and other forces" (194; translation modified). Cinema, as a function of the postal, is thus an element within a host of media apparatuses—some of which are in the process of transformation—that will inevitably transform cinema. However much desire or theoretical argument, including ours, might seek to foresee a future position for cinema, or for film theory, within those apparatuses, no amount of desire or theory can determine and destine the future of cinema in anything other than the most provisional sense. That desire and that theory, become institutions, can of course install a certain form of or position for cinema, within a given historical context and time frame; but cinema will never be restricted to that. Like desire, like theory, like any mediated form that has no natural origin but functions within the domain of the technē, cinema will remain after all that, and after all this, to be rewritten.

WORKS CITED

WORKS BY JACQUES DERRIDA

"But, beyond . . . (Open Letter to Ann McClintock and Rob Nixon)." *Critical Inquiry* 13 (1986), 155–70.

Dissemination. Translated by Barbara Johnson. Chicago: University of Chicago Press, 1982.

L'Ecriture et la différence. Paris: Seuil, 1967.

"Entre crochets." *Digraphe*, no. 8 (1976), 97–114.

The Ear of the Other. Edited by Christie V. McDonald. Translated by Avital Ronell and Peggy Kamuf. New York: Schocken Books, 1985.

"Economimesis." In *Mimesis: Des articulations*, edited by Sylviane Agacinski et al., 55–93. Paris: Aubier-Flammarion, 1975.

Feu la cendre/Ciò che resta del fuoco. Florence: Sansoni, 1984.

"Fors." *Georgia Review* 31 (1977), 64–116.

Glas. Translated by John P. Leavey and Richard Rand. Lincoln: University of Nebraska Press, 1986.

"Ja, ou le faux-bond." *Digraphe*, no. 11 (1977), 83–121.

"The Law of Genre." In *Glyph* 7, 202–29. Baltimore: The Johns Hopkins University Press, 1980.

"The Laws of Reflection: Nelson Mandela, in Admiration." In *For Nelson Mandela*, edited by Jacques Derrida and Mustapha Tleli, 13–42. New York: Seaver Books/ Henry Holt and Co., 1987.

"Limited Inc." In *Glyph 2*, 162–254. Baltimore: The Johns Hopkins University Press, 1977.

"Living On: Border Lines." In *Deconstruction and Criticism*, edited by Harold Bloom et al., 97–103. New York: Seabury Press, 1979.

Margins of Philosophy. Translated by Alan Bass. Chicago: University of Chicago Press, 1982.

"Me—Psychoanalysis." *Diacritics* 9, no. 1 (1979), 4–12.

"My Chances/*Mes Chances*: A Rendezvous with Some Epicurean Stereophonies." In *Taking Chances: Derrida, Psychoanalysis and Literature*, edited by Joseph H. Smith and William Kerrigan, 1–32. Baltimore: The Johns Hopkins University Press, 1984.

"No Apocalypse, Not Now (full speed ahead, seven missiles, seven missives)." *Diacritics* 14, no. 2 (1984), 20–31.

Of Grammatology. Translated by Gayatri Spivak. Baltimore: The Johns Hopkins University Press, 1974.

"Pas." In *Parages*, 19–116. Paris: Galilée, 1986.

Positions. Translated by Alan Bass. Chicago: University of Chicago Press, 1981.

"The Principle of Reason: The University in the Eyes of Its Pupils." *Diacritics* 13, no. 3 (1983), 3–20.

The Post Card: From Socrates to Freud and Beyond. Translated by Alan Bass. Chicago: University of Chicago Press, 1987.

Psyché: Inventions de l'autre. Paris: Galilée, 1987.

"Racism's Last Word." *Critical Inquiry* 12 (1985), 290–99.

Signéponge/Signsponge. Translated by Richard Rand. New York: Columbia University Press, 1984.

Speech and Phenomena. Translated by David Allison. Evanston: Northwestern University Press, 1973.

Spurs: Nietzsche's Styles. Translated by Barbara Harlow. Chicago: University of Chicago Press, 1979.

The Truth in Painting. Translated by Geoff Bennington and Ian McLeod. Chicago: University of Chicago Press, 1987.

Writing and Difference. Translated by Alan Bass. Chicago: University of Chicago Press, 1978.

Derrida, Jacques, and Christie V. McDonald. "Choreographies." *Diacritics* 12, no. 2 (1982), 66–76.

OTHER WORKS CITED

Anderson, Joseph, and Barbara Anderson. "Motion Perception in Motion Pictures." In *The Cinematic Apparatus*, edited by Teresa de Lauretis and Stephen Heath, 76–95. New York: St. Martin's Press, 1980.

Andrew, J. Dudley. *Concepts in Film Theory.* New York: Oxford University Press, 1984.

———. *Film in the Aura of Art.* Princeton: Princeton University Press, 1984.

Althusser, Louis, and Etienne Balibar. *Reading Capital.* Translated by Ben Brewster. London: Verso, 1979.

Armes, Roy. *Patterns of Realism.* Totowa, N.J.: A. S. Barnes, 1971.

Balkin, J. M. "Deconstructive Practice and Legal Theory." *Yale Law Review* 96 (1987), 743–86.

Barthes, Roland. *Camera Lucida: Reflections on Photography.* Translated by Richard Howard. New York: Hill and Wang, 1981.

———. *La Chambre claire.* Paris: Cahiers du cinéma/Gallimard/ Seuil, 1980.

———. "The Discourse of History." Translated by Stephen Bann, in *Comparative Criticism: A Yearbook*, 3:3–20, edited by E. S. Schaffer. Cambridge: Cambridge University Press, 1981.

———. *Image—Music—Text.* Translated by Stephen Heath. New York: Hill and Wang, 1977.

Bass, Alan. "The Double Game." In *Taking Chances: Derrida, Psychoanalysis and Literature*, edited by Joseph H. Smith and William Kerrigan, 66–85. Baltimore: The Johns Hopkins University Press, 1984.

Baudry, Jean-Louis. "The Apparatus: Metapsychological Approaches to the Impression of Reality in Cinema." In *Narrative, Apparatus, Ideology*, edited by Philip Rosen, 299–318. New York: Columbia University Press, 1986.

———. "Writing, Fiction, Ideology." *Afterimage*, no. 5 (1974), 23–39.

Bazin, André. "The Evolution of the Western." In *What Is Cinema?* Translated by Hugh Gray, 2:149–57. Berkeley: University of California Press, 1971.

———. "The Ontology of the Photographic Image." In *What Is Cinema?* Translated by Hugh Gray, 1:9–16. Berkeley: University of California Press, 1967.

Bellour, Raymond. "Le Blocage symbolique." *Communications*, no. 23 (1975), 235–350.

Benjamin, Walter. "The Work of Art in the Age of Mechanical Reproduction." In *Illuminations*, edited by Hannah Arendt, 217–51. New York: Schocken Books, 1969.

Berger, Peter L. and Thomas Luckmann. *The Social Construction of Reality*. New York: Doubleday, 1966.

Bordwell, David, Janet Staiger, and Kristin Thompson. *The Classical Hollywood Cinema: Film Style and Mode of Production to 1960*. New York: Columbia University Press, 1985.

Brunette, Peter. *Roberto Rossellini*. New York: Oxford University Press, 1987.

Cahiers du cinéma collective. "John Ford's *Young Mr. Lincoln*." In *Movies and Methods: An Anthology*, edited by Bill Nichols, 492–529. Berkeley: University of California Press, 1976.

Caughie, J., ed. *Theories of Authorship*. London and New York: Routledge & Kegan Paul, 1981.

Chatman, Seymour. *Antonioni; Or, the Surface of the World*. Berkeley: University of California Press, 1985.

———. *Story and Discourse: Narrative Structure in Fiction and Film*. Ithaca: Cornell University Press, 1978.

Collet, Jean. *Le Cinéma de François Truffaut*. Paris: Pierre Lherminier Editeur, 1977.

Comolli, Jean-Louis. "Technique and Ideology: Camera, Perspective, Depth of Field (Part I)." In *Movies and Methods (Vol II): An Anthology*, edited by Bill Nichols, 40–57. Berkeley: University of California Press, 1985. And in *Narrative, Apparatus, Ideology: A Film Theory Reader*, parts 3 and 4, edited by Philip Rosen, 421–43. New York: Columbia University Press, 1986.

——— and Jean Narboni. "Cinema/Ideology/Criticism." In *Movies and Methods: An Anthology*, edited by Bill Nichols, 22–30. Berkeley: University of California Press, 1976.

Conley, Tom. "A Trace of Style." In *Displacement: Derrida and After*, edited by Mark Krupnick, 74–92. Bloomington: Indiana University Press, 1983.

Cook, David. *A History of Narrative Film*. New York: Norton, 1981.

Crary, Jonathan. "Techniques of the Observer." In *October*, no. 45 (Fall 1988), 3–35.

Crisp, Colin G. *François Truffaut*. London: November Books, 1972.

Culler, Jonathan. *On Deconstruction*. Ithaca: Cornell University Press, 1982.

de Lauretis, Teresa. *Alice Doesn't: Feminism Semiotics Cinema*. Bloomington: Indiana University Press, 1984.

de Man, Paul. "Hegel on the Sublime." In *Displacement: Derrida and After*, edited by Mark Krupnick, 139–53. Bloomington: Indiana University Press, 1983.

de Saussure, Ferdinand. *Course in General Linguistics*. Translated by Wade Baskin. New York: McGraw Hill, 1966.

Doane, Mary Ann. "The Voice in the Cinema: The Articulation of Body and Space." In *Narrative, Apparatus, Ideology*, edited by Philip Rosen, 335–48. New York: Columbia University Press, 1986.

Eagleton, Terry. *Literary Theory: An Introduction*. Minneapolis: University of Minnesota Press, 1983.

———. *Walter Benjamin, or, Towards a Revolutionary Criticism*. London: Verso, 1981.

Ellis, Jack C. *A History of Film*. 2nd ed. Englewood Cliffs, N.J.: Prentice-Hall, 1985.

Etats généraux de la philosophie. Paris: Flammarion, 1979.

Fell, John L. *A History of Film*. New York: Holt, Rinehart and Winston, 1979.

Felman, Shoshana. *Jacques Lacan and the Adventure of Insight*. Cambridge: Harvard University Press, 1987.

Fischer, Hanns, et al. *François Truffaut*. Munich: Carl Hanser Verlag, 1974.

Frow, John. *Marxism and Literary History*. Cambridge: Harvard University Press, 1986.

Frug, Gerald E. "The Ideology of Bureaucracy in American Law." *Harvard Law Review* 97 (1984), 1277–1388.

Gallop, Jane. *The Daughter's Seduction: Feminism and Psychoanalysis*. Ithaca: Cornell University Press, 1982.

———. *Reading Lacan*. Ithaca: Cornell University Press, 1985.

Garner, Shirley Nelson, Claire Kahane, and Madelon Sprengnether, eds. *The (M)Other Tongue: Essays in Feminist Psychoanalytic Interpretation*. Ithaca: Cornell University Press, 1985.

Gasché, Rodolphe. "Deconstruction as Criticism." In *Glyph 6*, 117–216. Baltimore: The Johns Hopkins University Press, 1979.

———. *The Tain of the Mirror: Derrida and the Philosophy of Reflection*. Cambridge: Harvard University Press, 1986.

Giannetti, Louis D. *Understanding Movies*. 3rd ed. Englewood Cliffs, N.J.: Prentice-Hall, 1982.

Gleick, James. *Chaos: Making a New Science*. New York: Viking, 1987.

Heath, Stephen. "Difference." *Screen* 19, no. 3 (1978), 51–112.

———. *Questions of Cinema*. Bloomington: Indiana University Press, 1981.

Heidegger, Martin. *The Question Concerning Technology and Other Essays.* Translated by William Lovitt. New York: Harper and Row, 1977.

Henderson, Brian. *A Critique of Film Theory.* New York: E.P. Dutton, 1980.

Irigaray, Luce. *This Sex Which Is Not One.* Translated by Catherine Porter with Carolyn Burke. Ithaca: Cornell University Press, 1985.

Jakobson, Roman. "The Dominant." In *Readings in Russian Poetics: Formalist and Structuralist Views*, edited by Ladislav Matejka and Krystyna Pomorska, 82–87. Cambridge: MIT Press, 1971.

Jameson, Fredric. *The Political Unconscious: Narrative as a Socially Symbolic Act.* Ithaca: Cornell University Press, 1980.

Jardine, Alice. *Gynesis: Configurations of Woman and Modernity.* Ithaca: Cornell University Press, 1985.

Johnson, Barbara. *The Critical Difference.* Baltimore and London: The Johns Hopkins University Press, 1980.

———. *A World of Difference.* Baltimore: The Johns Hopkins University Press, 1987.

Kawin, Bruce F. *How Movies Work.* New York: Macmillan, 1987.

Kitses, Jim. *Horizons West.* Bloomington: Indiana University Press, 1969.

Kofman, Sarah. *Camera obscura: De l'idéologie.* Paris: Galilée, 1973.

———. *Lectures de Derrida.* Paris: Galilée, 1984.

Kolker, Robert. *Bernardo Bertolucci.* New York: Oxford University Press, 1985.

Kracauer, Siegfried. *From Caligari to Hitler.* Princeton: Princeton University Press, 1971.

Kuntzel, Thierry. "The Film-Work." *Enclitic* 2, no. 1 (1976), 38–61.

———. "The Film-Work, 2." *Camera Obscura*, no. 5 (1980), 6–69.

Lacoue-Labarthe, Philippe, and Jean-Luc Nancy, eds. *Les Fins de l'homme: A partir du travail de Jacques Derrida.* Paris: Galilée, 1981.

Leitch, Vincent. *Deconstructive Criticism: An Advanced Introduction.* New York: Columbia University Press, 1983.

MacCabe, Colin. *Tracking the Signifier.* Minneapolis: University of Minnesota Press, 1985.

MacCannell, Juliet Flower. *Figuring Lacan: Criticism and the Cultural Unconscious.* Lincoln: University of Nebraska Press, 1986.

McClintock, Ann, and Rob Nixon. "No Names Apart: The Separation of Word and History in Derrida's 'Le Dernier Mot du Racisme.'" *Critical Inquiry* 13 (1986), 140–54.

McHoul, Alec, and David Wills. "The Late(r) Barthes: Constituting fragmenting subjects," *Boundary 2* 14, nos. 1–2 (1985–86), 261–78.

———. *Writing Pynchon: Strategies in Fictional Analysis.* London: Macmillan Press, 1989.

Macksey, Richard, and Eugenio Donato, eds. *The Structuralist Controversy.* Baltimore: The Johns Hopkins University Press, 1972.

Magny, Joël. "Epiphanie du réel: André Bazin et le cinéma," *CinémAction*, no. 20 (1982), 42–53.

Marks, Elaine, and Isabelle Courtivron, eds. *New French Feminisms.* Amherst: University of Massachusetts Press, 1980.

Metz, Christian. *Essais sur la signification au cinéma.* Vol. 2. Paris: Klincksieck, 1972.

———. *Film Language.* Translated by Michael Taylor. New York: Oxford University Press, 1974.

———. *The Imaginary Signifier.* Bloomington: Indiana University Press, 1982.

———. *Langage et cinéma* (Nouvelle édition augmentée d'une postface). Paris: Editions Albatros, 1977.

———. *Language and Cinema.* The Hague: Mouton, 1974.

———. "Sur mon travail." In *Essais sémiotiques,* 167–72. Paris: Klincksieck, 1977.

Miller, J. Hillis. "The Search for Grounds in Literary Study." In *Rhetoric and Form: Deconstruction at Yale,* edited by Robert Con Davis and Ronald Schleifer, 19–36. Norman: University of Oklahoma Press, 1985.

Monaco, James. *The New Wave: Truffaut, Godard, Chabrol, Rohmer, Rivette.* New York: Oxford University Press, 1976.

Nichols, Bill. *Ideology and the Image.* Bloomington: Indiana University Press, 1981.

Norris, Christopher. *Deconstruction: Theory and Practice.* London and New York: Methuen, 1982.

———. *Derrida.* Cambridge: Harvard University Press, 1987.

Oswald, Laura. "The Subject in question: New Directions in semiotics and cinema." *Semiotica* 48, nos. 3/4 (1984), 293–317.

———. "Semiotics and/or deconstruction: In quest of cinema." *Semiotica* 60, nos. 3/4 (1986), 315–41.

Oudart, Jean-Pierre. "Cinema and Suture." *Screen* 18, no. 4 (1977–78), 35–47.

Peller, Gary. "The Metaphysics of American Law." *California Law Review* 73 (1985), 1151–1290.

Polan, Dana. " 'Desire shifts the Differance': Figural Poetics and Figural Politics in the Film Theory of Marie-Claire Ropars." *Camera Obscura,* no. 12 (1984), 67–89.

Plissart, Marie-Françoise, and Jacques Derrida. *Right of Inspection.* Translated by David Wills. *Art & Text,* no. 32 (1989), 10–18.

Robinson, David. *The History of World Cinema.* New York: Stein and Day, 1981.

Rodowick, David. "The Figure and the Text." *Diacritics* 15, no. 1 (1985), 34–50.

Ropars-Wuilleumier, Marie-Claire. "The Disembodied Voice (*India Song*)." *Yale French Studies,* no. 60 (1980), 241–68.

———. "The Graphic in Filmic Writing: *A bout de souffle,* or the Erratic Alphabet." *Enclitic* 5, no. 2/6, no. 1 (1981–82), 147–61.

———. *Le Texte divisé.* Paris: Presses Universitaires de France, 1981.

Rose, Jacqueline. "Introduction—II." In *Feminine Sexuality: Jacques Lacan and the école freudienne,* edited by Juliet Mitchell and Jacqueline Rose, 27–57. New York: Norton, 1983.

Rosen, Philip. "The Politics of the Sign and Film Theory." *October*, no. 17 (1981), 2–21.

Ryan, Michael. "Deconstruction and Social Theory." In *Displacement: Derrida and After*, edited by Mark Krupnick, 154–68. Bloomington: Indiana University Press, 1983.

——. *Marxism and Deconstruction*. Baltimore: The Johns Hopkins University Press, 1982.

Samuels, Charles Thomas. *Encountering Directors*. New York: G. P. Putnam's Sons, 1972.

Searle, John R. "Reiterating the Differences: A Reply to Derrida." In *Glyph 1*, 198–208. Baltimore: The Johns Hopkins University Press, 1977.

Schatz, Thomas. *Hollywood Genres*. New York: Random House, 1981.

"SCS Statement on Creative Rights." *Cinema Journal* 27, no. 2 (1988), 5–7.

Silverman, Kaja. *The Subject of Semiotics*. New York: Oxford University Press, 1983.

Spivak, Gayatri Chakravorty. *In Other Worlds: Essays in Cultural Politics*. New York: Routledge, 1987.

Staff, Frank. *The Picture Postcard and its Origins*. London: Lutterworth Press, 1979.

Stanford Law Review 36, nos. 1–2 (1984).

Studlar, Gaylyn. "Masochism and the Perverse Pleasures of the Cinema." *Movies and Methods (Vol. II): An Anthology*, edited by Bill Nichols, 602–21. Berkeley: University of California Press, 1985.

Thompson, Kristin. "The Concept of Cinematic Excess." In *Narrative, Apparatus, Ideology: A Film Theory Reader*, edited by Philip Rosen, 130–42. New York: Columbia University Press, 1986.

Tudor, Andrew. *Theories of Film*. New York: Viking Press, 1973.

Turim, Maureen Cheryn. *Abstractions in Avant-Garde Films*. Ann Arbor: UMI Research Press, 1985.

Ulmer, Gregory. *Applied Grammatology*. Baltimore: The Johns Hopkins University Press, 1985.

——. "Sounding the Unconscious." In *Glossary*, by John P. Leavey Jr., 23–129 (right-hand pages only). Lincoln: University of Nebraska Press, 1986.

Usai, Paolo Cherchi. "The Unfortunate Spectator." *Sight and Sound* (Summer 1987), 170–74.

Warminski, Andrzej. *Readings in Interpretation: Hölderlin, Hegel, Heidegger*. Minneapolis: University of Minnesota Press, 1987.

White, Hayden. *The Content of the Form*. Baltimore: The Johns Hopkins University Press, 1987.

Wills, David. "Deposition: Introduction to *Right of Inspection* [*Droit de regards*]." *Art & Text*, no. 32 (1989), 10–18.

——. "Post/Card/Match/Book/*Envois*/Derrida." *SubStance*, no. 43 (1984), 19–38.

——. "Supreme Court." *Diacritics* 18, no. 3 (1988), 20–31.

INDEX

Abraham, Nicolas, 18n
Adami, Valerio, 121, 126–28
adestination, 64, 180–89, 194, 196–98
Allen, Woody, 123, 191–92
anagram, 83, 99, 127, 131, 152; anagram-maticality, 82–83, 86–94, 99, 112, 121
analogy, 68–69, 72–73, 102, 107, 166; an-alogicality, 88, 93; analogical represen-tation, 72–73, 92–93, 105, 112, 141
Antonioni, Michelangelo, 44–45
apartheid, 27–28
apostrophe, 28, 169–71, 197
Arrivée d'un train en gare de la Ciotat, 70
auteurism, 44–45, 49–50, 64, 185
author, 5, 13, 45, 148–50, 191–92; death of, 64–66, 75, 115, 120. *See also* inten-tionality; signature

Balàzs, Bela, 184
Bataille, Georges, 116
Belmondo, Jean-Paul, 146n
Benveniste, Emile, 55n, 128, 133n
Bergman, Ingmar, 37
Bertolucci, Bernardo, 45
Beuys, Joseph, 125
Bicycle Thieves, 70n
binarism, 109, 140–46, 154–56, 160–70
Blanchot, Maurice, 48n, 120
Blow-up, 184
Blue Velvet, 139, 141–71
Bouquet, Carole, 135n
Breathless, 131–33
Brecht, Bertolt, 160
Bride Wore Black, The, 139–70
Bridge on the River Kwai, The, 144
Brief Encounter, 144

Canterbury Tales, 123
cartouche, 119, 177–79
Chaplin, Charles, 39
chiasmus, 105, 113, 117–18, 127, 137, 169–71
citationality. *See* iterability
Citizen Kane, 139
colorization, 191–92

communication: language as system of, 7–8, 9–10, 86–87, 159–61; science of, 8, 68; telecommunications, 26, 183–87. *See also* adestination; postal; technol-ogy
context, 8, 14, 57, 63, 87–88, 90, 99, 197; in Benjamin, 174–75; in *Blue Velvet*, 145, 153–55

death, 116, 161, 173–74, 179; in *The Bride*, 140, 144, 156, 164–70; in pho-tography, 113–16. *See also* author
deconstruction, 11–13, 72, 136, 139, 157, 188, 196; in America, 5, 21–23, 28–29, 91; as double operation, 11–13, 25, 91–92, 96; and feminism, 20, 32, 95–98 (*see also* feminism); and film history, 34–45; and hermeneutic circle, 44n; and hier-archical thinking, 8–10, 18, 20, 23, 32, 51, 57, 102, 106–7, 146; and history, 22–23, 29–30; and institutions, 24–27, 126, 135–37, 154, 188–91; and legal theory, 8n; and literary studies, 16, 20–21, 24–25, 80–83, 94; and Marxism, 15–16, 21–22, 29; and mimesis, 68–73, 77–78, 83–85; and name of Derrida, 3–6, 59; and pedagogy, 26, 195n; and pol-itics, 21–32, 174–75, 188–89. *See also* logocentrism; metaphysics
Deleuze, Gilles, 20n
Deneuve, Catherine, 146
De Sica, Vittorio, 37, 70n
différance, 4–5, 12–13, 60, 78, 96, 97–98, 118, 181; in *Blue Velvet*, 149, 165
dissemination, 13, 18, 64, 67, 90, 117–18, 196; in Ropars, 130, 132–34. *See also* signature
Diva, 151n
Dreyer, Carl, 184
Duras, Marguerite, 63, 76, 86n, 89, 119, 130

Eisenstein, Sergei, 67, 116, 119, 125, 128–29, 132
Edipo Re, 123

empiricism, 145n, 167n; in film history, 40–44

erasure, 11–12, 118; vs. correction, 149, 165–71

essentialization. *See* totalization

excess, 57–58, 69, 89, 123; in Barthes, 66–67, 109; in *Blue Velvet*, 155–59, 169

expressionism, German, 37–39

feminism, 20n, 32; and film theory, 18–20, 54–56, 58, 76, 153–55. *See also* positioning

figuration. *See* rhetoric

First Name Carmen, 86n

Ford, John, 15n, 124

frame, 13, 48, 66, 99, 101–18, 140, 179

Freud, Sigmund, 15n, 16, 18n, 19n, 20, 119n, 128, 134, 153n, 155, 173, 180, 182–83, 188–90. *See also* psychoanalysis

Genet, Jean, 14, 120, 124, 193

Genette, Gérard, 50n, 57

genre, 45–51, 140–50, 151n, 154–70

Gianni Schicchi, 152

Godard, Jean-Luc, 86, 123, 130

Gold Rush, The, 39

Hartman, Geoffrey, 21

Hegel, G.W.F., 14, 18, 28, 110, 120, 193

Herrmann, Bernard, 150, 152, 162n

hieroglyph, 99, 119, 125–26, 129, 131–34, 140

Hitchcock, Alfred, 122–23, 150–54, 168

Hoffmann, E.T.A., 153n

Hollywood, 17, 21, 40–43, 49, 51n, 129

Huston, John, 123

hymen, 60, 95–97, 105, 112, 144, 157n; in "Double Session," 78–83, 92; screen as, 85–86, 89

India Song, 63, 76, 89, 91, 119, 130–33

inheritance, 4, 182, 188–90, 196–97

intentionality, 58, 64–66, 119, 121–22, 176; in "Double Session," 81n; of film, 124; in Truffaut, 142, 168

invagination, 46–47, 50, 96, 105–6, 118, 122, 127; in *The Bride*, 166

iterability, 86–88, 93

Johnny Guitar, 146n

Jules and Jim, 166

Kafka, Franz, 190

Kant, Immanuel, 9, 28, 100–102, 148, 166

Keats, John, 166

Lacan, Jacques, 15–19, 21, 55, 97, 116, 125, 155, 172, 180–81. *See also* psychoanalysis

Leiris, Michel, 159n

Lifeboat, 123

logocentrism, 4–12, 42, 110, 172, 194, 196; in Benjamin, 176; and "beyond," 91, 125, 186; in *Blue Velvet*, 159; and narrative, 123, 193; and realism, 68, 74, 184. *See also* metaphysics

Lumière (brothers), 70

Lynch, David, 139

Lyotard, Jean-François, 66n

M, 134

Macherey, Pierre, 15

Mallarmé, Stéphane, 60, 79–85, 92–94, 114n

Manon of the Springs, 110

Marnie, 152, 154, 168

Marx Brothers (The), 195

matchbox, 79, 126n

media, 21, 26, 67–68, 172–76, 195–98

metaphysics, 6–7, 10, 53, 78, 93, 97, 197; and ideology, 29–32; and perception, 74n; and realism, 78, 88, 106–7. *See also* logocentrism

mimesis, 69, 80–86, 92–94, 107, 117, 129

mise en abyme, 69, 92, 137, 152, 156

Mississippi Mermaid, 146n, 148

monocular perspective, 15, 106–7, 108–9, 112

Most Dangerous Game, The, 134

Mulvey, Laura, 155

Murders in the Rue Morgue, The, 137

naming, 27, 66, 89, 119–24, 130, 153n, 163–71. *See also* signature

Narboni, Jean, 15

narrative, 106, 108–9; in *Blue Velvet*, 155–57; in *Breathless* and *India Song*, 89, 130–33; in *The Bride*, 154, 168; cinema, 38, 54–55, 61, 75–76, 97; film history as, 35–37, 39, 44–45; and writing effects, 67, 123–24, 135, 186, 191, 193

natural. *See* original

neorealism. *See* realism
Nietzsche, Friedrich, 25, 29, 74, 119n
North by Northwest, 122

Olmi, Ermanno, 37
Open City, 37
origin, 10, 57, 62, 64, 77, 85, 159, 182;
  originary, 7–8, 90, 103, 128, 134, 137,
  171, 194
original, 47, 68, 74, 88; cf. copy, 69, 73–
  75, 154, 174, 176–79; as natural vs. art/
  artificial, 148, 172–79, 182
Ossessione, 37

Paisan, 37
parergon, 9, 60, 78, 100–102, 140, 148,
  179
Paris, Matthew, 194, 197
Pasolini, Pier Paolo, 123
Peau douce, La, 158
periodization: in film history, 36–38
Persephone, 159n
pharmakon, 9, 60, 65, 78, 81n, 96, 179
Plato, 9, 65, 72, 80, 82–85, 173–74, 179,
  187–89, 194–95, 197
play, 14, 66, 82, 91–92, 95–96, 133, 161;
  wordplay, 13–14, 134, 145
Pleynet, Marcelin, 15
Poe, Edgar Allan, 18, 137, 180
Ponge, Francis, 91, 120, 124
positioning, 135, 157n, 180, 182, 185–86,
  196; feminist critique of, 55, 152–53; of
  spectator, 17–18, 30, 190, 196
postal, 172, 175, 180–90, 192–93, 196–98
postcard, 79, 125, 126n, 172, 184–85,
  193–97
psychoanalysis, 52, 56–58, 76, 105, 163,
  172, 180, 196; and *Blue Velvet*, 151–57;
  of cinematic apparatus, 72–73, 116; as
  institution, 188–91; and photography,
  174–75. *See also* Freud, Sigmund; Lacan, Jacques; positioning
Puccini, Giacomo, 152
punctum, 67, 111–14, 117

Ray, Nicholas, 146n
reading, 5, 34n, 88–92, 118, 122, 132–37,
  142; *Blue Velvet*, 145–63, 167–71; and
  intentionality, 64–66; and interpretation, 57–59
realism, 16–17, 29, 83, 85, 94, 106–7,

109–10, 190; in Bazin, 68–78; in *The
  Bride*, 158–64; of close-up, 184; Italian
  neorealism, 36–37, 74
Rear Window, 150, 152
rebus, 119, 125–26, 134, 145, 159, 161,
  169–71
Renoir, Jean, 123–24
repetition, 23, 47, 50, 68–69, 86–87, 194–
  95; reproduction as, 174–78. *See also* iterability
reversibility, 87, 136, 178, 194, 196–97
rhetoric, 22, 75, 88, 117, 137, 146, 197;
  Derrida's, 78–79, 125, 126n; figuration
  as, 56–58, 157, 188
Rossellini, Isabella, 167, 169
Rossellini, Roberto, 37
Rousseau, Jean-Jacques, 8–9, 83
Rules of the Game, The, 123

Saussure, Ferdinand de, 6–7, 10–11, 53,
  119, 128
semiology. *See* semiotics
semiotics, 50–55, 61, 62, 90, 106–8, 132,
  135, 177; and postal, 188, 192; semiotic
  politics, 24, 29–30
Seurat, Georges, 101
signature, 4, 13, 66, 119–24, 139, 150,
  190; in Adami, 127–28; in *Blue Velvet*,
  145, 161, 169; in *India Song*, 130; in Titus-Carmel, 178–79; in Truffaut, 142
Smellovision, 110, 124
Socrates, 6, 80, 84, 179, 183–84, 187–89,
  194–95, 197
Sollers, Philippe, 80
Son nom de Venise dans Calcutta désert, 63
Stolen Kisses, 148
structuralism, 11, 33n, 50–58, 65, 108,
  140–42
studium, 111–14
subject, 9–10, 30–31, 53–56, 145; in
  Barthes, 112; in Baudry, 61, 72–73,
  116; as identity, 183, 185–86; in Lacan,
  17–20
supplement, 60, 96, 174; logic of, 8–9,
  26, 42, 51, 150; *punctum* as, 112–13; in
  realism, 73–74, 77–78

technē, 99, 115, 177, 192, 196–98; vs.
  physis, 172–74, 179; as postal, 181–84,
  187
technology, 24, 172–78, 181, 183–87,

technology (*cont.*)
    191–93, 195–96; high-, 76, 93, 180–81,
    186–87; and rhetoric, 136–37
telecommunications. *See* communication
teleology, 18, 78, 88, 181, 186; in film
    history, 35, 40, 44–45
Tetto, Il, 37
title, 48, 87, 101, 125, 131, 178; in *Blue
    Velvet*, 145, 161–65; in *The Bride*, 140,
    166, 168; Derrida's practice of, 82, 127,
    134–35
Titus-Carmel, Gérard, 176–79
Torok, Maria, 18n
totalization, 52–53, 168, 195; essentializa-
    tion as, 36–37, 44, 58, 134; in film his-
    tory, 33–38, 41, 43–44
trace, 4, 7, 23, 60, 78, 105, 171; image as,
    68, 75, 93, 134. *See also* trait
trait, 46–49, 127
Treasure of the Sierra Madre, The, 123
Truffaut, François, 139–70
truth, 6–10, 18, 153, 169, 190, 198; in
    Plato, 80–82, 84; the visual as, 88, 126.
    See also logocentrism
tympan, 78–79, 157–59

Umberto D, 37
umbrella, 79, 126n

undecidability, 24, 121, 123, 142, 152n; in
    Blue Velvet, 141–49, 157n, 167–71; hy-
    men as, 83, 95, 96; as political, 28–29
university, 23–26
Updike, John, 192n

Van Gogh, Vincent, 135n, 165
violence, 27, 34, 43, 67n, 95–96, 111,
    137; in *Blue Velvet*, 147–49, 153, 157–
    61, 165–71; in *The Bride*, 144, 152,
    166–70
Visconti, Luchino, 37
von Sternberg, Josef, 124

Welles, Orson, 124, 139
Woolrich, Cornell, 150, 154, 160
wordplay. *See* play
writing, 9–10, 82, 173, 195; in *Blue Vel-
    vet*, 157–61, 165–71; in *Breathless*, 130–
    34; cinema as, 60–64, 75–78, 84, 88–89,
    98; pictorial, 100, 117, 119, 125, 137,
    193; *punctum* as, 112, 114–15; signature
    as, 120–23, 142, 150n; vs. speech, 8–10,
    61–62, 87, 161; technology as, 173–76

Young Mr. Lincoln, 15n